ONE FOOT IN WASHINGTON

ONE FOOT IN WASHINGTON

The Perilous Life of a Senator's Wife

BY ELLEN PROXMIRE

ROBERT B. LUCE, INC.   Washington, D.C.

ONE FOOT IN WASHINGTON

COPYRIGHT © 1963 BY ROBERT B. LUCE, INC.

LIBRARY OF CONGRESS CATALOG CARD NUMBER: 63-20858

MANUFACTURED IN THE UNITED STATES OF AMERICA

VAN REES PRESS • NEW YORK

To BILL

TABLE OF CONTENTS

ONE FOOT IN WASHINGTON

Chapter I

GETTING THERE
IS HALF THE FUN

My name is Ellen Proxmire. My husband is a United States Senator. This means I am one of ninety-two women in America who lead a very special kind of life. Instead of one home to care for, most of us have at least two; instead of a regular dinner hour, we must have a meal ready whenever our wandering legislator comes home; instead of normal two-week summer vacations, we must snatch our holidays when we can; instead of the usual eight hours of uninterrupted sleep, we are constantly awakened by a ringing phone; instead of being able to plan confidently for the future as most people do in terms of their careers, we must stew and worry about the next bout with the voters. Uncertainty becomes a way of life.

There are innumerable other "insteads" that will emerge as our story is told. Though I will write of experiences that all official families share, I am going to talk primarily about Bill and Ellen Proxmire, their five children, their harried, challenging and thoroughly unpredictable life. It is a story full of fun and promise, disappointments and demands, excitement and variety. My hope is that it will be meaningful to all those who are interested in politics as a career, and to all those who wish to know more about the kind of lives their elected officials lead. This glimpse of the daily reality for a political family will, I hope, result in a clearer picture and a more balanced account of the structure and pressures of political life.

This is how it all began for us.

My husband had twice been the Democratic candidate for Governor of Wisconsin, in 1952 and 1954. I had been deeply involved in the work of the Wisconsin Democratic Party since 1950, participating on every level from precinct committeewoman to Executive Secretary, the only full-time, paid position in the state organization. Naturally Bill and I had come to know each other well, for we worked together on every phase of political activity.

In his capacity as a member of the Wisconsin delegation to the Democratic National Convention in July of 1956 and in my capacity as Secretary of the state party, we went to Chicago for the mayhem and festivities that always accompany the convulsive act of nominating a Presidential candidate. As if we didn't have enough to do that week (we were each working twenty-hour days to fulfill our responsibilities), we took a walk one night in Grant Park, talked about our lives (we were both divorced and each of us had two children), and decided at that time to be married.

It seemed so natural and proper, in the light of our feelings for each other and our mutual interest in politics and in children. Neither of us, of course, had a shred of an idea of what the future really held.

We left Chicago and that frenzied week, and more or less went our separate ways for three and a half months. Because Bill was the Democratic candidate for Governor for the third time and I was holding the top position in the party office, we felt that announcing our engagement would perhaps prejudice the election in some way and once again remind the voters that we had both been divorced.

We worked very hard, saw little of each other, and lost the election in November. This was Bill's third try, and everyone immediately assumed he had struck out for good. After all, how could a three-time loser even *consider* running again?

Bill and I were quietly married on December 1, 1956, with only our families present. We snatched a weekend honeymoon in Chicago and then hurried back to our farmhouse on the out-skirts of Madison to settle down. Bill concentrated on his print-ing business, which had been sadly neglected during the cam-paign, and I concentrated on building a satisfactory family life for my two girls, Mary Ellen and Jan Cathy, and Bill's two children, Ted and Cici. I continued to work in the party headquarters half-time. Life became routine and predictable, what with Bill's regular hours, weekends at home, and little in the way of extra-curricular demands.

Then just before six o'clock on the balmy evening of May 2, 1957, the phone rang. A friend was calling to say that she had just spoken to a nurse she knew in Washington who was sta-tioned at the Bethesda Naval Hospital. Joseph R. McCarthy of Wisconsin was dead. Rumors about his failing health had been numerous for weeks, but there had been no hard news until now about his condition. We were taken completely by surprise. McCarthy had been such a controversial figure, had given his name to an era, had been so much a part of the American con-sciousness for so long, it was hard to believe that he was gone. When Bill walked in the door promptly at six (it was the last time he ever walked in our door at six on the dot), I could tell by his face that he had heard the news, too. Soon after, he told me he had decided to seek McCarthy's seat if a special election was called.

For weeks the Governor kept everyone speculating about his

3

plans. Finally he set August 27 as the date for a special election to fill the unexpired term of Senator McCarthy. The party primaries would precede it by four weeks.

Candidates appeared on the scene as fast as wild spring onions pop up on an otherwise smooth, untroubled lawn. The Republicans had seven men in their primary, but the Democratic contest involved only my husband and the Senior Congressman in the Wisconsin Democratic delegation, the Honorable Clement Zablocki of Milwaukee.

As *Life* magazine reported at the time, "All these men are vying for a big political prize—the late Joseph McCarthy's seat in the Senate. The outcome will not upset the Senate's Democratic majority (now 49–46), but it will undoubtedly be taken as an indication of President Eisenhower's popularity."

The eyes of the nation were on Wisconsin. After the two primaries were over, they focused on Republican Governor Walter J. Kohler (the man who had beaten my husband twice) and on William Proxmire for the final countdown.

Time reported that Kohler was the "early favorite to win"— and that Bill was a "chronic candidate who has yet to win statewide office." They went on to pick Kohler as the favorite because "Yaleman Proxmire, who preserves the common touch by staying in $2.50 hotel rooms and writing speeches on a typewriter in the back of his Chevrolet campaign car, is also classed in Wisconsin among the political sideshows." (Little did they know then that Bill stayed in $2.50 rooms because that was all we could afford, and that even after he became a United States Senator he would still drive a Chevrolet.)

At the time those words were written the prospects for overturning these predictions were indeed slim. The summer of 1957 was hot and steamy, especially in the areas where we had to concentrate—the cities. Many of the Democrats who had worked so valiantly since 1949 to build a strong new party organization and elect candidates against great odds were tired and discour-

4

aged. Nineteen fifty-six and Bill's third loss for the governorship had seemed to confirm their feeling that he simply could not win. In addition, there were disappointed Democrats in Milwaukee who had been stung by Zablocki's defeat in the primary. Money was scarce and optimism nonexistent.

We had no official headquarters, no paid staff personnel, no billboards, and practically no time to accomplish the impossible. Our kitchen was turned into a makeshift office. The children were corralled into everything from answering the phone to stuffing envelopes to running errands to delivering pamphlets door-to-door.

Volunteers drove Bill around, took over the fund-raising effort, such as it was, and kept all the campaign records. TV and radio spots were hurriedly recorded and distributed, where and when depending on the amount of money in the hands of our advertising agency. Cash was in such short supply and so uncertain in arriving that I found myself making daily trips to the bus depot to put checks on the Greyhound for Milwaukee. Our adman in Milwaukee would meet the bus and take the check in hand. Then, and only then, could time be bought.

The skills Bill had perfected since his first Wisconsin campaign in 1950 were put to the test. He hit the issues hard and squarely. He drove night and day, campaigning at county fairs, shopping centers, farm meetings, baseball games, church picnics and union meetings. He countered the "three-time loser" charge by saying, "My opponent doesn't know what it is to lose. I do. And I'll welcome the support of voters who do too. I'll take the losers. I'll take the debtors. I'll take those who've lost in love, or baseball, or in business. I'll take the Milwaukee Braves. The next Senator from Wisconsin should be one who has known defeat."

We learned this "loser" twist from another "loser" who had turned his losses to a victory. One Sunday afternoon when Bill and I were gloomily contemplating the last three weeks of the election, a long-distance phone call came to our farmhouse in

Blooming Grove. It was the soft Southern voice of Senator Ralph Yarborough, saying he too had lost three elections for Governor and he too had run in a special election just that year for the U.S. Senate—and won. He mentioned this "loser" story to us and said finally, "Opal and I are waiting to welcome you to Washington." This story, this advice and this encouragement came at just the right time for us and I think meant more to Bill than anything else that happened during the course of this incredible campaign.

On election morning we awoke early and headed for our polling place to vote. Photographers were on hand to take the usual "voting" pictures of the candidate and his wife. The ballot was simple, just two names, so the actual procedure took only a split second. We parked the children with friends and headed for Milwaukee.

On the way we stopped at Racine and Kenosha to greet those who were working at phone banks to get out the Democratic vote. Later we did the same thing at phone banks in Milwaukee.

One of the unwritten rules for a candidate on election day is to keep moving. It helps the time to go more quickly and even last-minute work sometimes helps. Sleep was impossible, even though our fatigue had turned to a persistent numbness. Late in the afternoon, Bill dropped me at our hotel and went on to make a few more calls. He promised to pick me up at six o'clock, for we had made plans to go to dinner with two friends who wanted to spend the early part of election evening with us.

Just before Bill was to return, I inspected the small room that had been set up to contain the election-night activity—celebration or wake. In the 1956 governor's race we had been somewhat optimistic about the outcome, so our plans for a celebration had been gay and substantial. In the end, the sadness and disappointment of that evening had only been heightened by the large room, the blaring band and the lavish supply of food. This time we took a small place with no extras. As I stood in the empty room which

6

was adorned only by a small radio and a bare bar, a friend from Sheboygan joined me. Just then the early returns began to come over the wire. (In Wisconsin some of the rural polls close at six o'clock, so returns begin to sift in quickly.) As I listened to those first results I could hardly believe what I heard—Bill was ahead!

Throughout the evening his lead remained constant. Previous Democratic candidates had had to wait until the bitter end to be sure about victory or defeat, because only the big-city returns, coming in last, are substantial enough to reverse the negative up-state trend. In 1954 it was four in the morning before we knew for sure that Bill had lost by one-half a percentage point. This time we didn't have to wait to know he was winning.

I will never forget Bill's face, nor the glow I felt when he picked me up for dinner that night. He cautioned me not to be overly optimistic and tried (unsuccessfully) to caution me on my high spirits. But I *knew*, and I soared with pride in him and in a job well done.

We settled down with our friends for dinner and our last quiet moment for many a day to come. Though we hadn't left word, someone found us even before our meal was served. It was the Milwaukee *Journal* calling to inquire about Bill's reaction to the favorable trend. He commented briefly, we ate quickly and returned to the hotel. Not even the slow rain which had begun could dampen the joy and good wishes that filled the evening. At one point an old and devoted supporter of Bill's was standing in the lobby, and on seeing Bill leapt forward, tackled and hugged him with unrestrained glee. A crowd had begun to gather and we shook hands all around.

At 9:30 we set out on a tour of television and radio stations for interviews. For the first time in our lives we had a police escort, reporters trailing us, and hangers-on who seemed to materialize out of the night. A reporter and photographer from *Life* had come up from the bureau in Chicago, just on the chance that there might be an unusual story. They stuck to us like burrs for five days.

Once the broadcasts were completed we returned to a mob scene at the Wisconsin Hotel. The roof seemed literally in the process of being unhinged as we entered the now packed and jubilant room. The victory fête was totally uninhibited. All those present had worked long and hard for the success of the Democratic candidates. The fact that we had tasted defeat so often made the cup of victory undeniably more sweet.

Proxmire campaign signs had been torn down from car tops and building walls; new signs saying "HAPPY DAYS ARE HERE AGAIN" and "HURRAY FOR PROXMIRE" had been hastily sketched. Party workers and well-wishers kissed, hugged, pumped hands and danced in the streets long into the night. In the midst of the confusion Bill was called to the phone over and over again; Adlai Stevenson, Lyndon Johnson, Estes Kefauver, and members of our families were among the callers.

It was clear that many of the merrymakers found the victory hard to believe. As the Milwaukee *Sentinel* said, "They remembered with a twinge of conscience, perhaps—that they had been ready to ditch Proxmire only a few weeks ago because they felt he had shown himself to be a political horse who would never make it down the home stretch."

About 1:00 A.M. we wound our way through a sea of outstretched hands and left the hall of celebration to go to our hotel room. Sleep even then was impossible. There were reporters waiting outside the room. Inside, the phones rang all night and telegrams poured in, in an astonishing stream. Hundreds were piled high on the coffee table, and more were slid under the door all through the night.

Nevertheless, in the relative exclusion from the outside world, we tried to collect our thoughts in order to contemplate what lay ahead. That moment of combined elation, exhaustion, and expectation is hard to describe, but neither Bill nor I will ever forget it.

We snatched a few hours of troubled sleep and were up at 5:30 A.M. to go to four plant gates. A "plant gate" probably doesn't mean much to the ordinary citizen, but it has played an enormously significant role in my husband's career. At factory gates throughout Wisconsin Bill has always greeted workers as they arrive in the morning or leave in the afternoon. This has been a regular part of his daily planning, in and out of campaign years, since 1950. It means getting up at 5:30 A.M. and sometimes earlier, standing outdoors in all kinds of weather for two hours or more, and shaking hands often with as many as 3,000 men and women before breakfast. Since this had been his practice during and between campaigns, he felt he should continue it the morning after the election—this time to thank those who had helped him win his new office.

To each person who passed, he said, "Hello. I'm Bill Proxmire, and I want to thank you for your support." Many of the workers seemed amazed that Bill and I would take the time to greet them *after* we had won! With us on the tour was our faithful friend Gerry Bruno, a factory worker himself, who had accompanied Bill on hundreds of such appearances. Today he commented that he truly felt lost because there was no campaign literature to hand out.

We returned at last to the hotel for breakfast and an attempt to decide what was next on our schedule. Just as we finished eating we were told that reservations had been made for us on a 4:30 P.M. flight to Washington. We absolutely had to go, because Bill had to be sworn in before Congress adjourned. My first response to this news was a flood of tears at leaving Wisconsin without seeing my children (I could just imagine how many questions were in their minds), and concern because I didn't "have anything to wear"—a typically feminine reaction, campaign manager or no campaign manager.

Thus ended the most momentous day in our lives—Election Day, August 27, 1957. With a small weekend bag in hand, we departed for the airport and the first of many days in Washington.

It was a glorious trip. As we entered the plane cabin, the stewardess presented us with a huge cake inscribed "Happy Landings." We settled in our seats with stacks of newspapers to fill the two and a half hours of the flight. Of course there were interruptions: congratulations from the passengers, pictures snapped of Bill working and drinking milk (the *Life* reporters were still with us), and jovial conversation with Philleo Nash, State Chairman of the Democratic Party in Wisconsin, who was accompanying us to Washington.

I still have many of the newspaper accounts of the victory, and they are as enchanting reading for me now as they were then.

"Astounding landslide victory of Bill Proxmire in Tuesday's special election can justifiably be regarded as one of the most significant developments in Wisconsin politics in modern times." (*The Capitol Times*, Madison, Wisconsin.)

"The extent of Bill Proxmire's victory on Tuesday was amazing. This was the very first time that the Democrats had won a top office [Senator or Governor] in Wisconsin since Civil War days except in times of national crisis [depression or war] or violent controversy within the state. On the state level, Wisconsin has been little less solidly Republican than Vermont or New Hampshire." (The Milwaukee *Journal*.)

"The political change in Wisconsin is as welcome as anything that has happened in a Senate election since the beginning of the century. Bill Proxmire persisted in taking his case directly to the voters in the smallest Wisconsin towns as well as in the large cities in the belief that eventually the political education of the people would bring a civic rejuvenation. Wisconsin has elected a man pre-eminently qualified, by his views and by his insistence on talking sense on the issues, to sit in the Senate. For the first time in a generation Wisconsin has returned to its great tradition of the Bob La Follettes, father and son. That heritage of progressivism is Wisconsin's great gift to the nation." (The St. Louis *Post-Dispatch*.)

We arrived in Washington just as the Senate was staging one of its most bizarre performances. Senator Strom Thurmond of South Carolina was in the midst of a twenty-four-hour filibuster. Though the hour was late, everyone was up and about, and a large and impressive contingent of Senators awaited us at the foot of the plane ramp, among them Lyndon Johnson and Ralph Yarborough of Texas, Hubert Humphrey of Minnesota, Estes Kefauver of Tennessee, Mike Mansfield of Montana, as well as the Democratic House delegation from Wisconsin. My parents were somewhere in the throng, as were my sister and several personal friends who had come to the airport to greet us. We barely had a chance for a hug before we were whisked to the Capitol in a big black limousine, the start of a whirlwind four days.

I was deposited in the office of the Secretary of the Senate while Bill went to the floor of the Senate. His arrival set off a furious squabble between Democratic Majority Leader Johnson and Republican Minority Leader William Knowland of California. Knowland had refused to consent to Bill's swearing-in, saying it would have to wait until Wisconsin's Governor Thomson sent a telegram Thursday confirming Bill's election. The argument raged for twenty-five minutes. Johnson lost. The swearing-in would have to wait until Thursday. Bill returned to the office of the Secretary of the Senate to be greeted by individual members as they left the floor.

I, meanwhile, had already been interviewed by several of the local women's page reporters and had discussed my plight in leaving Wisconsin so hurriedly. We had been living out of the same small overnight bag since Tuesday morning. I had an extra pair of shoes, a black dress and no hat. Bill's extra shirt was no longer presentable and for some reason he had no tie to go with the extra suit he had brought along. These were the small, niggling problems we contemplated on the long ride to my parents' home in Bethesda.

It was agreed that I would borrow some of my sister's clothes to see me through the week, that my father would pick up a new shirt for Bill on his way home from his job in the Patent Office on Thursday, and that we would *borrow* a tie for the swearing-in!

At 12:10 P.M. on Thursday, Bill was sworn in by Vice President Nixon. For us, this brief ceremony was the climax of years of hope and effort. At the same time it was a beginning—a momentous beginning of a new career and a new life for both of us.

After Bill took the oath, we attended a luncheon in our honor in the historic old Supreme Court Chamber off the Senate floor. Lyndon Johnson was host.

Later in the afternoon, Bill held his first press conference. Some thirty reporters, many of whose names we had known for years, crowded into the office of the Secretary of the Senate. I still recall my pride in the success of this, the first of Bill's confrontations with the nation's top press people. I thought he handled the questions with deftness and knowledge. These were qualities I knew he possessed, but when a man is only a candidate, and a three-time loser at that, his views are seldom taken seriously. I remember at that moment I thought of the comments of one Wisconsin paper: "William Proxmire's public life has consisted of perennial campaigning for one office or another and one term in the Wisconsin Assembly—a term distinguished only by his ceaseless, unconvincing oratory, and a sheaf of bills so patently introduced only for propaganda purposes that he could not even interest his own party colleagues in them. He is a cold-blooded calculator who came from Illinois, picked Wisconsin for his oyster and is driven by an overweening personal ambition for title and power."

What a contrast this kind of analysis was to the fact of this press conference. It was generally agreed that Bill made a big hit that day. I will never forget May Craig's comment (she's the well-known correspondent for the [Republican] Portland, Maine, *Press-Herald*.) "Those two kids are pure gold. That's the most attractive couple I can remember in Washington." Whether her words were warranted or not, they certainly went a long way toward soothing the sting of many years of epithets.

After the press conference Bill was briefed by Senators Clark and Humphrey on upcoming legislation. Then we headed for Bethesda and a quick change before a reception sponsored by the Washington Committee for William Proxmire.

On arriving at my parents' door we discovered not only that we were without a key, but that the door was locked and no one was home. The new Senator from Wisconsin unceremoniously climbed in a side window.

Once inside, we dressed in ten minutes and left. As we discovered later, my mother and father, who are totally unaccustomed to anything more than a sprinkling of phonecalls in one day, had fled the premises in order to have a bite to eat in peace. It was four in the afternoon before Mother had gotten to the breakfast dishes, thanks to the tyranny of electronics, so in order that neither of them would go hungry they had gone elsewhere for supper.

That Friday the Senate adjourned for the year. Suddenly we discovered that an office was ready for our occupancy, and that we had to set up some kind of a staff before returning to Wisconsin. Even though we considered ourselves "political professionals," this was the first of many discoveries that there was much to learn.

Bill found that his suite, Room 432, Old Senate Office Building, was just across the hall and a few doors away from that of Senator Alexander Wiley, his Republican colleague from Wisconsin. Senate workmen had mounted a brand-new gold-lettered sign saying "Mr. Proxmire" even before we arrived. The office had belonged to Senator Henry M. Jackson of Washington, who had moved into the late Senator McCarthy's office the day Bill was elected.

I had never before seen phones with five buttons flashing and five lines ringing all at once. I had never seen employees lined up in a hall waiting for interviews, and I certainly didn't expect them that soon after arriving in Washington. And I had never seen 4,000 unopened letters lying in piles on desks and in baskets. It was an absolutely appalling project to contemplate at any time, much less in our frazzled state.

Nonetheless we settled down to dig out from under. Another Senator lent us a couple of girls to answer the phones, and Bill and I began to interview applicants. Somehow we put together the nucleus of a staff, that Friday and Saturday. Supplies were ordered, some of the mail was handled and the rest postponed until a less hectic time.

Though we had planned to return to Madison on Saturday night, ABC had asked the two of us to appear on a nationwide TV show, *Open Hearing*. During the course of the program Bill was asked to discuss the nation's farm problem, to give his views on John Foster Dulles, Joe McCarthy, and foreign aid; to analyze the Wisconsin election and the future of the Democratic Party in Wisconsin.

Not being familiar with time and distance in Washington, we discovered to our horror after the TV show that we had not allowed enough time to get to the airport from the station. A phonecall was made ahead to the airlines, a police escort was provided, and we raced toward Virginia at top speed. The plane was loaded and waiting when we got there, so we entered via the

14

baggage compartment—a totally fitting *finis* to our four hectic days in Washington.

I should have been used to surprises by this time, but our reception in Madison was more thrilling than anything that happened since election night. More than a thousand friends and neighbors had gathered at the airport to welcome us home. The Mayor and his wife presented me with a bouquet of red roses, and I had some idea what a new Miss America must feel like. Bill commented that we were a bit weary after the events of the past five days, but this reception topped them all.

After the brief ceremony, we shook a few of the outstretched hands and quickly sought out our children, who had been brought to the airport for the festivities. A caravan of cars escorted us most of the way home. Kind friends had scrubbed the house from top to bottom, filled the refrigerator, and prepared an informal reception in our mammoth kitchen. The sign stuck on the back door was in perfect harmony with all that had gone before. It read: "THE GLORY IS NOT IN NEVER FAILING, BUT IN RISING EVERY TIME YOU FALL."

We visited and post-mortemed until we could no longer stand. The dishes were done quietly behind our backs, and it was not until the last friend left that we floated down to earth. We were at home.

The morning after our return to Madison, and for many mornings thereafter, we concentrated on answering the mountains of mail that awaited us in bushel baskets in the corner of the kitchen. Bill held several press conferences, made hurried trips to Washington, and took a ten-day trip to Germany during the fall. I found a house in Washington that we could rent furnished for eight months (Bill had to run again in 1958 for a full six-year term), and made preparations for the move.

Yet all was not sweetness and light. Critical press comment

began before the election was more than a week past. This is expected and necessary in politics, but it was quite a jolt after such a rosy week. Because Bill had been asked to go to Germany as a member of the Senate delegation to the opening of the Bundestag, his trip was termed "a free ride for Proxmire even before his seat is warm." Even though he had been able to participate in only three roll-calls during the 1957 legislative session, a story appeared in a Wisconsin paper under the headline, "Where's the 'Economy' Proxmire Said He'd Work For?" The article pointed out that Bill had promised in the campaign to do many things for the people, but strict economy was to be his watchword. It then went on to say that he had voted for approval of the Joint House-Senate Conference Report on the foreign aid appropriation bill for fiscal 1958.

All this is not to argue the points one way or the other. It is just to demonstrate the fact of life that wherever goes a politician go the pen and point of view not only of those who agree with him, but of those who are anxious for the opportunity to carry home a scalp. Bill learned the lesson without even having the traditional "honeymoon" period.

The fall exertions behind us, Bill and I packed our 1956 Chevy with all it could hold in the way of clothes, records, and personal articles for the family and started the drive to Washington. The children remained in Madison for the few days it would take us for the drive and the initial settling. Then all four of them flew to our borrowed home in Bethesda for Christmas.

After Wisconsin Christmases it was a dramatic change to have 75-degree weather for the holiday season. Bill met the kids at the airport, and all insisted on a detour to the Washington Monument before going to the house. In the inimitable way of tourists, the five of them—including Bill—walked the whole way down.

After the holidays the girls were entered in school, the new Senate session began, and we gradually began the adjustment to a new way of life. I had many surprises. Our house was about

16

ten miles from the Capitol, the whole distance through heavy traffic, so trips back and forth were often tedious. Evening mealtimes were unpredictable, and opportunities for the whole family to eat together were infrequent.

Because Bill had to run for office again in the fall of 1958, he soon began regular weekend trips back to Wisconsin. In all, he spent 156 days in Wisconsin in 1958 during the eight-month session without missing a single roll-call vote on the floor of the Senate. Often this meant taking a Sunday flight from Milwaukee at midnight, arriving in Washington between three and four in the morning, then spending the rest of the night on the couch in his office rather than make the trip to Bethesda.

The mere fact of these constant trips to Wisconsin was a jolt to the way of life I had expected, and quite different from the way many Senators operate. A great number of Senators do not find it necessary to return home more than two or three times a year. If their seats are relatively safe, this additional burden on their pocketbooks and family life is not required. But it was a "must" in our case, and we learned to accept the inconvenience. I should like to point out, too, that a Senator is only reimbursed for three such trips, so the cost of the additional travel comes out of personal income.

I was in the last months of pregnancy during the first half of 1958, so my activity was limited. Our first son, William Wayne, was born on July third and died on July fourth—a tragic blow to both of us and to the older children. But there was little time for sorrow and disappointment.

As soon as I felt healthy again, I moved a desk into Bill's office in the Senate and began to set up the campaign in earnest. There was money to raise, itineraries to plan, positions on issues to solidify and an organization to set up. August was terribly late in the normal run of campaigns to get under way, but we had to make the best of the time we had.

Before the Senate session ended on August 24, we had done

much of the preliminary planning for the campaign in Washington. The night of the adjournment of Congress the Senate was in session until 4:00 A.M., so we were two tired people when we set out for the turnpike, once again with the overloaded Chevy, arriving in Wisconsin twelve hours later.

For the second time in a year our house became a campaign headquarters. The situation was somewhat improved this time. We had better equipment; my husband's secretary, Nancy Barkla, moved in with us for the two-month period, and the job of getting volunteers was simplified by the fact that Bill was a U.S. Senator, not just a perennial candidate. Nancy handled all the Senate correspondence and the typing of press releases, and I was responsible for organization work and campaign details. We built car-top signs in our garage, chauffeured visiting newsmen in and out of Madison, cooked meals for unexpected guests, and provided a haven of sorts for the many itinerants who flitted through Madison during the course of the campaign.

Bill was constantly on the move. A typical campaign day for him began with a plant gate appearance in Madison at 6:25 A.M. and ended back in Madison at 10:15 P.M. with a live five-minute radio broadcast. In between he toured Baraboo, Portage, Waupun and Beaver Dam, addressed a Democratic breakfast, a Kiwanis luncheon, held a question-and-answer period with a Chamber of Commerce group, did a live radio interview, taped an interview with the League of Women Voters, attended a farm auction and a home auction, visited numerous stores in the five cities and by the best available count at the time, shook hands with at least 2,595 people. Whatever hour he arrived home (and many evenings it was later than 10:30), he was prepared to arise again the next morning at 6:00 A.M. to start all over again. Many who watched him campaign termed his technique "Operation Handshake"—and it is obvious why.

There were incidents galore to demonstrate the flavor of that hectic time. One morning I recall awakening to the clatter of coffee cups and the systematic bang of cupboard doors in the kitchen. It was only six in the morning, and I couldn't imagine who was downstairs. Nancy and I both heard the noise at the same time; we hastily dressed (I'm sure we looked it) and hurried to the kitchen to find the famous columnist Marquis Childs searching the premises for the makings of a cup of coffee. Our advance man had neglected to tell us that Mr. Childs was to spend the day with Bill in order to write a campaign color story. He insisted on beginning at the beginning, which meant plant gates in Madison; hence the pre-dawn arrival at our house.

Childs' day was to end with a flight from Wausau to Madison. I felt so distressed about the kind of welcome he had had in our home (he never did get any coffee—only an apple) that I went to the airport in Madison to meet his plane. I continue to hope that this bit of attention at the tag end of the day helped to soften his impression of what must have appeared to him a barbaric way of life.

There were other crises and disasters along the way. For some reason the wrong kind of glue had been used for the back of car-top signs; hundreds of them completely dissolved in the first rain. At one point our house became a sick bay for fallen campaign warriors. Press releases often failed to reach their destinations on time. Occasionally I had to substitute for Bill when he couldn't fulfill a speaking engagement, and for me that was always a trauma. I would rather have a tooth pulled than make a speech.

Despite all the missteps and oversights, the campaign somehow began to jell. To me a campaign is like a monstrous machine with hundreds of parts; at first it seems to fly to pieces and go in ten directions at once. Then suddenly everything clicks into place, there is harmony and technical perfection. You can feel it as each day relentlessly brings you closer to the climax.

Election Day, 1958, was much like the one that had preceded

it in August, 1957. On the way to the regular calls we always pay that day, Bill wrote both victory and defeat statements.

He won again, just as substantially, percentage-wise, as he had done the time before. At last he was a six-year Senator with an unquestionable mandate. We looked ahead to a more permanent kind of life in Washington and the chance to learn the workings of the Senate on a more realistic, less haphazard basis.

Before describing what our new life was like, I think it appropriate to answer a few of the questions that people constantly toss our way. They ask, "Why does anyone want to be a politician?" "Why does your husband want this kind of job—one that is full of uncertainty, unfairness and frequent personal inconvenience?" "What is the attraction and fascination the Senate holds for your husband?" These are legitimate questions that can only be answered by briefly describing my husband, his interests, goals, and personality. It wouldn't be fair for me to make this kind of an analysis, so I will rely on an interpretation of Bill which appeared in the *Wall Street Journal* of August 30, 1957.

"When Wisconsin's new Democratic Senator was in prep school, he was voted not the 'most likely to succeed' but the 'biggest grind.' By his recent victory, however, William Proxmire demonstrated that the two can be almost synonymous. For his surprise landslide success followed almost a decade of a steady grind toward major public office.

"It would be surprising if this personality trait didn't mark Mr. Proxmire's career in the Senate. 'Indefatigable,' 'devoted,' 'studious,' 'persistent' are a few words that go into the concept of 'grind.' And the direction in which these traits are likely to be turned is worth some examination."

The article noted that Bill was concerned about the plight of the farmer in America, that he was interested in championing the cause of the small businessman in this country, that he felt foreign aid was necessary and important (but that careful scrutiny to avoid wasted American dollars was essential), that aid to educa-

20

tion has been underemphasized, and that "if the Democratic Party is to merit support in the future as the real champion of those who deserve justice, it must fight for the right to vote for those who are today denied it.

"A look at the life of William Proxmire underscores the picture of an intelligent man with a slow but relentless approach to winning his goals.

"At Hill Preparatory School in Pennsylvania, he kept his nose in his books most of the time. He wasn't much of a mixer and to this day is somewhat of a 'loner.' Having graduated from Yale in 1938 Mr. Proxmire moved to Harvard Business School from which he graduated with distinction in 1940. He enlisted in the Army in 1941 and was stationed part of the time in Washington, D.C.

"While in the capital, Mr. Proxmire reports, his interest in government grew, and by the time he left the service he apparently was seriously considering public life.

"He returned to Harvard in 1946, this time going to Harvard School of Public Administration. He got a Master's Degree and taught for a year, a freshman class of comparative government and political theory while working on a doctorate. But he never wrote his dissertation. Instead he started writing letters to various liberal papers across the country, with his typical searching, thorough questions aimed at finding the area of greatest opportunity for an aspiring young politico.

"He narrowed his search to New Mexico, California and Wisconsin. He finally chose the latter and as an entering wedge went to the office of the liberal Madison *Capitol Times* in 1949 and sought a job as a reporter. After a rather brief newspaper career during which he made some political contacts he left the *Capitol Times* to run a 'Union Labor News' program in Madison.

"He then left his radio job for his first fling at public office. He ran for the state assembly to which he was elected for the usual two-year term.

"Ever since then William Proxmire has been campaigning for some office, quietly shaking hands, cementing fences and pressing on toward his goals when even his friends said he was all but finished.

"Obviously the Democrats in the Senate will find they have acquired a determined colleague and the Republicans a tough competitor." *

This article answers many of the whys about Bill and does much to explain his fitness for his chosen career. He finds life's purpose in hard work and in climbing what seem to be impossible mountains; he likes variety and tackling thorny problems; he has strong convictions and a deep desire to be of service. In the Senate all these qualities can be put to use. Bill's unswerving devotion to the achievement of this goal is the real reason we are in Washington and why I have a story to tell.

* Copyright © 1957, *The Wall Street Journal.*

Chapter II

DURING ALTERATIONS—
BUSINESS AS USUAL

January 5, 1959, dawned cold and clear as our B&O train from Chicago pulled into Union Station in Washington where we were at last ready to settle down. I dropped Bill at the office and went on to the house we had purchased in December on a flying trip of five days. The moving van was waiting when I arrived.

One gesture Bill and I had made to convenience in our daily lives was choosing a home in the suburban Cleveland Park section which borders on Rock Creek Park. The house we picked out was about four and a half miles from the Capitol, situated on a small lot with room for neither a driveway nor a garage. Shopping, schools, churches and bus-lines were all within easy walking distance, yet the neighborhood was quiet and comfortably residential.

Cleveland Park was named after President Grover Cleveland, who picked it as the site of his summer home. Though today there is scarcely a plot of ground left vacant in the area, the fact is that this section was once considered "the country," and 900-acre estates were not uncommon. It also seems incredible that as recently as 1904, there wasn't a house or building from the

Calvert Street Bridge to the foot of our street, half a mile up Connecticut Avenue.

After getting the children registered in their new schools, I began the task of setting the things we had brought with us in some kind of order. Despite my efforts, something always seemed to be missing when we needed it, and the rest of January became a nightmare of unpacked books, harsh ceiling lights where lamps were missing, burned food on an unfamiliar stove, meals eaten on a borrowed card table, and mad scramblings through bottom-less boxes looking for galoshes on rainy days, a flooded basement when exposed pipes froze and burst, and all the myriad inconveniences involved in this type of upheaval.

Hardly had we begun to have that settled-in feeling when the roof blew off our new-found peace. Bill, who had become deeply concerned over the concentration of power in the Senate, launched an assault on the revered but sometimes autocratic leadership of Majority Leader Lyndon Johnson. He decried the disappearance of frequent party conferences at which the Democratic legislative program could be discussed and hammered out. In addition, it became obvious soon after the first session that the Majority Leader was exercising his greatest power to determine what legislation should or should not be considered on the floor of the Senate.

Bill felt that Johnson was running the Senate under a system which could only be called "achievement without discord." The Majority Leader would keep a piece of legislation from the floor until backstage bargaining for votes had completely stripped it of controversy. Then it would be whipped to quick passage, lengthy debate would be scorned, and night sessions would frequently be forced in order to tire the legislators into acquiescence. Both Democrats and Republicans who cooperated would be rewarded with priorities for pet measures and other favors within the Majority Leader's gift.

In his February 22 speech Bill noted that the Senate, established by the Founding Fathers to proceed with more caution, discretion and wisdom than the House of Representatives, had lapsed into lethargy under this system of continual compromise, accommodation and negotiation.

He said, "Initiative and responsibility appear to begin and end with the Majority Leader. There is no place for Senators outside his inner circle. We get no real report from the leadership, and we don't even have an elementary knowledge of when his power is to be used, and why."

Bill's outspoken stand had an immediate and dramatic effect on our daily lives. Controversy not only breeds conversation, it means a lot of extra work. Office mail became astoundingly heavy, phonecalls were incessant, interviews with newsmen from all over the country piled on top of each other, and much midnight oil was burned tying up the loose ends.

One Sunday afternoon, our office staff was busy mimeographing and collating a lengthy press release when Bill dropped into the back room to offer his services. One person suggested that what they really needed more than anything else was a good supply of hot coffee. So Bill obligingly made the trek to a nearby delicatessen and returned with paper cups of steaming coffee stacked on a bun tray. He had all the creams and sugars right, too!

That was the same Sunday afternoon that Jan, our ten-year-old, decided to try out a new bike. She and Mary Ellen and two friends had taken the five-mile ride to visit their grandparents without mishap. But on the return trip, Jan forgot that her new home was located halfway down a steep hill and that hand brakes didn't work as quickly as pedal brakes. She ended up at the bottom of the hill cracked against a tree. Her chin and knees were badly cut up, the bike was bent out of shape, and her new overalls were minus the bottom half. I later made them into shorts.

When Bill got home from the office he found Jan and me missing. We spent the rest of the late afternoon in the emergency room at George Washington Hospital getting sewed up. Sometimes I think our Senatorial men think all the crises arise under the dome of the Capitol. They forget we have our own home-grown variety often enough.

Once again we were forced to renew our preoccupation with press commentary. Some newspapers said that Bill should be hailed as a hero for having the courage to buck the Senate "Establishment"—especially when the Majority Party was his own. Others were highly critical, terming his speech irreverent, unfair, headline-hunting, and, what's more, a total failure. There were wry jokes, too: one columnist said there had been two Farewell Addresses that day: Washington's and Proxmire's (George Washington's Farewell Address is traditionally read to the Senate and the House on his birthday every year). A local commentator, referring to the Proxmire-Johnson differences, said: "Boss Johnson got a noisy ovation at a big Democratic rally recently. Even Senator Proxmire rattled his chains in the slave quarters." We received a letter from a Texas critic of Johnson to the effect that he was raising money to build a one-hundred-foot statue of William Proxmire in Johnson City, Lyndon's home town. Governor Pat Brown of California, in a highly amusing and successful speech before the Gridiron Club's annual dinner that year, said, "Lyndon Johnson believed in the divine right of kings, but then along came 'Fidel' Proxmire. Nevertheless you have to give that Proxmire fellow the credit he deserves. Like Notre Dame, he plays a tough schedule." A headline that particularly amused us read, "BILLY THE KID TAKES ON THE FASTEST GUN IN THE SENATE."

The Johnson affair provided me with my first lesson in a long string of many to come—the core of that lesson symbolized by

26

shattered peace of mind. If your husband is controversial (and most of the men who have been successful in historical terms are controversial during their careers), you have to develop and survive a new emotional state of being. There is pride mixed with concern for consequences, there is the need for a relaxed, self-assured outward appearance despite churning inner discomfort, there are many nights of a new kind of sleep from which you awaken exhausted and restless, there is anxiety because of the strain on your husband, and some hesitation in your relationship with others. Because most Senators' wives follow the news closely, you wonder whether or not you will be accepted in the same warm way as before.

As I see it, the political wife must acquire many of the skills of an accomplished surf-boarder; she must ride the crests of waves of success without too much abandon, accept the necessity of many a quiet, unspectacular lowpoint, approach dangerous eddies with confidence in herself and her husband, and with just enough apprehension to assure success. She must try to learn control, without erasing completely the possibility of honest emotion. It is so easy in the world of politics to be hysterical about everything—about your chances, about your opposition, about the press, about cranks who write and demand the impossible, about the frequent unfairness of it all.

I had to learn very early in Bill's career that politics is a game of give-and-take, and that learning to "roll with the punches" is the only way to survive. By demanding of yourself this kind of discipline, you eventually develop an ability to accept almost anything that comes along as a fact of your existence. At least, I always try to keep this goal before me. I still feel the palpitations, the cold hands, the burning sensation in the pit of my stomach when I see that once again we are to be in the eye of the hurricane, but there really is a sunny side to all this. Losing your appetite is still the easiest way to diet, and participation in active politics is a sure-fire cure for overweight, overpopulation and overconfidence.

After the Johnson controversy had left the front pages, the real proportions of Senate life began to take shape. Bill immediately began making speeches in many parts of the country, adding to the complication and unpredictability of his schedule. I decided to take an active part in Bill's daily life in the Senate, so I began spending several days a week in the office and many hours of those days sitting in the galleries following the debate on the floor. My work in the office revolved around answering letters of a social and political nature, writing a bi-weekly column for Wisconsin newspapers, working on the newsletter from time to time, and talking to some of the visitors who came to the Capitol from our home state. During each fall I worked full-time overseeing the operation of the office while Bill was in Wisconsin, and one year I substituted for Bill's personal secretary for a five-week period when she was out on maternity leave. The staff always jokes about giving me the real "dogs" to answer.

The girls felt settled in their schools for the first time in years (they had been in three different school systems during the previous two years). I adjusted our family daily routine to include the kind of a dinner that would be served to the children at six and to Bill whenever he happened to arrive. We became accustomed to many middle-of-the-night phonecalls.

Our social life seemed to be little removed from our political one, as indicated by the kinds of things we did during the first six months in Washington. The Women's National Press Club's "Welcome to Congress" dinner is always held on opening day. We attended our first one in 1959. There was a banquet given by the Credit Union National Association and a reception by Agnes Meyer, then wife of the publisher of the Washington *Post*, in honor of Adlai Stevenson; a luncheon at the Richard Harknesses' for the Gridiron guests; and a reception at the Senator Paul

Douglases'. We began to meet and get to know people, to become acquainted with many of the greatest minds of our time—people who over the years have become fast friends. The opportunity to do this does not lie in going out frantically, seeing and being seen at balls, banquets and parties, but in quiet conversation during relaxed evenings.

We discovered that the Washington social whirl can keep you on the run all day every day if you let it. For the Diplomatic Corps and military personnel, there is a constantly packed social calendar, but for Congressional families socializing is truly optional.

During June and the first half of July, we, like every other Congressional family, fell victim to the old Washington game of guessing when Congress would adjourn. More experienced and wiser wives made plans either to return to their home states or to take their children to some vacation spot for the summer, regardless of adjournment dates, tentative or otherwise. I listened to one optimistic voice of responsibility who said we would be through by July fifteenth. July fifteenth came and went. Then a columnist stated that he had the "word" that we wouldn't shut up shop until September fifteenth. So the few plans we had made for at least two weeks in Wisconsin before the opening of school had to be remade. Two of the older children were scheduled to go to camp in Wisconsin, so I had to make arrangements for someone else to get them there.

In one way, we were fortunate: there was a recreation program run by the District at two nearby playgrounds, with baseball, ping-pong, and an occasional swimming meet. I had to drive ten miles to Virginia each way for a day of swimming where facilities were good for all the children—certainly a far cry from the easy access of Wisconsin lakes.

On damp days—downpour is really a better description of Washington precipitation—we would sight-see. I was determined that we would not be one of those Washington families that live here for years without seeing any of the historical attractions.

There are a few places that we liked best and have returned to again and again. One of these is Ford's Theater on Tenth Street where Lincoln was shot. At the theater, which is now a museum, we saw furniture from the Lincoln home in Springfield, some of the rails he split, his boots, china from the White House, the flag in which his coffin was wrapped for its last journey, and samples of his early writing.

We went to the Lee Mansion and Arlington National Cemetery, directly across the Potomac in Virginia. The home of Robert E. Lee has a fascinating history. One year after the Declaration of Independence was signed, George Washington's stepson, John Parke Custis, purchased 1,100 acres of land in Virginia, overlooking the Potomac. Here he built a mansion destined to become a national shrine. Young Custis married the daughter of one of Virginia's oldest families, Mary Lee Fitzhugh. Their daughter, Mary Ann Randolph Custis, married a West Point graduate and scion of one of the state's first families, Robert E. Lee. Arlington was inherited by the Lees and it was here that Lee made the most awesome decision of his life: to defend his beloved Virginia and the Confederacy.

The view from the Lee home is unquestionably the most breathtaking in Washington. From the front portico the entire city can be seen. The serenity and beauty of the mansion is now so complete, it seemed hard for us to believe as we stood there that this estate was once an armed camp with military headquarters established in the house itself. When Virginia seceded from the Union, the Lee family dismantled the house and moved to Richmond. The federal government later took over the property and set aside four hundred and eight acres as a National Cemetery. In 1929 the government undertook restoration of the property, and a great deal of the original furniture was traced. We especially enjoyed the children's playroom, full of tiny dolls, cribs and old-fashioned playthings, and the brick-floored kitchen with its simple but ingenious equipment.

On the way to the Tomb of the Unknown Soldier we drove through the natural beauty of Arlington National Cemetery, the acres and acres that surround Lee Mansion. The youngsters were enthralled by the pomp, the horses, the caissons, the twenty-one-gun salute and taps. The cemetery has about twenty-two burials a day, so on almost any visit one can be seen. A lone sentry stands guard by the Unknown Soldier's grave twenty-four hours a day, each guard having a one-hour tour of duty.

A visit to another famous house took us farther back into history. Mount Vernon, the home of our first President, is on the Virginia shore of the Potomac, nineteen miles from Washington. It is thought that Washington's father built the house. It began as only a story-and-a-half structure, but two later additions brought it to its present size. During one of General Washington's winters at home he himself designed and planted the grounds and the garden, which has been maintained as he carefully planned it.

We were especially delighted to learn that the Mount Vernon Ladies Association keeps fresh flowers in every room of this exquisite colonial house. Many of its pieces of furniture, the desk, the globe, many of the books, are the originals. The children said as we walked through the grounds that they could almost feel what it was like to live there. Thoughts of gracious living, rolling hills to ride over, and peace and quiet in general, evidently appealed to them.

Driving home after one of these sight-seeing trips we usually talk about the great variety and contrast found in Washington's architecture. In the space of a brief drive we can be taken back to colonial days, swept to the Orient at the Islamic Center which was built by twelve Moslem countries, charmed by the classic Greek design of the Supreme Court building and by Italian Renaissance architecture at the Congressional Library, or be disappointed and distressed by the blocks of crowded row houses with bare patches of dirt lining the sidewalks, broken window-panes, tattered curtains and dilapidated furniture. To my way of thinking, the contrast brings you up more sharply in Washington than in any other city because it is so devastating. Millions upon millions have obviously been spent restoring historical sites, constructing marble mausoleums for everything from fish to fine paintings, and erecting ugly, sprawling office buildings. But very little has been done about living quarters for the low-income families—mostly Negro—who make up about half of our population. The effort and expenditure that have gone into federal building have made the nation's capital one of the most beautiful cities in the world, but federal neglect has spawned some of the most dismal slums to be found anywhere. I am in despair whenever such trips remind me of how so many people have been neglected.

One of our favorite places to visit is the Children's Chapel at the Washington National Cathedral. Everything in the chapel is scaled to size for little people, and since it is in our neighborhood we can stop there often.

During the rest of that first summer the children read books, dropped in to their father's office frequently, and each evening after dinner took part in a quiz session on the day's work or visit. There were the usual objections when we first broached the idea of making summer somewhat educational, but eventually, I think, all of the children learned to appreciate the discipline.

Each summer since, we have kept the hope alive that somehow we will be able to get home before September; since this has yet to be the case, at least we have learned a little about history and a lot about patience.

Patience and discipline seem to me to be the qualities most necessary for survival in politics and the natural end result of our lives of perpetual inconvenience. Two homes to worry about, dinner hours that are never definite, social engagements which, even in your own home, have to be made on a tentative basis because late sessions often interfere—all make planning impossible, whether for a vacation or a birthday party. All this adds up to constant daily uncertainty and personal inconvenience. This uncertainty is just as much a part of political life as the speeches, press releases, campaigning and applause. Much of its burden falls on the shoulders of the political wife, for it is her role patiently to mesh all the jagged pieces of discord and demand into the kind of a life that looks whole to the outside world.

Chapter III

AFLOAT IN THE
GOLDFISH BOWL

I sometimes think that goldfish in a bowl are much better off than the public figures they resemble. Though the fish's every move can be scrutinized from every angle, people observe them only as things of beauty or objects of scientific interest. Those who study their silky movements from outside the glass don't criticize what they are wearing, what they do, what they say, what they mean, nor do they ask the fish lots of questions, or expect them to do much more than entertain. For political fish, life is truly lived in a glass bowl, but with all the necessary human results added.

"Glamor" is the quality most people associate with life in the public eye, whether it be that of a movie star, a sports figure or a politician. According to Webster, "glamor" suggests magic, elusive charm, something exciting or cloaked with fascinating allure. After a close look at the realities of public life, it would be surprising to me if this kind of an interpretation were possible, at least as far as our particular experience is concerned.

I recall one two-week period in the spring of 1960 that was certainly exciting and unpredictable, but the words "frustrating," "exhausting," "demanding" and in the end, "satisfying," would much more nearly fit the facts.

Bill was scheduled to make a speech in Providence, Rhode Island, that busy spring. (He will accept out-of-town speaking dates, provided they do not interfere with roll-call votes on the floor. That often means frantic rides to the airport to catch the last possible plane that will satisfy the arrival time for the speech at the other end.) On this particular trip to Providence, bad weather forced his plane (which was to land in New York) on to Boston, unsuccessfully, and then, finally, to Hartford, Connecticut. Hurried calls related Bill's plight to those who expected him; there were more plane arrangements that didn't work out, and the long day ended with a dreary train trip back to Washington. Bill arrived home at 5:00 A.M., heavy-bearded and cross, undelivered speech still in his breast pocket. A talk at a Smith College mock convention two days later was almost a repeat of the same situation. Impending floods delayed the trip to the college, but Bill arrived just in time to give a twenty-minute speech and then make an ungraceful dash to the airport for the return flight home.

The trip back to Wisconsin for the Easter recess was then delayed two days because of predicted roll-calls that never materialized. Once the plane reservations were made with certainty, an unexpected hearing came up to delay the flight another six hours.

I recall that at the same time Senators Hubert Humphrey and John F. Kennedy were engaged in an excruciating Presidential primary campaign in Wisconsin. (And how well we knew those high school auditoriums and plant gates they visited! Whenever we see either the President or Senator Humphrey they never fail to remind us of their Wisconsin ordeal—the icy roads, the plant gates, the brutal schedule that is accepted and expected in the Midwestern political arena.) Months of the most arduous campaigning had resulted in what newspaper commentators termed an "indecisive victory" for both. But the lines of weariness around their eyes and the new wrinkles in their brows attested to the fact that the campaign had been something less than "glamorous."

It is hard to be glamorous when you haven't had time to have your suit pressed or your shoes shined or when your clothing is uncomfortably hot on an unexpectedly warm day. This happened to me on a campaign trip to California in November of 1960. I had never been to California before, so was not prepared for the 80-degree weather that greeted us during the three-day trip. Bill made nineteen speeches in ten different towns. At one point we found ourselves in Sacramento where Bill was to give a talk to some college students. In the inimitable way of Californians, it turned out to be an outdoor affair. The platform faced the peak of the afternoon sun, and the backdrop was a shiny metal that intensified the heat. My heavy wool dress practically had to be wrung out by the time Bill had finished his speech. Six hours and two speeches later, I finally had an opportunity to shower and change for the next appearance.

It is hard to have a ready smile and the right answers when you have had only three hours' sleep. It is even harder sometimes to remember what town you're in when you have been in six others earlier the same day, or to recall the names of people you know well when you've seen hundreds of other faces in the space of a few hours.

This constant exposure and perpetual public scrutiny in the middle of the goldfish bowl means that political families are faced with a number of unique dilemmas. Dilemmas are everyday occurrences for many mature people in demanding professions, but I think it can honestly be said that politicians face them with greater frequency than anyone else. This is a side of elective life that had never occurred to me until we had been in Washington a year or two, and now that the two have grown to six these dilemmas seem to appear with mushrooming frequency.

Stimson Bullitt put it very well when he said: "A politician must serve several masters and serve them well. He tries to reconcile the never-ending conflicts between the things he is supposed to do: the duty to obey the wishes of his constituents and to follow his conscience or judgment; the duty to do the right thing, and the necessity to stay in office to get the right things done." *

For example: what should be the daily routine of a Senator? Should he be on the floor listening to or taking part in debate, or in committe studying legislation in detail; in his office answering mail, or in the reception room greeting constituents? On a number of occasions when I have taken visiting firemen to the gallery, there is almost always an automatic reaction to the sparse population on the floor of the Senate. People just can't understand why every single Senator is not on the floor while the Senate is in session. This puts the burden of explanation on political wives, who must try to justify the situation.

For the average Senator, a full day could be devoted to any one of the above-mentioned pursuits, so decisions on allocation of time are perpetual. This is the toughest and most persistent dilemma of all: the best use of time in each working day.

A more severe and pressing dilemma revolves around the extent to which help is given a constituent. Since most federal departments have become enormous, impersonal labyrinths, quite often the Congressman is the only person to whom a citizen may turn for help. But walking the fine line between demanding Congressional privilege and being satisfied with normal fair treatment is a difficult path for many people to follow.

Innumerable other dilemmas confront Washington politicians every waking hour. Many fall into the humorous category.

* Stimson Bullitt, *What It Means to Be a Politician.* Copyright © 1959 by Stimson Bullitt. Reprinted by permission of Doubleday & Company, Inc.

If you drive a bright new car you are either too well paid or too extravagant. If you drive an old klunk (our 1956 Chevy had 127,000 miles on it when we finally had its dilapidated carcass tugged to the salesroom in 1962), people comment that this is too undignified a vehicle for one in your exalted position.

If you spend time among your constituents, people inquire, "Why aren't you in Washington doing your job?"; if you are in Washington for roll-calls (after all, a Senator's job is to vote and be recorded) at the time of an important local party function, home state officials and others in attendance immediately assume you are abandoning them for the delights of Washington.

If you turn out as much mail as your office staff can possibly produce, constituents and newspapers sometimes complain about the use of the franking privilege; if you are late in answering a letter, you unquestionably hear about your inefficiency.

If you entertained all the people who come to see you from your home state you could do nothing else; but if you don't happen to be around when a certain group comes by, you're not being hospitable, and obviously have ceased to care about the folks back home.

Early in Bill's career in Washington, we devised a system whereby we hoped to make everyone feel welcome, even if it happened that Bill was not available. Each person who came to our office to say hello was asked to sign a guest book. If Bill was in his office and free to come out for a minute, a check was put by the names of the people he had seen and talked to. Many, of course, could not be personally greeted. So he wrote a personal letter to all those he had not seen, expressing his regret that he had missed them.

One day the system backfired. Two reporters happened to come to Washington for a visit. Bill did see them, and I did take them to the gallery and on a personal tour of the Capitol. Somehow their names were not checked off in the guest book, and after returning to Wisconsin they received a note expressing Bill's disappointment in not being able to see them while they were in Washington. He was smacked with a derisive editorial that not only complained about the inefficiency of his office, but made him look quite foolish and incompetent in his efforts to make people feel at home. After all, said the paper, he couldn't even remember whom he had seen!

When it comes to taking a stand on specific issues, the dilemmas are eternal and an official's voting record puts him in the middle of another kind of goldfish bowl. If he votes to cut a military appropriation he is accused of weakening the national defense; if he votes automatically for all the budget requests of each and every agency and department, then the tag of "extravagant spender" follows as surely as the night the day. If he votes for a cut in the total of a particular program, then he is obviously insincere and hypocritical if he decides to vote for the bill anyway on final passage. On the other hand, if he has fought for a cut, and it fails to pass during the legislative process, and he feels in good conscience that he cannot vote for the bill in final form, the public assumption is that he must be against the program in essence or in any form. In between, every one of the interested parties associated with a particular piece of legislation is lobbying for all he is worth. A legislator faces the daily dilemma of inevitable alienation of those constituents who are affected or those whose desires and objectives are not in the public interest.

An elected official's personal finances, too, are necessarily a matter of public interest and concern. This is sometimes hard for a wife to accept, but she must learn to recognize this fact of life in the goldfish bowl. The nation's press has covered often and in great detail examples of nepotism, rented front porches, and possible and often real Congressional conflicts of interest. This is news and it should be. Rarely, though, is the other side of the coin presented.

The purpose of much of this sort of publicity is to prove that the average Congressman profits well from his tenure on Capitol Hill. I can only cite from our own limited stay in Washington, but so far I think it would be fair to say that being in government is not exactly the road to riches. It could be described more accurately as "financial brinkmanship," or an expensive hobby on a Senator's annual salary of $22,500.

Attention is always concentrated on the "fringe benefits" of being in the Senate or in the House. It is pointed out that Congressmen are reimbursed for traveling between their home towns and Washington. They do get twenty cents a mile compared to the common figure of nine or ten cents in private industry. As far as this statement goes, it is true. But the implication is that this is the case for *all trips* back home. Actually, Congressmen are reimbursed at the rate of twenty cents a mile for *one round trip* and, in addition, for two round trips in the actual amount of the transportation-ticket vouchers presented. Bill has averaged eighteen or twenty trips back to Wisconsin every year since he was elected, and I travel with him four or five of these times. All of these expenses come out of our pocket.

The people from our home state expect and should have frequent radio and television reports about what is going on in Washington. This is an essential part of keeping in touch. The cost of these films and recordings, including mailing expenses, averages $1,000 a year, and once totaled $3,500. None of this cost is underwritten by the expense money allotted to a federal official.

The government defrays $600 of the cost of running a home office; Bill's home office expenses during the year and a half he had one ran more than twice as much as the amount received.

Bill annually runs over his allotment for long-distance calls, telegrams and first-class postage, as do most Congressmen. Before the end of each fiscal year his budget for stationery and office supplies is always completely flattened, and the paper necessary to complete the year's work comes out of our personal income.

In 1963, the people of Wisconsin failed to understand Bill's need for a substantially well-paid staff man in Wisconsin. The fact that the man Bill chose was a straight-A graduate student at the same time made it even more impossible for them to understand. Even though he was performing his job honestly and with worthwhile results for the people of Wisconsin, his presence on the payroll became an overemphasized and potentially damaging political issue. Because we live in a goldfish bowl, and the salaries of those who work for us are public record, this fact was fair game for the press and for the opposition party who wanted to make an issue out of it. They had been looking for some chink in Bill's armor for ten years. The situation got completely out of hand, the facts were distorted and, as a result, the gentleman in question was denied his degree, his effectiveness was severely impaired, and Bill's reputation was in danger.

To once again restore balance to the situation and to make it clear that Senator Proxmire was not using federal staff money for a questionable purpose, Bill repaid to the federal government the amount that our staff man had been paid for the previous eight months. This was a jolt to the educational kitty for our children, for it amounted to more than $9,000, but Bill felt it necessary to restore some measure of sanity to the political picture. He had done nothing unethical or immoral, he had not absconded with public money, but in the light of the recent Congressional disclosures of conflict of interest and even outright bribery, the people seemed in the mood to lump all legislators together—on the lowest shelf of human behavior.

It was an expensive decision, but just another in a long series of expensive decisions that every political family must make.

Bill and I feel strongly that abuses of the public trust must be countered with effective legislation; that Congressmen should be required to make public their financial dealings, their sources of income, and their stock transactions, particularly where a possible conflict of interest is involved. But we also feel that people are often misled into believing that all public officials feather their nests whenever the opportunity arises. It is my belief that a politician would much rather leave behind a good name and a record of service than take with him a pot of gold. Other fields are without question greener—with money, that is.

All this emphasis on knowing the last detail about the private lives of people who hold public office puts an extra burden on the political wife, one that didn't exist before the days of rapid communication, television, mass magazines and instant coverage. She must look well dressed without being too elegant; she must have practical but interesting clothes; and she must be properly attired for everything from a county fair to an elegant dinner at the White House. I have found that living in Washington requires somewhat dressier clothes than in Madison, but I have also learned not to worry about it too much. Clothes with simple lines that can serve for both afternoon and evening, dresses with jackets, and comfortable shoes seem to be the answer. Lavish wardrobes are out of the question for most of us, so we solve the problem by convincing ourselves that, after all, our husbands aren't in Washington for the purpose of justifying our fashion sense, and that this aspect of life in the public eye is truly a fringe matter.

Being a celebrity and having to live in Washington adds to our housing problem, too. We must maintain an establishment in our home state in order to convince the people there that we really haven't abandoned them forever for the glamorous whirl by the banks of the Potomac—but you can't just let a house sit unoccupied for six years. So most Congressional families rent their property back home and split their lives in two by living in both places. Bill and I rent our house in Madison, and live year-round (or at least the children and I live year-round) in Washington. Caution must be taken in the selection of the Washington house, too. There are naturally certain considerations, such as proximity to schools and the condition of the plumbing, but I'm afraid that the main considerations for many of us are the cost and the location. For certain Senators, a home mustn't be too big, too expensive, or in too exclusive a neighborhood. If it were, it would undoubtedly be said that the Senator had abandoned the implicit simplicity of his roots for big-city sophistication.

I try to keep our house in a state of relative neatness, despite the uncertainty of juvenile behavior and the unpredictability of our schedule. Our house is big enough for twelve at a sitdown dinner, thirty for a cocktail party, or sixty if we have a summertime informal buffet using the recreation room and backyard. It is adequate for our needs without being extravagant, and about all I can handle as a housewife with political leanings and an unhandy husband—unhandy in availability as well as mechanical talent.

I will say this—our existence inside the goldfish bowl keeps our faculties sharply honed, our shoes properly shined, and our sense of humor constantly cultivated. A Member of Congress is expected to know and understand everything from complex economic theory to baseball batting averages, from what to do about tattered District of Columbia textbooks to the refugee problem in Hong Kong, from social security to small business, from precinct organization to who's going to get the next postmaster's appointment. Their wives must be authorities on Caroline Kennedy's playmates, on how to raise money for a charity, on the best places to eat in Washington, and on budgeting the family resources.

Today, I think, the demands are greater than ever before on those who have chosen a public life. We are expected to make a good impression on camera as well as in person. We are expected to be well informed on myriad issues spanning the spectrum from personal and local to international, and perhaps, at some future date, even celestial affairs.

Our every move is scrutinized by friend and foe alike. Our personal lives are free from neither public impact nor private criticism.

This is as it should be, for it is part of the price we pay when we choose this way of life. It is understood and accepted. And maybe that is why our profession is considered "glamorous"— because the stakes are so high and the demands so great.

Whether you are Mrs. Richard Nixon traveling in Siberia or Poland, Mrs. Lyndon Johnson visiting Greece or Italy, Mrs. Hubert Humphrey campaigning in a small Minnesota town or a West Virginia coal mine, or Mrs. Kennedy touring in England or India, you strive to leave a personal impression on your public as well as giving them something to ponder. It isn't a glamorous life in the usual definition, but it is stimulating, satisfying and rewarding.

You learn hope, patience, and the ability to enjoy to the fullest the infrequent quiet family times that do occasionally materialize.

To put it quite simply: One night the ten-year-old in our family said in her turn at an original grace before dinner: "Thank you for having us all together for dinner this time. Take care of Dad on his trip tomorrow—and, by the way, where did you say you were going this time?"

Our daily problem-solving and performance in public can be the process of government in its best sense. It means constant compromise, sifting, winnowing and deciding, within the framework of personal conviction, accumulated knowledge and constituent representation. It takes steady nerves and often great courage, and the perennial hope is that when the time comes to push the handles on the voting machines the people back home will know what we did and why.

Chapter IV

HOME FROM THE HILL

Former Senator Theodore F. Green of Rhode Island used to say with a twinkle that a Congressman never had to eat a single meal at his own expense if he didn't want to. And he was not far from wrong.

Entertaining and being entertained in Washington runs the gamut from almost production-line affairs to the simplest and most straightforward meetings with people. For a new Senate wife, the first few months in Washington can be a nightmare, since everyone who has had any connection with her husband's campaign wants to have a dinner or cocktail party, all top officials entertain the new members, party organizations throw a shindig to show off their new prize, hostesses with a reputation for little else make sure via a luncheon or dinner party that they have the opportunity to look you over. It is all very confusing at first. Most Washington entertainment is so much more lavish than anything many of us have witnessed before—what with servants, groaning buffet tables and sometimes even strolling strings—that the average Senate wife waits months before attempting anything on her own.

Not knowing which invitations to accept makes the first months in Washington especially trying. There are a variety of "circuits" here, other than the electrical type. There is the "banquet circuit," the "cocktail circuit," the "embassy circuit," the "luncheon circuit" and after-hours events galore. Conventions are in town at the rate of several a week. If you just kept up with *them*, you would always have a place to eat lunch, a place to drink cocktails, and a banquet every evening.

Embassies entertain continually for the never-ending stream of foreign officials who pay calls on Washington. Congressional figures are always included in the invitation lists.

The cocktail party is the accepted way for many people to entertain. It is easy in terms of preparation, several hundred people can be run in and out in a relatively short time, and scores of social obligations can be settled at one fell swoop.

It must be admitted that the pace and the opportunities, if followed, require a strong stomach, a loud voice, steady nerves, good feet, and a lot of discretion about alcoholic beverages.

Bill and I decided early in the game that we would try to avoid endless party-going. It's not that we don't like people; we just find that people by the hundreds, all talking at once and milling around, are not our cup of tea. Each day a Senator must see people in large numbers. During a campaign he must see them in even larger numbers. For us this resulted in the inevitable decision that social life should be relaxing and modest.

When we lived in Madison we preferred buffet serving if the guest list was larger than ten. If we had a sitdown dinner, we would make it family-style with Bill doing the serving. That always limited the number of courses, but it was more than adequate for the life we led. Hiring people to serve was almost unheard of before Washington. Here there is a large pool of such help available, and it is not unusual to begin to recognize familiar faces among waiters as you move from house to house. Sometimes this way you can even tell what firm catered the meal.

The first adjustment we had to make was the hour of the

46

dinner party itself. In the Midwest, most dinner parties begin at 6:00 or 6:30. In Washington the working day begins later and ends later so that the earliest convenient hour to invite people is 7:30 P.M. Most hostesses, however, set 8:00 P.M. as the time of arrival for dinner parties. That seems a little late to us (it means you seldom eat before 9:30) so we have stuck to the 7:30 hour.

I still serve buffet-style, but make it a seated buffet. People serve themselves from the sideboard, and placecards indicate the seating at the dinner table. My children are pressed into service to pick up dinner plates, and Bill serves dessert from his place. We have coffee and after-dinner drinks in the living room.

Even though this is the simplest of procedures, it seems to take a lot of planning and preparation. First comes the decision about whom to invite.

Since I seldom have more than twelve for dinner, I try to follow this pattern: two other Senate couples, perhaps a member of our staff, a couple of newsmen and maybe a government official. I must admit I felt some trepidation when I worked out a guest list which included Mr. and Mrs. Chester Bowles, the James Restons, Senator and Mrs. John F. Kennedy, Senator and Mrs. Joseph Clark and the Walter Lippmanns for one of our first parties—but it turned out to be one of the most interesting evenings of our lives. I decided then and there that good, lively conversation is much more important than whether or not everything is served professionally or the menu is long, rich and complicated. (My children love to recall that evening and their conversation with the Kennedys. They point with pride to the chair where the Senator sat, and still comment about Mrs. Kennedy's thoughtful interest in their doings—not to mention her pink dress and glorious mink coat!)

After the invitations are out I start to stew about the menu. For some reason I decide almost every time I have a dinner party that this is the time to experiment with a new recipe. This

47

philosophy, coupled with my way of doing things, has often resulted in disaster, but I usually find out in time to substitute. Even some recipes from a White House cookbook have failed for me.

As an hors d'oeuvre I usually serve hot cheese balls that can be made and frozen ahead of time. They only need a few minutes in a hot oven after the guests have arrived. Most people have come around to the point of view that there are too many extra calories in pre-meal nibbling, so a single hors d'oeuvre is more than sufficient.

My main course is usually either chicken Tetrazzini, veal paprika, lasagna, or a seafood casserole. In the summer I often cook a large roast beef and serve it cold with a horseradish-sour cream sauce. The meal is rounded out with a vegetable, a large green salad, and home-made rolls which my mother contributes. For dessert I rely on a sherbet ring with fresh fruit, *schaum tortes* (which can be made ahead of time), or a lemon ice-box dessert.

If I am particularly rushed, I set the table as much as two days ahead of time. Flower arrangements can be done early, too, as can the polishing of silver and glassware. This method is a little dangerous if you have a nosy cat, or a toddler who can reach high enough to disarrange the place settings (and we have both), but despite these drawbacks my system has served me well.

Up until very recently, Bill and I usually did the dishes ourselves after the guests were gone. We liked this time to unwind and discuss the evening. But I finally came to the conclusion that I much preferred not confronting heaps of unwashed glasses, mountains of silver and well-depleted serving dishes at midnight. So now I have a girl come in to clean up as the evening goes along, and it's made a great difference in my disposition.

Our entertaining has fallen into something of a pattern by this time. We will have about six dinner parties, spread throughout the spring and summer. (I don't entertain in the fall because Bill is always in Wisconsin.) In June I give a party for the members of our staff and their wives. This is usually outdoors, and strictly a buffet. Then on New Year's Eve we have a few friends in for champagne and *Quiche Lorraine*. This is a "ten 'til—" and the only Proxmire function that bears any relation to a cocktail party. But people come and go, so the house is never crowded at any one time.

Of course, many Senators' wives entertain in other ways. If their lives were somewhat formal before they came to Washington they would naturally live and entertain more formally here. The real lesson I have learned from our experience is that a Senate wife is free to entertain in the manner most suitable to her home, her taste, her background and her inclinations. There are no "musts" or expected procedures. Moreover, I have found that people are enchanted to learn that a Senator's wife can cook after all.

There is a little-known occasion on which Senate wives entertain *en masse:* when we invite the First Lady to be our guest once a year in the spring. Our Senate Red Cross unit meets from January to June each Tuesday to roll bandages for hospital use. Luncheon at this time is simply coffee and sandwiches. But once a year we plan something very special.

Up until 1963, our big luncheon was held in the historic Old Supreme Court Chamber in the Capitol. With a little embellishment this chamber can be a magnificent room. It is semicircular, with a range of Ionic marble columns along the walls. Busts of ten former Chief Justices are placed around the room, and the gilded eagle that used to look down over the Vice President's Chair when the room was the Senate Chamber (from 1810 to 1859) is still in the center of the east wall. In 1935, the Supreme Court moved to its own magnificent building, and since then the room has been largely used for receptions.

49

Our 1959 luncheon for Mrs. Eisenhower had as its theme a salute to Alaska and Hawaii. Two large stars made of white flowers hung over the Justices' bench which now serves as the head table. Bright blue stars were used as plate doilies, and at each place was a fifty-star flag. The salmon had been flown in from Alaska and the fruit from Hawaii. That year, because the occasion had been postponed, it served as a farewell lunch for all of us, as well as a tribute to Mrs. Eisenhower.

In 1961 we entertained Mrs. John F. Kennedy—a former "Senate Lady" herself—for the first time. For this lunch, pink was the theme. Deep rose azalea plants stood at the door and on each end of the court bench. The tablecloths, napkins and menus were several shades of pink and rose. (By some happy coincidence, Mrs. Kennedy and her sister-in-law, Mrs. Robert Kennedy, arrived dressed in mauve-pink suits.) The head table was circular and stood in the middle of the Chamber. Fanning out from it were ten rectangular tables each with a centerpiece of pink and rose carnations. Because of Mrs. Kennedy's interest in French cuisine and in the arts, the menu was in French and the gift we gave her was a huge book of famous paintings published by the National Gallery of Art.

Mrs. Lyndon Johnson, as President of the Senate Ladies, gave the welcoming remarks, saying, "There is always special excitement in the air when we have a brand-new First Lady, as we have today. We want to say to Mrs. Kennedy, 'How delighted we are to have you with us! You have been in residence only three months, but already we—and American women everywhere—are impressed with the imaginative ideas, the gifted hand and the enchanting manner in which you have set about to make the most beloved house in America the most beautiful and gracious.'" Mrs. Kennedy responded with a graceful little speech in which she thanked us all for making her transition from Senate Lady to First Lady such an easy one. She promised to make every effort to "outdo" us when we were to be her guests later in the year.

In 1962 our luncheon for the First Lady was on May Day. The centerpieces were apricot-colored candles which served as symbols of Maypoles. Apricot and yellow streamers trailed to each place, at the ends of which were individual corsages of carnations for the 109 guests. Topping the Maypole on each of the eleven tables was an orchid flown in by Mrs. Hiram Fong, wife of the Senator from Hawaii, the evening before the luncheon. She also provided the Islands' famous macadamia nuts. The main course this time was New England boiled lobster with cold asparagus *vinaigrette*. The meal ended with fresh strawberries from Maryland's Eastern Shore, floating in thick Guernsey cream from a nearby Virginia farm.

On this occasion, Mrs. Johnson reminded us of the many historic figures who had sat in the room we then occupied—men such as Daniel Webster, Henry Clay, and Alexander Hamilton. In the early 1800's, part of the room was used as the Senate Chamber, too. Her description of the lively debate that took place then on the subject of whether or not Senators should wear wigs and robes while in session was charming and extremely interesting.

At the end of her talk Mrs. Johnson presented the First Lady with a book on Brumidi, the Italian artist whose decorations and murals cover many of the walls of official buildings in our nation's capital. Mrs. Kennedy seemed especially happy with the gift, and commented that this luncheon each year made her homesick for the less turbulent years when she, too, was a Senate wife and a "Red Cross Lady."

Senate wives from various parts of the country take part in the planning of these occasions, and the results are always worth remembering and writing about. Everyone who has ever been a Senate wife is included; thus invitations go out to some 132 women in addition to those whose husbands are currently in the

Senate. Many of these ex-Senate Ladies come from great distances. Two who invariably come every year are Mrs. A. O. Stanley of Kentucky, whose husband arrived in Washington as a Congressman in 1903 (he later was elected to the Senate), and Mrs. J. Hamilton Lewis of Illinois, whose husband took office in 1913. The luncheon always provides fond memories for those of us whose husbands are presently in the Senate and, I am sure, nostalgia for those who were here many years ago. I guess that is why they continue to come back.

Another form of entertaining with which many Senate wives become involved is the planning of big banquets, whether they are political functions, women's conventions or fund-raising events. Most housewives in this modern age, myself included, find the prospect of feeding twelve for dinner a major undertaking, and are thrown into a virtual panic if faced with feeding even twenty at a time. How do you suppose it feels to be responsible for feeding three thousand simultaneously? In order to find out, I worked on the planning of several banquets and have dug out the details of this sort of enormous undertaking.

I discovered, first of all, that the efforts of many individuals must be coordinated in order to supply and serve this small army of hungry people—in addition to a *maitre d'*, there are a chef, a steward, a sales manager who is responsible for the physical arrangements, a baker, a pastry chef, a headwaiter who must train more than two hundred waiters and waitresses for each event, a banquet captain, a banquet steward, a "food controller" and a "food checker."

Once the menu is decided upon (after consultation with the sponsors of the dinner), the wheels begin to turn to produce the proper food at the proper time in the proper amounts and at the proper temperatures. The first requirement is having sufficient equipment to handle this quantity of food.

In most households, the planning of kitchen and serving

equipment is geared to the average number of people served each day. At hotels where banquets are common occurrences, the management of kitchen facilities is a truly formidable operation. There are rotating ovens to prepare meats, sixty-to-one-hundred-gallon steam kettles for soups and sauces, huge coffee urns and rolling wagons which hold a hundred plates at one time. These wagons maintain a steady temperature of 140 degrees and can keep food for hot service for as long as an hour.

Having spent many a forty-hour week at banquet tables over the past few years, I consider myself something of an expert—on the eating end. I have yet to go to one when the food was served at the time stated on the program. I therefore was especially interested to learn how this food is kept hot without losing its quality.

If filet mignon is chosen for the main course (what lucky banquet-goers these—no creamed chicken!) the man responsible for meat selection goes out to the stockyards, selects and stamps the meat, and sees that it is properly aged. It is then frozen until the day of the dinner. If fresh fruit cocktail is the first course, the following items must be hand-prepared if three thousand people are to be served—a hundred cases of oranges, a hundred cases of grapefruits, fifty bunches of bananas, fifty cases of apples and five hundred pounds of grapes, cherries and pears! One hundred and seventy-five gallons of coffee are required.

As in most political undertakings, there are many pitfalls and endless details in this kind of professional cookery. Patience is required when constantly dealing with unfamiliar groups; there must always be a touch of originality to attract new interest, and sometimes there must be boldness and the willingness to gamble to achieve an innovation.

As Christopher Morley said, "Life is hunger, and for every emptiness caters its own just food." It takes food to produce the thought that nourishes, develops and sustains society. Many an important decision has been made at table, whether a banquet for several thousand, a business lunch, or a family get-together. Eating and the relaxation it provides seem to make the world go 'round.

An atmosphere of pleasure and relaxation as an impetus to constructive conversation is the real goal of Senate wives when they entertain. The setting can be one's own dining room, with home-cooked food and simple service, or with servants hired for the night and more elaborate menus.

Even "accidents" can often be turned to good advantage. I am reminded of a Senate wife who gave a dinner party for some visiting editors from her home state. She had carefully thought out the menu and done all the shopping herself; a competent cook arrived on schedule to prepare the dinner. The Senator's lady had chosen as a vegetable braised artichoke hearts and had purchased seven boxes of them, frozen. She trusted the cook, who, she felt, needed no instruction as to their preparation.

When the dinner was being served the hostess discovered to her horror that the cook had emptied seventeen jars of her precious marinated artichoke hearts, which she kept on hand for canapés, and was serving *them* as the vegetable of the evening. The editors commented on the unusual flavoring used to season this rare vegetable. Without admitting error, the Senate wife blithely thanked her guests for the compliment, and indicated that on this evening she was fortunate to have had with her an especially talented cook.

The setting for a dinner or luncheon can be a place such as the famous F Street Club, the most elegant spot to eat in Washington, according to our experience. Here fifty or more guests can be served a truly memorable meal, exquisitely and expensively prepared, yet the atmosphere remains warm and old-fashioned.

By trial and error, each Senate wife finds her own favorite way of entertaining. Though we try to keep social schedules as uncomplicated as possible, mix-ups do occur. I arrived at the Walter Lippmanns' for a reception one Sunday, only to discover I had the right day but the wrong week. And Senator Paul Douglas called at *our* house one evening twenty-four hours before the time of a dinner party to which he had been invited.

This kind of thing adds a certain amount of surprise and informality to what might appear to the ordinary observer a stiff and brutally institutionalized form of socializing. We do have a good time, and we do have many of the same problems that wives have everywhere when they are having a dinner party. The added "plus" is that Washington entertaining involves participants from all over the world, each with a different point of view and much to contribute. With today's jet planes and speedy communication the world is as small as a state used to be in terms of travel. This has helped give substance beyond that of caloric consumption to each social gathering, and thus lifted entertaining out of the realm of drudgery or light fun into the sphere of real warmth and mutual understanding.

Chapter V

"THE PLEASURE
OF YOUR COMPANY..."

W HEN WE first arrived in Washington, protocol to me was just a word out of old-fashioned romances or newspaper accounts of royal doings. Its rules and restrictions seemed so out of place in modern America that I had never really given its existence much thought. However, every Senate wife must familiarize herself with what is expected of her soon after settling down in Washington, and protocol becomes part of her existence, even though it does have its humorous aspects.

If, as in my own case, your previous way of life has been informal and unordered (disorderly might be a better word), it is hard to get used to this rigid type of formality. In Wisconsin, Bill and I had never even had printed stationery, much less printed calling cards. We had never used placecards at table, much less were we concerned about the "rank" of our guests or who was to be seated to our right or left. Bill didn't own a dress suit (as common a uniform in Washington as the conservative business suit), much less would he ever have had occasion to wear one. (It is hard for some Easterners to comprehend the existence of a year's social calendar without a single "black-tie" event, but in Wisconsin he never attended or was invited to a full-dress affair, even as a candidate for high office.) And I sincerely doubt that before the election we had ever received a printed invitation to anything other than a wedding or graduation. (Invitations to the White House are not only printed, they are in engraved script—including your name!)

Now, social life was to be run by a new rule book. In the spirit of "when in Rome . . . ," I set about to do research on it as seriously as any student. Mastering the ins and outs of protocol wasn't quite as hard as learning a foreign language, but almost.

Before World War II there were specified "calling days" when Cabinet, Senate, and Supreme Court homes and the Embassies were open to callers. And "making a call" meant just that and only that. When a card was left at the East Gate of the White House, the caller never expected to go beyond the gate. Between 1900 and 1940, Congressional wives spent as many as three days a week "calling on" the homes they were expected to and the other three days sitting at home waiting for people to call on them. It must have been frightfully stiff and uncomfortable, especially since the whole procedure was so regimented.

There are no longer any special days to make calls, but some people still expect the new Congressional wife to leave her card at the White House, at the door of the Vice President's home, at the homes of the majority leader, of members of the home state Congressional delegation and of her husband's fellow committee members. So far no one has left a card at our house, nor have I followed the rules in this way, but for those who really wish to be formal about things, this is how it's done.

Moreover, according to the rules, there is a certain way in which to leave cards. In order to indicate that cards have been delivered in person, their upper right-hand corners should be turned down. Traditionally, a woman should leave one of her own cards for each lady in the house and one of her husband's cards for each adult member of the family, male or female. For example, if I were to "call" at the White House, I would leave *one* of my cards and *two* of Bill's.

Social procedure in its strictest form differs in many ways from that followed "back home." In Washington, a husband precedes his wife down a receiving line. In the Midwest that would be considered terribly rude!

In Washington, a newcomer is responsible for making first calls; whereas in the average "home town," long-time residents customarily call on the newcomer to extend welcome.

Back home the *purpose* of a call is to become personally acquainted; in Washington, if a Congressional wife follows strict procedure and "makes calls," she never expects to see the person on whom she is calling. Here, if an honor guest is of sufficient rank he leaves a party *first*. Back home, the honor guest is expected to stay until the last dog is hung!

Despite the rather archaic quality of much of this social rigmarole, there are quite a few rules that are still followed to the letter—particularly when an invitation to the White House appears in the mailbox.

In the first place, an invitation to the home of the President and First Lady is considered a "must," unless illness or some other emergency interferes. The invitation itself is beautiful enough to frame, with its United States seal in gold, its handwritten engraved script and the fine texture of the stock. An "admit card" is enclosed with every invitation. It must be preserved and presented to the sentry at the gate indicated. In addition there is a small card which says "black tie" or "white tie" and another card with the RSVP information. Usually you are asked to reply to the Social Secretary of the White House. Secondly, it is not considered either polite or politic to be late to a White House function; everyone more or less arrives *en masse* and later departs as a group.

The one occasion when Bill and I attended a formal White

House dinner we were almost late! It wouldn't have mattered so much if we were just going to an ordinary dinner party, but I knew the "rules," and, what's more, had looked forward to this night with great anticipation. As it happened, we had been unable to attend the first dinner to which we were invited, in November, 1961—the now famous one at which Pablo Casals performed— for I had just given birth to our son Douglas. So when the invitation arrived for the dinner honoring André Malraux, the French Minister of Culture, I was determined that we would go, and my plans were geared to making it an unharried, spectacular evening.

Bill's staff was instructed to shoo him out of the office in plenty of time to arrive home by 7:15. That would give him a good twenty-five minutes to bathe, dress, and get to the White House by eight. I had carefully laid out his dress clothes and was positive I had checked on all the necessities.

I then proceeded to get dressed in order to be ready ahead of time. In 1960 I had appeared in a *Life* magazine picture story showing Congressional wives modeling the latest fashions. As a surprise, Bill had bought me the dress I wore in a lovely color picture for that article. It was a long red brocade gown, the only long dress I owned. As I zipped it up the back, much to my horror the zipper absolutely disintegrated. Mary Ellen, my fifteen-year-old, was desperately trying to sew me into the dress when my husband arrived home at twenty to eight.

Bill was rushing around and I was bordering on hysteria when he discovered that I had gathered together everything he needed except his black bow tie. We began frantically scrambling through drawers and closets, but couldn't find it anywhere. Bill jumped in the car, drove down the street to a tailor shop, bought another one, returned and picked me up, and we were off at last. I insisted that Bill stand close behind me all evening for fear the amateur patch-up job wouldn't hold. My nervousness about all this slightly dampened my enthusiasm for the marvelous food served that night, but despite everything, we had a good time.

We were the last of the 150 guests to arrive. From a silver bowl a military aide handed us our table numbers, and then immediately ushered us into the East Room where the line of guests was forming. At a formal dinner of this kind an aide announces each guest as he passes through from the foyer. The Kennedys have dispensed with a receiving line for large receptions, but they do employ it at formal dinners for visiting dignitaries. It was the line-up of guests and the glorious gowns that drew my attention this time rather than the new look of many of the White House rooms. Recognizable on sight—and thrilling to see—were famous faces from the world of the theater and literature: Julie Harris, Tennessee Williams, John Hersey, Geraldine Page, Charles and Anne Lindbergh, Agnes deMille and her husband, Mr. and Mrs. Arthur Miller, Thornton Wilder, Adlai Stevenson, Leonard Bernstein, Irwin Shaw and George Balanchine, to name a few.

I remember that Geraldine Page wore a flowing white Grecian chiffon dress, and that Mrs. Kennedy looked exquisite in a hot-pink strapless gown by Dior. All the men looked about the same in their "black-tie" uniform, but I do recall one congressman who wore an Austrian emerald-green jacket with brass buttons and a ruffled shirt. Seeing him, Bill felt downright conservative in his plain-front shirt, midnight-blue suit, and the patent leather shoes he had worn in his Yale days some twenty-three years before.

We greeted the President and his wife as we passed through the receiving line, chatting for a minute with them about the President's scheduled trip to Milwaukee the next day. We told him how excited everyone at home was about his visit, the first one he had made to our state since before Election Day.

Twelve small tables had been set up in the State Dining Room and five in the Blue Room. If it had been a royal affair, it couldn't have been more beautiful. I will never forget the gleaming crystal, the gold-plated flatware, the lovely spring flowers and the soft music that accompanied the meal. Dinner was French and superb. It began with jellied consommé *madrilène* with caviar and sour cream, and ended with cream puffs.

One of my dinner partners talked to me about the theater, a delight for me because usually it's politics from first course to last. The other of my partners was from the French Embassy. Though I majored in French in college, it is decidedly rusty, but we had fun talking about the places he had been in the United States and what else he wanted to see before his tour in Washington was over. There is a certain procedure followed at more formal dinner parties in Washington that was new to me. Somewhere between the main course and the salad, those sitting next to each other at table "switch partners," so to speak, and chat with the guest on their other side. Sometimes I forget as I get immersed in an interesting conversation, but that is the procedure that is expected. Bill and I try to remember.

There were toasts both humorous and serious by M. Malraux and the President. The President gave his toast first, and I recall it was one of the most interesting and humorous I have ever heard. He said:

"Ladies and Gentlemen: I want to express a very warm welcome to all of you, and particularly to our distinguished guests, Monsieur and Madame Malraux.

"This will be the first speech about relations between France and the United States that does not include a tribute to General Lafayette. It seems that almost every Frenchman who comes to the United States feels that Lafayette was a rather confused sort of ineffectual, elderly figure, hovering over French politics, and is astonished to find that we regard him as a golden, young, romantic figure—next to George Washington, our most distinguished citizen. Therefore he will not be mentioned, but instead I will mention a predecessor of mine, John Adams, who was our first President to live in the White House and whose prayer on occupancy is written here. John Adams asked that on his grave-stone be written, 'He kept the peace with France.'

"I am very glad to welcome here some of our most distin-guished artists. This is becoming a sort of eating place for artists. But they never ask us out. I want to tell you how very pleased we are to have so many distinguished writers and artists and actresses and creative thinkers.

"You know, one of the great myths of American life is that nothing is pleasanter or easier than lying around all day and painting a picture or writing a book and leading a rather easy life. In my opinion, the ultimate in self-discipline is creative work. Those of us who work in an office every day are actually the real gentle livers of American society...

"... We regard [M. Malraux] as an honored guest in this country, as participants in the cultural stream, and also as admir-ers of those who travel the far horizons of human destiny...

"I know that there are sometimes difficulties in life but I hope that those who live in both our countries realize how fortunate we are in the last two decades to be associated in the great effort with him. And we are glad to have Monsieur Malraux and Ma-dame Malraux here because we believe that they will go back to France and say a kind word for the United States—and its President.

"So I hope you will drink to all of us, in the sense that you are leaders in our free society—and particularly to our distinguished leader whom we are very glad to have with us tonight—and most especially to drink to the President of France, General de Gaulle."

After coffee all of us moved into the marble foyer to mingle, sip champagne and listen to the Air Force Strolling Strings. I en-joyed this method of handling after-dinner activity much more than the more formal and frequently used system of separating the men from the women for after-dinner drinks and coffee.

Even though the musical program didn't get under way until well after 11:00 P.M., all the assembled guests quickly fell under the spell of the exquisite music-making. Eugene Istomin, Isaac Stern and Leonard Rose superbly performed a Schubert trio.

The President and Mrs. Kennedy stayed downstairs until 12:45, making this night one of the latest official affairs I had heard of at the White House.

It was an evening to remember, one far removed from the ordinary simplicity of our everyday lives and for that reason very special. Since there were only three Senators and one Congressman present that night, subjects other than politics were discussed, and we had an opportunity to forget, if only briefly, the struggles of the day, to mingle with those who have devoted their lives to other fields of endeavor, and to be reminded of those who have passed before through the door of the White House.

There are other types of White House functions we have attended—five luncheons given by the First Lady for the wives of Senators, and several Congressional receptions. Each of these has its own quality, and each demonstrates the varied nature of White House entertaining.

I remember reading somewhere that Mrs. Eisenhower's favorite color is pink. At her 1959 lunch there were pink azaleas, pink snapdragons, pink tulips, pink tablecloths and a real fountain (not pink) in the center of the State Dining Room. As a memento of the occasion, each of us received a souvenir pink engraving of the White House mounted on gold. The food was simple and multi-colored. For the first course we were served cold consommé. Then came breaded veal, fresh asparagus and rice. For dessert there was a lemon mold topped with cherries. People frequently ask me if the food at the White House is good, and I can truthfully say it is outstandingly so. I have never had finer food, more beautifully prepared and served, anywhere.

Mrs. Eisenhower rarely spoke in public, but at her 1960

luncheon, which was a "farewell" occasion, she did. She spoke briefly of how much she had enjoyed her association with the wives of Senators over the eight years she and her husband had been in the White House. She concluded with a quiet, obviously heartfelt "God bless you *all*."

To the music of the Marine Band, all of us left the White House that afternoon to return to the problems of traffic jams, meals to be planned, letters to be answered and a very important year—a Presidential election year—to be lived. I couldn't help but wonder then which of the women present would be sitting at the head table as First Lady the following year, for all the prospective ones were with us that day—Mrs. Hubert Humphrey, Mrs. Lyndon Johnson, Mrs. Stuart Symington, Mrs. Richard Nixon, and Mrs. John F. Kennedy. Mrs. Kennedy had been seated at my table of ten that year, together with Mrs. Charles McNary, whose husband had been Senator from Oregon from 1917 to 1944, and Mrs. Owen Brewster of Maine. They and I discussed future possibilities. Mrs. Kennedy refused to look that far ahead, and I don't blame her. After all, there were still the National Conventions and the arduous campaign to go through. Since she was also expecting a child at the time, I can imagine that just the prospect of all that lay ahead was so staggering as not to bear thinking about.

But the Democratic Convention *did* nominate John F. Kennedy for the Presidency, he *did* win the election that fall, and it was Mrs. Kennedy—now the mother of a husky son—who greeted us in the Blue Room at the annual Senate Luncheon in 1961. I noted several changes as soon as I arrived. Instead of using the more formal Pennsylvania Avenue entrance, we were met at the Southwest Gate and thus were allowed to enjoy the lush expanse of lawn, the fountains and the curved walk on the way in. Instead of formal placecards, each of us drew a table number out of a silver bowl in the entrance hall. Instead of having a head table, Mrs. Kennedy sat among us at one of the thirteen tables. Not knowing who would sit with the First Lady added an element of anticipation and surprise to the occasion. Mrs. Lyndon Johnson and the Cabinet wives each sat at a table as a kind of hostess, so the distant head table was no more. It was a fine change.

And instead of every head carrying some gay, flowered spring creation, I noticed that many were hatless. That reminded me of the time Mrs. Kennedy had sat at my table in 1960. She had whispered to me that the large black velvet bow attached to the front of her bouffant coiffure was a last-minute gesture to proper attire for a White House luncheon, since she hadn't been able to find a hat. Thus is fashion set.

Spring and a light, informal touch were evident in both the decor and the menu. The magnificent green and gold State Dining Room was sparkling with white tablecloths, green and gold china and centerpieces of yellow and white Shasta daisies. The engraved menu cards at each place told us that we were to have cold lobster, capon, tiny browned potatoes, green beans and almonds, pineapple sherbet and cookies. Demitasses were served in the Blue Room after lunch. Once again we had been treated to a brief glimpse of a lovely fairyland. Though informality was evident in the many hatless heads and the loose bouquets of spring flowers, the occasion was elegant and memorable.

Each year, the President and his wife give a reception for all the members of the House and Senate and their wives. Since about a thousand people usually attend, these functions have an entirely different character from the luncheons and formal dinners. But just as in the luncheons, these receptions reflect the new look of the New Frontier.

Before 1961, most Members of Congress usually regarded these "must" affairs as chores which involved wearing white-tie-and-tails (which many had to rent for the occasion) and standing wearily in line before a long walk through a formal receiving line. This took up most of the two and a half hours allotted to the reception, and guests felt fortunate to get close enough to the punch bowl to see that there actually was one.

Now, black tie has replaced white tie for men's formal dress, and short dresses are allowed. The receiving line has disappeared and guests are permitted to move freely through the Blue, Red, and Green Rooms, the East Room and the State Dining Room.

I especially recall the reception in 1962. Banks of colorful spring flowers brightened every corner. There was music in the East Room for those who wanted to dance. Buffet tables running the full length of both the East Room and the State Dining Room were laden with hearty, exquisitely prepared food. Silver trays were piled with cold roast beef, smoked salmon, turkey, *paté de foie gras* and ham. Crystal bowls filled with ice held mounds of raw vegetables. There was champagne punch and a great variety of French pastry on tiered trays. Horns-of-plenty overflowing with fresh fruit provided the centerpiece. The only other decorations took the form of whole hams glazed in white, turkeys draped with fruit, and pheasants with feathers, each sitting on their respective trays of meat.

Despite the fact that many of us have been acquainted with the President and First Lady for years, there is a noticeable and altogether natural difference in the freedom one now feels in conversation with them. They attempt, and succeed eminently, to offset this by talking about subjects that are particularly close to the person with whom they are conversing. Their skill and thoughtfulness in this area makes everyone relax and almost forget the impressive surroundings.

Embassy parties are another category of affair that falls within the context of the word "official." There are more than a hundred embassies in Washington now, so there is endless choice among luncheons, cocktail parties, garden parties and even midnight buffets after the opening of a play. Even though each one of them is in its way a fascinating occasion, we seldom have time to sample all the available "fruit."

Embassy luncheons here and there around town are one aspect of social life that I usually pass up because most of them take three hours, thus making it impossible to use the rest of the day effectively. In addition, it is hard on the waistline to eat a full meal in the middle of the day.

However, I was lucky enough to be able to attend a luncheon given by Madame Avraham Harman, the wife of the Ambassador from Israel, early in 1963. Madame Harman had invited two other Senate wives, the wives of the Ambassadors from New Zealand, Togo, and Yugoslavia, Mrs. Ernest K. Lindley (wife of the columnist) and the superb South African singer, Miriam Makeba. With such a varied and imposing guest list there was little chit-chat, and much discussion of world travel and national customs.

The highlight of the afternoon was hearing Miriam Makeba describe her flight from hate-ridden South Africa. Harry Belafonte had heard her performance in a political film that had been made in secret in Johannesburg. He urged her to come to the United States for concerts with him, and she applied for a passport in 1957. Because Miss Makeba is a Negro and was politically controversial, it was two years before she was allowed to leave. After her departure, her participation in the film came to light, making it unlikely that she will ever be able to return home again. All her grief and despair for the plight of her people shines through her singing, which she demonstrated for us with an Israeli song, a Negro spiritual, and a South African song.

The delightful thing about official life in today's Washington is that, whereas the rules are still there, they are neither as binding nor as restrictive as they have been in the past. Vestiges remain to give us a framework within which to operate and to provide, occasionally, a taste of the pomp of earlier days. But it is

67

now possible for overburdened officials to relax, to get to know one another informally, and to participate in what is termed "proper" and "protocol" without dread or hesitation.

To prove this theory, the Women's National Press Club writes and stages a spoof each year that is truly professional and ticklingly funny. No one who plays a part in official life in Washington is allowed to escape, nor is any side of the Washington scene left unscathed. This occasion—like the all-stag Gridiron Dinner, about which we women hear—is the surest sign to me that there is truly an "officialdom," but that nobody, not even the President of the United States, is such a "sacred cow" that he can't be kidded a little.

Spoofing our Vice President's Texas-style entertaining, whether his guests be royalty, UN delegates, or a group of local ranchers, some Press Club members sang to the tune of "Home on the Range":

> "Home, home on the ranch
> Where the deer and convertibles roam
> Where the Senators play
> Where there's company all day
> And the stars above spell LBJ."

One can guarantee that when a barbecue is served on the banks of the Pendernales River, no one worries too much about rank.

And remembering the many changes in the White House since the occupancy of the Kennedys, a reporter impersonating "Jackie" sang to the tune of "There'll Be Some Changes Made":

> "I've made a change in the White
>   House—as you saw on TV
> My new decor is making history
> I'll redo the Mall and the Capitol too
> Re-hang Mellon's Gallery in Red,
>   White, and Blue."

There will always be dedications, unveilings, state visitors, and formal receptions, and there are invitations to all of these in each week's mail, but current practices have proven that they mustn't necessarily be rigid, cold affairs. They can become warm memories, glorious occasions far removed from the humdrum or hubbub of our daily lives.

Chapter VI

LEAVE IT TO
THE LADIES

SEVERAL TIMES when my husband has gone to Boston to make a speech, he has been met at the airport by a man who is known as the Mayor's "Official Greeter." Believe it or not, this is a specific job with specific responsibilities, and the gentleman has a printed calling card on which his name and title are inscribed.

It made me feel more useful when I heard that being an "Official Greeter" was a full-time job for a few appointed individuals in cities across the country, for it is about one-third of the job of Congressional wives, and a very important part of our role in Washington. Another third of our official time is spent, I would guess, in charity work for various organizations, and a final third in keeping informed on the issues of the day. The practice of meeting in a partisan way with our fellow Congressional wives enables us to learn from each other and keeps us up to date on new campaign ideas and the latest techniques for being effective helpers in our husbands' work. This adds an extra dimension to our lives and, we hope, to the lives of those around us.

Every spring Washington fairly bursts with everything from blossoms to broken heat records, from tourists to the DAR—

2,000 strong—from editors to visiting VIP's from all over the world.

Usually, sudden 90-degree heat brings out all the flowering shrubs in the city at once; it almost seems to happen overnight. The cherry blossoms, forsythia and crocus are first, and often, while they are still in bloom, out come the dogwood, the tulips and the azaleas. The abundance of brilliant color makes the city look its best for the million or more visitors who flood in from all parts of the country. Well over half of these are high school students who come here on their senior trip, an annual pilgrimage for most graduating classes from near and far.

Chartered busses clog the streets, gaily dressed groups of young people pour out of hotels and restaurants, tens of thousands of pictures are taken and the vendors who sell ice cream on a stick do a land-office business. Because a great many of the tourists who arrive in Washington head straight for the office of their Congressman or Senator, Congressional wives often bear the responsibility of showing them the town.

We become "Official Greeters" without the advantages of an expense account, a chauffeur-driven Cadillac, or a police escort. We have even had to figure out how Washington can be seen in one day.

My own experiences have taught me that it is best to start off in the cool of the early morning with a tour of the White House. A call from our office to the White House ahead of time will facilitate a special tour. Visitors are not allowed in the First Family's living quarters, but guides will take them through the main entrance, to the East Room where the President and his wife entertain on state occasions, through the Blue, Red, and Green Rooms and into the formal State Dining Room.

The next stop after the White House is usually the Washington Monument. From the pinnacle of this stark white shaft a panoramic view of Washington is yours at a glance. The hardier souls always want to climb the 898 steps to the top, but elevators are available for those who want to save their strength for the rest of the day.

The third stop on this "bare bones" tour is the Lincoln Memorial. This breathtaking marble temple on the brink of the Potomac River fills even the most blasé visitor with awe. As a child, when my parents took me to this, their favorite spot, I always begged to climb up in Lincoln's lap. I still have to resist the impulse.

If time allows, we drive around the Tidal Basin for a glimpse of the stunning Jefferson Memorial before heading to the more practical world of the Almighty Dollar—the Bureau of Engraving and Printing. Here each of our guests can see money being printed, trimmed and counted in staggering quantities. Youngsters always inquire whether or not free samples are distributed but, sad to say, this is one instance in which federal money is not available for the asking!

The sixth and last stop before lunch is the Federal Bureau of Investigation. Here is the splashiest government show in Washington, a tour that will explode any possible theories that crime pays. Special displays are built around the solution of front-page crimes. There are conducted tours of some of the labs, and a final stop down in the basement firing range where the FBI agents practice marksmanship. Here there are free samples of shell casings for those who want to take them home.

After luncheon, we suggest that the time between 1:30 and 3:00 P.M. be spent on Capitol Hill. This includes a tour of the Capitol itself, a ride on the shortest subway in the world (from the Capitol to the Senate Office Buildings), and short stops at the Supreme Court and the Library of Congress.

From the Capitol the tour then heads across the Potomac for Virginia. Along the route all the major government buildings can be seen. At a brief stop at the Pentagon we see the huge and busy concourse of the world's largest office building.

Our tour usually ends with a visit to the Lee Mansion, followed by the white stillness of Arlington National Cemetery and the Tombs of the Three Unknown Soldiers.

In the space of nine hours our guests can catch the flavor of this magnificent city and the workings of government it houses. No matter how brief the visit, most of our guests tell us they come away with a feeling of historic reverence for the past and a revealing glimpse into the exacting activity of the present. Many Congressional wives play a vital role in tourists' introduction to and memories of this very special city.

Besides helping those from our home states when they are in Washington, most of us, by inclination and interest, want to help those in need in the District. This type of Congressional participation takes many forms.

The Senate wives have a Red Cross group which meets regularly to fold bandages for local hospitals; there is a Congressional Circle for Friendship House, an interracial day-care center near Capitol Hill; many of us work in behalf of the Lighthouse for the Blind or for the Florence Crittenton Home for Unwed Mothers. We raise money, serve on committees, act as sponsors, donate old clothes or favorite recipes for bazaars, and make door-to-door calls for everything from the United Givers Fund to the Metropolitan Police Boys Club.

The two activities with which I am most deeply involved are the Senate Ladies Red Cross group and the Congressional Circle for Friendship House. Being a part of these groups allows us to make a contribution to local charities, much as we would do in our own home towns, and at the same time permits us to play a role that is, at least momentarily, outside the clamorous arena of partisan politics.

All Senate wives are invited to attend the weekly Tuesday meeting of the Senate Ladies Red Cross group as soon as they arrive in Washington. Each wife of a sitting Senator is automatically a member of the group and, once a member, is always maintained on the mailing list. Many of the wives whose husbands are no longer in the Senate (either retired, defeated, or deceased) attend the meetings regularly, so all of us have a chance to know those who preceded us and to learn from them.

As a matter of fact, I had never met a member of Wisconsin's illustrious La Follette family until I became acquainted with Mrs. Robert La Follette, Jr., in our Red Cross meetings. Though her home was in Wisconsin, she remained in Washington when her husband died in 1948. She, too, is now dead, but I treasure the conversations we had, the insights she gave me into the history of Wisconsin and also what is expected of those in public life.

A history of the Senate Ladies, as the organization of Senate wives is known, goes back to 1917. In that year, Mrs. Key Pittmann, wife of the late Senator from Nevada, issued the first call "in the service of our country" and twenty-five Senate wives responded.

Instead of meeting in the Capitol as they do now, the women gathered at Wadsworth House to sew and make surgical dressings one morning a week. After World War I, such close friendships had been formed that the regular Tuesday luncheons were continued. Some said at the time that the hours were filled with much talk and little work, but even though the war effort was a thing of the past, Red Cross activities never once were stopped. By 1938 the group had expanded so much that a sewing machine had to be bought and knitting was added to the list of skills expected of the Senate wives.

When the Second World War came to the United States that fateful day in December, 1941, the Senate Ladies were ready to go into action again. They decided this time to concentrate on surgical dressings for the Army and to meet two full days a week. The women became so expert that the Red Cross reported that the work of their unit was one of a very few efforts which did not have to be rechecked. Between January, 1942, and June, 1945, a total of 337,990 surgical dressings were made by the Senate Ladies, a task involving a total of 27,592 hours of work.

The minutes of the organization and the memorabilia going back to World War I include letters from such prominent women as Mrs. Woodrow Wilson, Mrs. Alben Barkley, Mrs. John Nance Garner and Mrs. Arthur Vandenberg. The gavel that is used today in conducting our meetings was presented by Frances Parkinson Keyes as a gift to the club when she was just beginning to test her literary wings. The sugar and cream pitchers we use were given to the organization by Mrs. Herbert Lehman when her husband left the Senate. All these are souvenirs of a historic as well as a sentimental nature—reminders that the present is securely linked to the past and that we have much in common with those who have preceded us.

Today the work goes on. Now we concentrate on surgical dressings for the Bethesda Naval Hospital outside Washington. Because of the extreme accuracy necessary, the hospital accepts only our output and that of one church group. Occasionally the comment is heard that the work is simple and unstimulating. To many it seems incredible that the wives of U.S. Senators would sit around once a week to fold bandages in this high-powered age. But I find the Senate Ladies group offers me one of the few opportunities I have to meet the other Senate wives informally, to share common problems, to visit unhurriedly in quiet surroundings, and at the same time perform some worthwhile service for others. It is unlikely that we would get to know each other this well if it weren't for these Tuesday meetings.

The work of Congressional wives at Friendship House is of a different variety. Basically, our efforts represent the desire to demonstrate here at home our ability to live together in understanding and felicity. For Friendship House is an interracial daycare center for seventy-five children from the ages of three to ten.

The historically fascinating building which houses this community center is located only a few blocks from the Capitol. The daily work of those who supervise this complicated undertaking is an "open opportunity for investment in friendship." The main goal of the work at Friendship House is to improve community and family life in the difficult neighborhood which surrounds it.

The house itself is one of the oldest in Washington. It was built before the Revolution and was originally a pioneer cabin in the midst of thick woods. During the War of 1812 it was used as a military hospital, and in 1815 Francis Scott Key bought it as his home. The house was subsequently owned first by Senator Clayton of Delaware, and then by Mrs. Emily Edson Briggs, one of the first women journalists in America. Famous visitors there have included George Washington, the Marquis de Lafayette, Daniel Webster, Henry Clay, John Calhoun and Abraham Lincoln.

Much of the historic charm still exists in the ivy-covered brickwork and the layout of the rooms. But today the ballroom is a theater, another large room the gym, and the stairway to the old "smoking porch" is now the central feature of the Children's Playroom. It is especially significant that a building so rich in tradition should be the home and symbol of tasks we must face today and in the future to improve the lot of mankind and to learn to live together in peace.

Friendship House is an oasis for several hundred families in a desert of deprivation, broken homes and bleak futures. The children who come each day frequently receive their only square meal in our dining room. Care which used to be primarily custodial in the earlier days of day-care centers, now emphasizes child development and guidance. Trained personnel do complete social histories of each child, and families are visited on a systematic basis.

Because sound development of children is the first step in helping them become self-reliant members of society, at Friendship House the emphasis is on the young. But there are also opportunities for adults to broaden their lives. There are after-school clubs and sports for teenagers (some of whom move their gangs from the street corners to the warm and friendly atmosphere of Friendship House), evening lecture programs, art and ceramics classes (often taught by Congressional wives), a book discussion group, the Capitol Hill Players, a monthly forum for the discussion of current issues, and an interracial community council which concerns itself with community planning.

Each month the Congressional Wives' Circle for Friendship House meets with the Director of the Center, and each year we plan a money-raising project which provides necessary funds (from $3,000 to $10,000) for expansion purposes, for needed furniture and personnel.

Our Friendship House and others like it can become the core around which we demonstrate the validity of our democratic ideals and thus become a real show-window for democracy. Here future members of the Peace Corps might well do some on-the-job training, for here I have seen it daily demonstrated that it is possible for people to unlearn their fears of one another.

My own interests have carried me into other pursuits above and beyond pure charity work. In 1961 the United Nations Information Center here in Washington desperately needed volunteer help. Since I enjoy doing research, I was asked to summarize for news distribution the participation of the United Nations in the Congo. Because the procedures at headquarters in New York tend to be complicated and wordy, it is hard to find a brief record of action on a particular subject. My assignment gave me an opportunity to read through the daily records of debate and action, to sift out the pertinent decisions, and to present the material in chronological form. I later did the same thing on the record of votes concerning the admission of Red China to the United Nations. This work was a new experience for me; since Bill concentrates on domestic economic affairs, my U.N. work enabled me to keep him informed about at least some of the latest developments on the international scene and to ease his burden of research and reading.

On the lighter side, Congressional wives are frequently called on to assist the Board of Trade when a local celebration is being planned. One such occasion is the spring Cherry Blossom Festival which annually brings throngs of visitors to Washington. Each of the fifty State Societies is responsible for selecting a Cherry Blossom Princess to represent it during the four-day gala. For the presentation of the princesses at the Cherry Blossom Lunch, tradition dictates that a Senator or a Congressman be asked to escort his state's princess down the runway when she is introduced for the first time. Naturally, none other than the wife of a Senator is asked to be the Chairman of the Escort Committee! It sounds simple enough, as do all these jobs when you are first approached, but there is many an obstacle between the invitation and the achievement.

When Mrs. Clair Engle of California was Chairman of the Committee, everything went smoothly until the week before the event. At that point Congressional leadership decided that this particular week was the time for an Easter recess. Mrs. Engle was left with the stupendous job of getting substitute escorts at the last minute, and with the more difficult task of calming irate mothers whose daughters had been deprived of what mama considered their inherent right—the presence of a Senator beside the little darling as she walked down the aisle.

I held the job of Committee Chairman for two years. One year everything went smoothly. The next year everything went wrong. According to customary procedure, I first scanned the Congressional Directory for the name of the Senior Senator from each state. (He is the first person asked to be the escort unless a princess is the daughter or granddaughter of a Senator or Representative.) After final selection of fifty escorts, each must receive a written request, asking that he respond by a certain date.

The second year I was Chairman, our deadline came and went with many responses not in. (Actually, it is difficult for any Senator to commit himself to a midday engagement.) I sat down to make phonecalls to round up the strays.

Finally I had a complete list. Everyone seemed happy. The day before the event each office was called again to make sure there hadn't been any last-minute changes. The night before the big event, I learned to my horror that a Joint Session of Congress had been called for noon the following day. There went my list of Congressional escorts—or so it seemed when I heard the news. The time of the luncheon was moved ahead, wires were sent to all fifty, and calls were made again the next morning. Somehow none of the princesses or anyone in the audience of a thousand was disappointed, but the unexpected had come mighty close to ruining months of planning and preparation—just another example of the sometimes perilous life of a political wife.

I have also been a Congressional liaison worker for the National Cultural Center, Chairman of the Speakers Bureau for the Women's Division of the Democratic National Committee during a campaign, editor of a small paper for Congressional wives, and the author of a column for Wisconsin newspapers. I am not alone in this last activity. Wives of six other Senators do the same. Together our columns appear in nearly two hundred newspapers around the country—mostly weeklies—but a few metropolitan dailies are included.

We cover a great variety of subjects in these columns. According to C. P. Trussell, who commented on our various columns in a New York *Times* article: "There is a minimum of chit-chat. Newly arrived politicians are pictured as they adjust themselves to Washington and word pictures take constituents into Senators' offices.

"Home state readers travel through the columns, with the wives when they accompany Senators to strange lands. Gardening tips come direct from top experts, and the difficulty of house-hold logistics for the wives of busy Congressmen is passed on to the home readers. Unusual tasks to which Senatorial staffs are assigned are revealed and there are descriptions of events they attend to which ordinary reporters are sometimes not invited."

Other Senatorial wives who have joined me in this type of "amateur reporting" are Mrs. Wallace F. Bennett of Utah, Mrs. Prescott Bush (wife of the former Senator from Connecticut), Mrs. John Sherman Cooper of Kentucky, Mrs. Jacob Javits of New York, and Mrs. Gale W. McGee of Wyoming.

Besides "doing," we gather to learn, too. One organization that provides this type of "education" for me is the Democratic Congressional Wives' Forum. It was organized in 1954 by a popular vote of Democratic Congressional wives who wanted a group meeting where they could discuss common problems and become better acquainted with one another. This organization, composed exclusively of Democratic Congressmen's wives, meets once a month during the Congressional sessions.

Our main objective is to promote understanding of legislative issues and political and campaign problems through informal discussion.

By hearing about the scattered responsibilities other wives have to live with regularly and about their own particular campaign hardships, we are better able to gain perspective on our own problems. At one meeting I recall in detail, six Congressional wives described their recent campaign trauma. Three of the speakers had been deeply involved in their husbands' campaigns in the South. The unexpected difficulties they encountered provided a new and harsh experience for them. They met opposition—both in the primaries and from a rising Republican movement—for the first time. The way each man met the new challenge was fascinating.

Mrs. Lister Hill, whose distinguished husband had been in

Congress for forty years, described the hard-campaigning Republican opposition they had faced—a photogenic couple who concentrated on TV (the wife was a former Miss Alabama). For the Hills, the entire pre-election effort was beset by mishaps. Mrs. Hill was on crutches throughout the campaign, having slipped and fallen just before leaving Washington in June; Lister had had to remain in Washington until three weeks before the election. Because of the short space of time left, they concentrated on television, on Lister's record and on a documentary film. It almost didn't work. For the first time in their forty years in public office, they almost lost an election. Mrs. Hill told us that "never had she been prouder of a victory."

The same pattern developed in two other Southern states. Carrie Davis, Representative Clifford Davis' wife, described her efforts in a Tennessee Congressional district and Mrs. Homer Thornberry in an Austin, Texas, Congressional district. They told of aprons made by and for the Ladies' Committees, special billboards with a clever twist, hundreds of "coffees," speeches by long-distance phones when the Congressman couldn't be at meetings, and the use of TV in an increasingly professional way.

To illustrate the unpredictable nature of their experiences, Mrs. Davis told of the time her husband said, "Carrie, I hope you won't be too upset, but it's getting around that *you* are ironing the aprons for the Davis committee. If it comes out tomorrow in the newspapers, don't lose heart; even if it isn't true, let's let it stand." Carrie laughed and then realized that they had seen so little of each other during the campaign that he couldn't possibly have known that ironing aprons was exactly what she *had* been doing every morning between 6:30 and 8:00 A.M.!

The wife of the new Democratic Senator from rock-ribbed Republican New Hampshire brought us the story of their unique adventures. Because they had had meager funds and little state-wide organization, Senator Tom McIntyre and his wife had had to rely on clever gimmicks and round-the-clock work. Instead of leaflets, they passed out packets of Chanel No. 5 at plant gates, county fairs and picnics. The picture of political busses, literature, and campaign headquarters reeking of perfume is almost comical, but it seemed to do the trick.

This exchange of ideas shows that there are as many gimmicks and fresh ideas as there are candidates and races. We learn from each other's experiences, add a dash of our own originality, and try to come up with something new and appealing. In these ways we can make some contribution to our husbands' careers.

It is easy to see why political wives in general and Congressional wives in particular occasionally feel like "split personalities." We recognize in ourselves daily the reality of the cartoon which depicts an irate wife accosting her husband over the evening newspaper with these words: "The trouble with you is that you live in a little world of your own—the Middle East crisis, the Far East crisis, Berlin, the national economy, segregation, integration, government, Laos—just a little world of your own!"

Chapter VII

CAPITAL PUNISHMENT

THERE are two subjects on which everyone considers himself an authority—politics and the weather. In fact, if it weren't for Washington's unpredictable weather, people here would have to talk about politics all the time—and that would be disastrous. Both winter and summer mercury are real factors in a politician's life here.

I grew up in Washington and somehow remembered in great detail mild winters, balmy days in January and even crocuses blooming in February. As luck would have it, several Washington winters since 1957 have been extremely severe and reminiscent of the bitterness and intensity of Wisconsin winters. My husband has never ceased to remind me of my predictions about the pleasant change in store for us, and it has grown into a regular family joke.

The most frequently heard question during the winter months is, "Why does Washington go to pieces every time it snows?" In order to find out from the source whether or not this is so and, if so, why, I talked to former Engineer Commissioner Frederick J. Clark and William Xanten, Superintendent of the Sanitation Division and head of the city's snow removal brigade.

Francis E. Twiss, the City's Chief Traffic Engineer, was also on hand.

These men claim that winter panic in Washington is due to three words—topography, temperature, and transportation. The capital city is laid out like a wheel. At the hub, where most of the people work, the land is low. All the spokes of the wheel (in other words, the avenues leading out of the city) are uphill. In addition, sixty percent of those working in the city live in the suburbs. This, then, leads to the second stumbling block—transportation. Some 800,000 cars cross the borders of the District every day. New York has its subways, Los Angeles has its freeways. Washington has neither, and a higher proportion of people than is usually the case in a metropolitan area drive cars to work. Parking is allowed on all streets at night, a fact which complicates snow removal.

Lastly, Washington is in a relatively mild climate, so when it does snow the mercury hovers between 25 and 33 degrees, with the subsequent melting and refreezing of heavy, wet snow which is harder to remove.

According to the average, Washington usually gets twenty inches of snow in fifteen separate storms each winter. But the worst and most eventful snow of all was in January, 1961, the day before John F. Kennedy was to be inaugurated as President of the United States.

After the arduous 1960 Presidential campaign, all of us were tired and more ready for a long vacation than for another major undertaking. But much to my surprise, I learned that a Presidential inaugural just doesn't happen. Hundreds of people work and plan for the event—and this time I happened to be one of them.

For those away from Washington, an inauguration is an impressive historic event to be watched on television or read about in the newspapers. For those of us on the scene it was the culmination of long weeks of a new kind of volunteer work. When I was asked to be chairman of one of the Inaugural Ball committees, I thought this would be like any other affair: a few weeks of work, a few meetings and then it would all be over. I couldn't have been more wrong. And it was largely the fault of that incredible snow that I was still involved with the ball committee until June.

The headquarters of the 1961 Inaugural Committee was on the fifth floor of an old office building in downtown Washington. Housed here were innumerable committees—the Ball Committee, the Governors' Reception Committee, the Parade Committee, the Medallion Committee, the Kennedy Liaison Committee (all of the individual events in which the appearance of the President-elect or members of his family was expected had to be approved and authorized through this committee which was in daily contact with the soon-to-be First Family), the Protocol Committee, the Housing Committee (it was responsible for seeing that every one of the visitors who was coming for the three days had a place to stay; this committee catalogued all the available hotel space, assigned the thousands of rooms, and then notified each individual about where he was to stay), the concessions, the press, the volunteers and so on *ad infinitum.*

Two facts struck me soon after my committee project began. The first was that ninety percent of the work being done for the Inaugural was done by volunteers; Congressional wives, secretaries working nights, lawyers, and interested citizens devoted most of their waking hours to seeing that each function was properly planned.

The second surprising fact was that this was not entirely a Democratic Party function, even if we were "in" at last after eight lean years. To be sure, most of the people working in the Washington area were Democrats, but the over-all enterprise was, in many respects, a non-partisan business venture with a total investment running well over $1½ million. This meant that citizens and businessmen in Washington had "put up" the money to get the Inaugural under way, had underwritten the daily expenditures, and hoped to get their money back when it was all over. The Chairman, Ed Foley, not only wanted them to be repaid in full, but hoped to have a surplus with which the next Inaugural Committee could get started. Each function, therefore, had to be carefully planned and supervised so that those who had invested in the committees' work would not end up in the red.

The event with which I was the most familiar was the Inaugural Ball—or rather Balls, plural, as it turned out. Basing our calculations on past history we expected at least 15,000 people to attend. The only building in Washington that will accommodate this number is scarcely a ballroom—it is the National Guard Armory. That was picked as the initial site, but it was still not big enough, and four hotel ballrooms had to be used to accommodate the overflow.

Another facet of the planning was the enormous problem of getting lists together; before the process was complete, some 40,000 invitations had been catalogued, alphabetized, checked and then *hand-addressed!* As it turned out, very few people seemed to be refusing our invitation, and we had counted on a large number doing so! When it became apparent that four more balls had to be scheduled, it involved additional work on decorations and music and, of course, created new problems of ensuring the security of the First Family at each place. It meant additional work on the assignment of box seats, too. I recall that four women worked all night long at one point, trying to meet the deadline.

My "little task" involved the design, purchase, and distribution of favors at each of the ball sites. We decided on a 14-karat gold-filled charm for the women guests and a silver one for the men. The charms would be engraved with pictures of the new President and Vice President. First, artists' designs had to be submitted and approved by both the committee and the subjects themselves. The bids for manufacture were taken from three firms, and at the last possible moment before time ran out the order was given for production. We had to keep revising the order upward, as acceptances poured in. We finally settled on 25,000. Each one had to be individually boxed and engraved on the back before shipment.

I was responsible for meeting the various busses with the shipments as they arrived (I seem to spend more time meeting busses, planes and trains than a mayor's Official Greeter!) and assigning Congressional wives in teams to supervise the distribution of the favors at each of the hotels. There had to be a policeman on duty in each place too, because the charms represented an investment of some $14,000.

At about 4:00 P.M. on the Thursday before the big day, a light snow began to fall. Hardly anyone paid much attention to it at first, but as the hours went by and the flakes got bigger and thicker, we knew we really had a blizzard on our hands. On an ordinary day this would have been enough of a disaster, but on this day with the city filled to the bursting point with out-of-town visitors all with some place to go, the complications that raced through all our minds were almost beyond comprehension.

Panic was an impossibility. The District Commissioners called in the Army, and overnight a magic transformation was worked on the parade route and the site of the inauguration itself.

In addition to the District's regular equipment, the Army sent in 3,000 men, six graders, eighteen front-end loaders, seven hundred plows, six wreckers and one hundred and fifty dump trucks. Their biggest contribution was removing the cars that were stalled on the streets. It seems hard to imagine, but about 183 automobiles were abandoned that night on Pennsylvania Avenue, some immobilized right in the middle of busy intersections. (Fifteen thousand truckloads of snow were shoveled off the main arteries downtown in the space of a few hours. The parade route and all of Washington's main streets were cleared by 11:00 A.M. on Inauguration Day.)

Many incidents occurred on that long and bitter night that were taken quite seriously at the time, but fortunately had satisfactory results. One poor private was working on snow removal, fell in a deep puddle of water, requested a new pair of pants, called for help, was ignored and continued to work until 6:00 A.M. in frozen clothing. A sergeant who was instructed to pay special attention to sanding the intersections did so simply by dumping a truckload of sand at each corner. There was the problem of finding a resting place for mules; of deciding what to do with a non-union-made 10,000-pound cake; of housing a large group of Indians in full regalia; of soothing the anger of wool manufacturers who couldn't understand why we didn't use woolen material to decorate the dance halls. We had to listen to the anguished disappointment of drill teams, bands, manufacturers and politicians who felt they just had to be in the parade. If all requests had been granted, the parade would have lasted two days instead of an already lengthy six hours.

Hotels were jammed to capacity; cots were set up in halls and lobbies, West Point cadets slept in thirty Pullman cars in Union Station; visitors were housed as far away as Richmond before the demand for space was satisfied. Sadly, many had to be told as they arrived at National Airport that if they had made no provision for housing before coming, the best thing for them to do was return home. And, even more sadly, many people arrived in Washington clutching only a souvenir invitation, thinking this would gain them admission to all the events scheduled for the week. Queues were so long at some places that many of the visitors never got inside the door at all. On Thursday night, musicians walked to Constitution Hall for a special Presidential concert and on arriving found an almost empty auditorium.

Those of us who had volunteered to help during the previous two months found that our careful planning just hadn't been careful enough. We were in despair as the crush at headquarters reached incredible proportions. I even resorted to turning up my coat collar and wearing dark glasses to avoid being recognized and accosted by desperate visitors who insisted that I help them get tickets. It was the first trip to Washington for many, and they had come totally unprepared. It was so sad, but I was truly helpless. Tickets just weren't available for *anything* at that point.

Many of the celebrated participants at the Gala the night before the inauguration never got to their hotels at all to change (Leonard Bernstein and Ethel Merman started for their hotels from the Armory rehearsal, saw it was impossible, stopped at the home of a stranger to make phonecalls and returned to the Armory for the performance in their traveling clothes); our office staff was driven to distraction by many of the visitors from Wisconsin who expected us to make their appointments at the hairdresser, depended on us to get them tickets to everything, and hoped we could find beds for them to sleep in.

At the ceremony and parade all of us looked like natives of the Klondike as we sat bundled up to the eyes in several layers of clothing. The parade had 32,000 marchers, fifty bands (from every state in the Union) and the most magnificent floats to be seen anywhere. President Kennedy graciously remained until the last unit from the Panama Canal Zone passed his reviewing stand.

Mary Ellen had been thrilled to be asked to ride on a stage-coach float dressed as a Western dance-hall girl. The plans sounded wonderful and glamorous when we first heard about them, but neither she nor I had visualized her sitting outdoors for five or six hours in 20-degree weather, dressed in a flimsy pink net dress and long black stockings. I had expected her to be angry, miserable and disappointed when she arrived home after the parade, but as it happened a famous TV Western star ("Cheyenne," no less!) had been assigned to ride on the stage-coach with the girls. He had entertained them the whole time they waited for the parade to start, bought them hot cocoa at the end of the line, and put them in cabs for home. She couldn't have been happier if she had sat in the President's reviewing stand and, in fact, hadn't even felt cold.

There were mighty few who stuck it out until the end, but we did. With numbed fingers and stiffened toes we headed home to prepare for the Inaugural Balls.

I quickly changed (into a short dress instead of the long one I had originally planned to wear) and headed for one of the hotels to finish off my project—the distribution of the favors. As I might have expected, dozens of the boxes were stranded in various bus stations along the East Coast, and we had only a portion of the charms we needed. Even the distribution of the ones we had was a problem. People wanted more than the two each couple was allotted; even though we thought we had provided ample guards and personnel, handfuls were stolen; the crush at the Armory got completely out of hand and before the evening was half gone the favors were removed from the entrance hall and locked in a safe. Meanwhile, back at the hotel, someone took issue with the reproduction of the Johnson profile on the charm and threw one at me, box and all! After the evening was history I found that I had several thousand charms left over, each of which had to be hand-addressed and mailed to the long list of those who had not gotten theirs. It was six months before the requests ceased arriving by mail or by phone.

It had been difficult to create the elegant atmosphere of a ball at the cavernous Armory, but some 25,000 people at five balls were able to dance a little, jostle a lot, sip champagne and stare at the new President and his Lady. At least it wasn't as bad as President Grant's ball, which was held in an unheated, temporary building. That night the champagne froze, the musicians' instruments were rendered useless by the cold, and the guests had to dance in their wraps.

History books tell us that one hundred years ago, Inauguration Day for President Lincoln dawned cloudy and raw, that row on row of solemn faces watched as he rode down Pennsylvania Avenue in a heavily guarded carriage, that there were no crowds, no bands, no cheers, no atmosphere of festivity and celebration. Inauguration, 1961, couldn't have been more different, despite the almost knock-out blow dealt to the city by Old Man Winter.

It is obvious now that it takes many long hours in the gray of fatigue and the most intense kind of effort to get a President inaugurated, but in the final analysis it was an historic moment, an event worthy of a great and free society. And the total effect of the week was a happy one. Out of it all, those of us who participated and the many thousands who watched will carry forever the memory of the spirit of the occasion and the belief that it was worth the effort. The President's message was appropriate and moving as a new era began: "The energy, the faith, the devotion which we bring to this endeavor will light our country and all who serve it, and the glow from that fire can truly light the world."

The weatherman cooperated and we had a glorious spring. But then came June, and with it the grim reality of a Washington summer. In late June the mercury climbed through the high 90's and hit 100 for seven days straight. The humidity sapped our strength. Sleep was difficult. Sessions of Congress reached long and tedious proportions. That year, Pentagon IBM machines caught fire, resulting in millions of dollars worth of damage, and thirty firemen were overcome by the fumes. Even in the air-conditioned chambers of the Capitol there was more heat than light. I remember being there the afternoon a short circuit in the Senate Chamber caused the lights to go out. For some time the foreign aid bill was debated with only dim shafts of sun filtering through the skylight in the ceiling.

It became then (as it always is) Washington's most trying time of year. Each summer, though, we look forward to the Fourth of July celebration and the kind of family fun it brings. Because of the longer sessions and the unpredictability of roll-calls, most Congressional fathers are here during the summer months more than they are during the rest of the year. On the Fourth we sometimes have a picnic, but we always attend the unforgettable celebration held annually on the Washington Monument grounds. We try to get there early enough to watch the crowd gather and to see the sunset over the Potomac.

In 1959, the Navy Band started off the evening and there were a few speeches by local officials. At 9:30 the display of fire-works got under way. The featured themes were the two new states of the Union—Hawaii and Alaska. While red, white, and blue searchlights played over the Washington Monument, the 150,000 spectators were treated to a truly remarkable display of pyrotechnics.

There were kayaks, pineapples, palm trees and igloos etched in flame. Even the contours of the new states were outlined with fire. The sky was filled with parasols of golden color, bursts of blue, red, and green and thunderous shots of sparkling white heat that brought gasps from the crowd.

In 1960 we saw the 49-star flags around the Monument lowered for the last time, and to replace them, fifty brand-new flags were raised.

We emphasize to the children that times of celebration like this should be times of rededication. In 1960 the United States was undergoing vilification and humiliation in too many countries. Our prestige had seldom seemed lower. We felt at the time that the fault lay not with the President, the Congress, the Secretary of State or our Ambassadors abroad, but with ourselves. We told them that many Americans seemed to have

92

forgotten what it means to sacrifice, to work with high purpose, for other people and toward goals besides those of material acquisition. The night when the birth of our nation is celebrated is a good time for all of us to redouble our efforts to rediscover the burning purpose that somehow has slipped by the wayside.

One of the ways to do this was suggested that night in a speech by George V. Allen, then Director of the United States Information Agency. He suggested that every American make it a personal duty to make a pilgrimage to Washington at least once in his lifetime, "to view with his own eyes the original Declaration of Independence and the Constitution of the United States and to take the Oath of Allegiance at least once in the Nation's Capital."

This sentiment was an appropriate starting-point for the children's growing understanding of why we have to stay in Washington each summer. Despite the lack of sailing and a comfortable temperature, there are ways to have both a delightful and a meaningful season.

All the children have become accustomed to going to the office frequently. They have come to know every policeman and guard, every elevator operator and many of the Senators, too. Cici even managed to have her picture taken with Vice President Nixon on one of her forays into the Capitol, and both she and Jan were treated to a bowl of ice cream by Senator John McClellan on one of their "hungry" afternoons. They feel completely at home in the Capitol, and often provide helping hands in our office. They can alphabetize, stuff envelopes, do filing and even a little typing. This knowledge has given them a greater understanding of what their father does as well as an increased interest in politics itself.

Though summer school has been on the agenda for all of them from time to time during several summers, two of the girls ride horseback a couple of afternoons a week and all our children swim at the nearby Sheraton-Park pool when the spirit strikes them. We have taken them occasionally to the most unusual theater anywhere, the Carter Barron amphitheater. This is truly one of the dividends for sticking out the "dog days" of August in Washington. This beautiful spot in the midst of deep woods provides a variety of entertainment—everything from rock'n'roll to opera and ballet and an occasional ice show.

I remember particularly the night we heard Harry Belafonte present a moving program of American and international folk songs, and the night Danny Kaye delighted everyone—at least he delighted the Proxmires—with his patter, songs, and rubber legs. Both evenings, thunderstorms threatened, then disappeared and a full moon burst through to make the setting magnificent.

Thus it seems that for Congressional families summertime can mean more than the usual warm-weather diversions. For some it means long periods of separation. I recall that in 1959 Mrs. Hubert Humphrey left early in the summer and took her children to their cottage in Minnesota. Mrs. Eugene McCarthy did the same. Mrs. Stuart Symington was in Nantucket and Mrs. John F. Kennedy was in Newport. Mrs. Tom Dodd had gone up to Connecticut with five of their six children, and Mrs. Albert Gore returned to her native state with her son to supervise the building of a new home, leaving her daughter to take care of the Senator.

Those of us who choose to stay here improvise baseball games and swimming excursions, feed our husbands and figure out ways to beat the heat. Of course, we would all prefer to be cruising the Caribbean or camping in the Rockies or basking on the Riviera. Who wouldn't? For those of us who come from areas such as Massachusetts, Wisconsin, Minnesota, Nevada, California and the Pacific Northwest where familiar lakes and shores beckon, it is a difficult choice. But being in Washington isn't necessarily a terrible sacrifice. By staying here we *do* avoid crowded highways filled with families in frantic search of camp-sites, restaurants, restrooms and motel space. We enjoy walking in from hot sidewalks to the cool high-ceilinged government buildings and museums with all their opportunity to listen, learn and investigate. We are especially lucky to be able to give the children an insight into how their country is governed by including them in the activity of the Senate. Moreover, we find yearly that summer social life in the capital is the most fun and the most informal of the year. There are family get-togethers around a pool, and family barbecues are more frequent than full-dress dinners.

Many is the time I have packed a regular picnic supper, left our un-air-conditioned house and, children in tow, gone up to Bill's office for an indoor, ant-free repast. When night has fallen and the Senate has finally adjourned after the late session usual at this time of the year, we leave the Capitol behind us and head for home through a quiet city. These evenings always pro-vide fond memories for us and for the children.

In political jargon, there are twelve "weathervane counties," and some elections are called "weathervane elections." The Washington weathervane (of the meteorological variety) seems to be erratic and unpredictable, and runs the gamut from frigid to equatorial, from exquisite to dismal. No matter what the ac-tuality, however, it, along with politics, is one of the favorite D.C. topics of discussion. The existence of this kind of a con-versational axis, with weather at one end and politics at the other, makes for ample table talk. The two tend to balance each other out, since no one can do much about either and no one can fully understand or appreciate either.

All of this goes to show that man is born with a chronic anxiety about the weather and about the men who govern him.

And that, as Ralph Waldo Emerson expressed it in *The Mountain and the Squirrel*,

> "All sorts of things and weather
> Must be taken in together
> To make up a year
> And a Sphere."

We political families lead constantly unpredictable and difficult lives, especially when the storm-warnings are going up. But as Cyril Connolly said, "Melancholy and remorse form the deep leaden keel which enables us to sail into the wind of reality; we run aground sooner than the flat-bottomed pleasure-lovers, but we venture out in weather that would sink them."

Chapter VIII

CIRCUS AND CEREMONY

W<small>HEN</small> <small>BILL</small> and I arrived in Washington that summer night in 1957 I spent part of the evening in the Family Gallery of the Senate observing the debate on the floor. That occasion was a memorable one for me because it was my first meeting with two Senators' wives who were also stationed at the family observation post. Mrs. Frank Church and Mrs. J. Strom Thurmond were old hands by that time, and this was the first of many hundreds of hours we would spend here together, exchanging views and following the action on the floor.

The most interesting times for the wives of Senators are an occasional filibuster or a night session that brings us down to the Capitol to witness some controversial debate or vote. Even though our husbands don't always vote together, we wives tally the votes as they are taken and congratulate the winning side without the slightest dent in our mutual friendship.

For me, the opening day of each Congressional session is a time of mixed feelings. It has a special quality—a combination of poignancy for the faces that have disappeared from the floor and interest in the new ones, welded together by an impressive ceremony which has been preserved from the past.

Members of Senators' families traditionally gather in the

97

Family Gallery to watch the Opening Day proceedings. About an hour before noon, the wives begin to enter, to exchange greetings and await the first bell. Reporters are allowed on the floor of the Senate before the convening bell, but as soon as it rings they rush off to pack the press gallery.

In 1960, a year that would witness one of the most hard-fought, bitterly partisan campaigns in history, I recall a remarkable feeling of peace and lack of rancor as the Senate Chaplain, Frederick Brown Harris, encouraged the members to "stretch out their horizons to meet and match the stupendous dimensions of these epic days." Battles, disagreements and temperamental outbursts were all in the future, and those of the preceding year were blurred in recollection.

I noticed a flurry of handshakes as the Senators welcomed each other back, much in the "first day of school" manner. There was a feeling of promise, excitement and change, not only because of the new decade, but in the dramatic appearance of each of the Presidential possibilities in that election year. Vice President Nixon, Senators Kennedy, Johnson, Humphrey and Symington appeared one by one on the floor. I sensed a special feeling of pride and admiration as the Senators cheered the return of Joseph O'Mahoney of Wyoming, who had been struck down by a massive stroke the previous June and was back in his seat for the first time. And, as usual, there was a feeling of loss for those whose chairs were empty, because of either death or defeat.

That year, the late Senator William Langer's familiar pale complexion and upright form were gone from the front-row desk on the Republican side—a desk he had occupied since our arrival in Washington. Senator Thurmond was missing from his seat next to Bill because his young and beautiful wife, whom I had met and liked on my first evening in the Gallery, had died that morning. My friendship with Jean Thurmond had been a

98

warm and satisfying one, and more than ever, that noon in 1960, I felt a sense of deep loss at her passing.

That occasion was as auspicious as any convening can be, but the session only lasted twenty-four minutes. I had the feeling then, and it remains with me still, that the Senate is in effect a great theater; the players come and go, but the shadows of those who have gone before are always present, felt and remembered, especially on each Opening Day.

In 1961, as in each odd year, the first order of business on Opening Day was the swearing-in of new Senators. The thirty-five who were new that year walked down the aisle in groups of four, accompanied for the most part by colleagues from their native states. This year, however, Senator Margaret Chase Smith of Maine decided to break precedent. She requested that Senator Maurine Neuberger of Oregon escort her down the aisle. The first two women Senators in history to win full terms for themselves walked arm-in-arm to the Vice President's desk and stood together while the oath was administered. The hundreds present stood to give them a rousing ovation.

My usual mixed feelings on Opening Day were heightened that January of 1961 when I glanced at the chair of the presiding officer. Vice President Nixon was sitting there, as he had been for eight years. He had been narrowly defeated for the Presidency the previous November, but he was still Vice President (and, consequently, President of the Senate) until the inauguration took place and he could turn over his gavel to Lyndon Johnson. I always find myself full of sympathy for those who have lost, but an extra portion for those who must appear in public and go through the motions of their job, if only briefly. Vice President Nixon was controlled and sure of himself as he presided over a complicated parliamentary problem; his demeanor was a reminder that all those involved in politics must be prepared to lose, but never to show it hurts.

99

Senator Allen Frear of Delaware appeared that day in the Gallery, rather than in the front-row seat on the Democratic side which he had occupied for twelve years. He and his wife Esther gave the impression that they couldn't bear to miss an Opening Day even though another man had won his seat.

Another vivid memory of that 1961 Opening Day was the swearing-in of Vice President-elect Johnson for his third term as Senator from Texas. Since he had also won election to the second highest office in the land, he immediately resigned from the Senate and escorted his replacement, William Blakeley, to the front to take the oath. For a brief moment there were three Senators from Texas on the floor. Johnson soon left to await his inauguration as Vice President—after having served for a quarter of a century in the legislative branch. He had been one of the most powerful and effective Majority Leaders the Senate had ever known. Despite Bill's earlier differences with him, I had great respect for his political skill and couldn't help but wonder how he felt about his new job. The change now was brought about swiftly and easily. Senator Mike Mansfield slid into the vacated Majority Leader's Chair and Senator Hubert Humphrey, the new Democratic Whip, joined him in the front row.

When such changes take place I always think of the desks themselves and of the men who have occupied them over the years. All of the desks in the Senate Chamber are of a design originated in 1819—and are surprisingly small. Forty-seven of the original forty-eight desks built after the Capitol was burned by the British are still in use today. The name "Daniel Webster" is clearly carved on the inside of the desk formerly used by Senator Styles Bridges of New Hampshire. The workmanship and skill that went into the construction of these desks are typical of the meticulous craftsmanship of early American workmen. The desks have portable tops, intricate wooden inlay on the sides, and hand-carved feet. The sand bottles used before the days of blotters and ball-point pens still remain. Even the desks which have been built since to accommodate the Senators from our new states were made by hand, despite our contemporary dependence on machine skills and assembly lines.

Bill's desk has a history, too. Clearly carved on the inside are the names of Charles A. Culberson, who served Texas starting in 1899, Hugo Black of Alabama, now a Supreme Court Justice, Matthew Neely of West Virginia, who served until his death in 1958, and Senator Herbert Lehman of New York. Its most recent occupant was Senator John F. Kennedy of Massachusetts. Although I have never seen a legislator wielding a penknife on the floor, I assume they must chip their names in the varnish during working hours—an offense for which many a schoolboy has been reprimanded!

Seeing these old-fashioned pieces of furniture that have survived so much time and so much history and the weight of so many books and papers makes me stop and think about those who have come and gone, just as each Opening Day does. In many instances the carved letters are all that remain as mementos of a public servant's life, while in others, they serve as reminders of monumental accomplishment.

On Opening Day there are usually no real surprises, no fireworks, no deathless speeches. But there is something about the atmosphere that draws me, other Senate wives, and hundreds like us back each year to look on. For the Senate—like a theater —has the quality of being a world separate and detached. There are no windows in the Chamber and no obvious contact with the outside world. The men return each year, some more worn than when they left, some with new ideas, some with no ideas, some with high aspirations and others with no greater ambition than to continue the good life they have known. I feel each January that it is well for us to enjoy the tradition of an old and revered institution without being bound by it, to welcome the new faces and to recognize that the rules and much of the procedure as well as the surroundings provide a link with the past and a solid framework for the future.

"The future" in 1960 would see a prolonged filibuster that would add a new dimension to the life Senators occasionally lead. As February slid into March, the papers were filled to overflowing with every aspect of the "extended debate" on the civil rights issue. Very little was written about what this meant for those of us who had husbands involved in the proceedings. I learned in a personal way what it meant to "live with a filibuster."

February 29 of any Leap Year traditionally results in a rash of stories about the eligible bachelors that remain in Washington, special parties to honor the day and the brief fling of many young ladies who take the opportunity to be Daisy Mae to their particular Li'l Abner. But in 1960, the 29th of February witnessed the preparation for a warlike siege in the Capitol of the United States; this news completely overshadowed romance.

Though some 115 hours of debate on this momentous issue had taken place in the Senate since the middle of February, little progress had been made. The Democratic and Republican leaders in the Senate decided that continuous sessions would begin at noon on the 29th. Huge green books weighing five pounds each and containing sixty-four amendments to the Civil Rights Bill were placed on each Senator's desk. The gavel fell and the parliamentary battle was under way.

The eighteen Senators from the Southern states were using the filibuster to delay a vote on an issue on which they were in the minority. In this way they hoped to "educate" the electorate —and their colleagues—and at the same time wear out their opposition so that a compromise would result.

In order to wear down their opponents, the Southern Senators would frequently call for quorums (the required presence of fifty-one Senators on the floor). If it took a long time to round up the fifty-one, the speaker thus was allowed a substantial rest, and the debate was necessarily prolonged. In order to cut this opportunity for rest to a minimum, it was necessary for fifty-one Senators to remain on hand to answer quickly to their names.

In order to thwart the Southern strategists, most opposing Senators slept in makeshift quarters in the Capitol. Forty cots were borrowed from the Army and set up in the Senate Appropriations Committee Room, the old Supreme Court Chamber and in the office of the President just off the Senate floor. The Senate Restaurant was kept open twenty-four hours a day; doorkeepers, policemen and elevator operators worked twelve-hour shifts and the wives of Senators gnashed their teeth.

We trooped to the Hill daily with vitamins, clean socks and shirts and watched the light at the top of the Capitol as it burned around the clock.

The Southern Senators had an easier time of it. They had been divided into shifts, with six men "on duty" every day, each of whom was expected to hold the floor for four hours. When a man had completed his stint, he had two days off to recuperate. Not so their opponents, who had to keep the watch and be ready for a quick trip to the Senate floor when the quorum buzzer sounded—whether it was two in the afternoon or two in the morning.

In spite of the carefully laid battle plans and strategy, and the deadly seriousness of the debate, I observed many amusing things. Stuart Symington, one of the most distinguished and elegantly dressed of all Senators, was spotted at a pre-dawn quorum call attired in a black turtle-neck pajama top underneath a handsomely tailored suit. One Senator who spied Stuart remarked that he looked like a cross between a minister and a prize-fighter. Senator Ernest Gruening of Alaska took to wearing brilliant orange slippers. And Senator Clinton Anderson of New Mexico, the Senate's leading sage on the intricacies of high finance, was seen carrying the book *How to Win at Gin Rummy* under his arm.

Faces grew wearier, tempers shorter, exchanges sharper as the mental and physical strain began to tell. We Senate wives welcomed our weary warriors home after eight weeks of siege, during which there had been one 125-hour period of consecutive debate. It had been an unusual drama, for a vital purpose, but we hoped that it wouldn't turn out to be common practice. We had witnessed a debate on an issue of the greatest importance, a debate which involved men who have much at stake in a nation watched by the world and which affected the lives of millions of Americans. It was an unsettling endurance contest, but one of the most remarkable phenomena of democratic government.

Another fascinating aspect of Senate procedure is an occasional night session. For those who find excitement in the processes of government and politics, there is nothing to match the drama of such an evening. The minute the door to the gallery is closed and I am settled in my seat, I sense the electricity, the tension and often the passion of democracy in action.

The night of the Strauss confirmation vote in 1959 was such an occasion. Lewis Strauss had been nominated by President Eisenhower to be Secretary of Commerce. He had always been a controversial figure, an outspoken person who had as many enemies as he had admirers. I brought Mary Ellen and a young friend of hers with me to the Senate gallery. We hoped to witness a vote, but the chances seemed slim when we arrived.

Senator Barry Goldwater had just begun what he called a "very extensive discussion of the Strauss matter." Vice President Nixon was presiding, the galleries were packed to capacity and the floor was crowded. Rumors fly on a night like this; from the jammed press gallery to the clerks clustered at the back of the Senate, questions buzzed: "Who are the missing three Senators?" "Have planes gone to pick them up?" "Will they get here in time?" "Will we be here all night?" For hours the speculation continued.

About the middle of the evening we went down to the Senate restaurant for soup and coffee and then returned to our seats, determined to stay the night. Bill finished his work in the office about 10:30 P.M.; Senator Paul Douglas had taken a nap; Senator Thruston Morton had appeared on the floor, having just arrived from Denver in time to vote; Senator Kefauver showed up in a midnight-blue tuxedo and Senator McClellan in a white dinner jacket; Senator Tom Martin of Iowa even left a sickbed in the Bethesda Naval Hospital to be on hand for the vote.

At 11:45 Senator Johnson announced that there would be a vote at 12:15 if no Senator objected. None did. The score cards and pencils came out, and not a soul stirred from his seat. In the middle of Senator Dirksen's speech, the time allotted to the pro-Strauss forces expired, and the clerk abruptly began to call the roll. As the roll-call droned on, it became apparent that the issue would be decided by one or two votes. There was an audible buzz when Senator Johnson voted "No" and a gasp when Senator Margaret Chase Smith, usually a strong Administration supporter, also voted "No." Suddenly it was over. The results: 46 for and 49 against the confirmation of Lewis Strauss.

As we headed home on that summer night, we commented on the drama we had witnessed, and on the personal tragedies that so often lie near the surface of the sea of politics. Anyone who has observed from such a vantage point knows that some day he may be on the casualty lists, too. To accept that fact is tough but essential.

An entirely different kind of occasion on Capitol Hill is a Joint Session of both Houses of Congress. Here both legislators and visitors watch, without participation. Each Congressman's office is allotted only one gallery ticket, so most often it is the fortunate Senate wife who has the opportunity to attend.

Of late these Joint Sessions have seemed to come in bunches. In the spring of 1960, President Alberto Lleras Camargo of

Colombia, French President de Gaulle and Madame de Gaulle, and the King and Queen of Nepal were here. For each of these visits the streets of Washington were ablaze with flags and the head of state addressed a Joint Session.

The procedure at a Joint Session is formal but fascinating. Television cameras line the wall facing the Speaker's rostrum. The guest galleries are filled to overflowing and tickets are as rare as emeralds.

First, the Doorkeeper of the House steps to the middle aisle and announces in a booming voice "The Members of the Senate," who file down to seats reserved for them.

Then come the members of the Diplomatic Corps and representatives of foreign governments, followed by the members of the Cabinet and the Justices of the Supreme Court.

For the French President's speech, everyone in the Chamber arose and cheered when Madame de Gaulle was escorted to her seat in the gallery accompanied by Mrs. Nixon and Madame Hervé Alphand, the beautiful wife of the French Ambassador.

De Gaulle himself received a stunning ovation as he approached the Speaker's rostrum, his severe countenance broken only once or twice by a fleeting smile. He spoke entirely in French, and throughout his twenty-five-minute speech referred only briefly to longhand notes. His performance impressed his audience of professionals, many of whom are accustomed to speeches "strictly from the script."

Not since General Douglas MacArthur's dramatic "Old Soldiers Never Die" speech in 1951 had a Joint Session been called to honor an American. But in February, 1962, following John Glenn's amazing space flight, precedent spanned a decade and a Joint Session was held to honor him and the others on the astronaut team. Even in these "cool" days of science and sophistication, an example of human courage can still capture the hearts and imaginations of men. Several Congressmen and Senators had brought their children to the floor with them, and they sat on their fathers' laps for the brief but unforgettable half-hour.

I sat in the gallery with Mrs. Ralph Yarborough, Mrs. J. Glenn Beall, and movie producer Otto Preminger. Not even Mr. Preminger's *Advise and Consent* in wide-screen VistaVision could equal this occasion for drama. When Colonel Glenn was announced by the Doorkeeper and proceeded to walk down the aisle, the entire House Chamber exploded with cheers and thunderous applause in unrestrained tumult. I noticed tears in many eyes—even Mr. Preminger's. Watching Glenn's performance that day was one of the truly great moments of my life.

At this moment the modern world seemed so overwhelming and so complex to me that after the speech I felt an uncontrollable desire to walk through the Capitol, not along the beaten tourist paths, but up long-forgotten stairways and deserted corridors, stopping in a gallery long since abandoned.

As I walked alone, details that I had never noticed before seemed to stand out in sharp focus: the reliance on American symbols in the sandstone columns located on the ground floor (Latrobe used corn, tobacco and cotton in place of the customary flutes); the simplicity of the original Senate Chamber; the marks left on walls, floors and columns by fire when the British burned the building in 1814 (though priceless documents and furniture were piled in what is now Statuary Hall and lit, much of the sturdy structure was left unharmed); the personal trademarks left by nameless workmen on the beautiful steps leading to what used to be the Ladies' Gallery when the House met in Statuary Hall; the graceful Goddess of History surveying the thousands who pass below her in that gallery, her exquisitely simple clock, vintage 1819, still keeping perfect time; the spot where John Quincy Adams was stricken and the couch in the office of the Clerk of the House where he lay down to die two days later; the only unretouched portrait of George Washington in existence, so real and detailed that he seems to speak to those who stand in front of him; the magnificent artwork executed at dizzy heights in the Rotunda by Brumidi, an immigrant Italian artist with a passionate love for America, his adopted country.

There were these things and many more to remind me of what is America, for the Capitol is America. The men who built and watched over this country surrounded me in every corridor, niche and corner. Relics of the past such as snuff boxes, quill pens, massive furniture and mirrors still remain, but they seem to blend harmoniously with air-conditioning, subway cars, shiny new marble and the bustle of modern life.

I remember thinking then that, as democracy is threatened around the world, we as a people must be strong within ourselves. We must believe in ourselves and live up to our great tradition, not by resisting change, but by meeting the challenge of the present, just as John Glenn did. The walk through the Capitol served to inspire me with the majesty of great men and to remember what they had accomplished. I recalled that it was only the toughest kind of thinking and the greatest courage and ingenuity that had made our way of life possible, and keeping it alive would require a full measure of the same.

I must confess that inspiration sometimes runs a bit dry as each year's session drones on. All of us feel like the proverbial dregs by the final night of a Congress. On September 14, 1959, for example, after a marathon twenty-one-hour session, the first half of the Eighty-Sixth Congress adjourned at 6:34 in the morning. I stuck it out until 2:00 A.M. and then headed for home. Bill, of course, stayed until the bitter end.

As last-night sessions go, this one was less than exciting. There were moments when tension and controversy broke through the surface, but most of the last hours were filled with routine business, last-minute insertions in the *Record* and the customary speeches of commendation for the Majority and Minority Leaders and the official reporters. Despite the languor, the galleries were filled to capacity when I left, and the press was amply represented. Because of the special nature of the final night, there is always the possibility of a filibuster developing, or some last-minute fireworks. On many a closing night Senator Wayne Morse has slipped a rose into his lapel—a sign that he is prepared to "speak at length" if necessary. For this reason those who have the stamina will stay and stay in hope of witnessing something exciting and memorable.

Mrs. Nixon and her oldest daughter, Tricia, were in the gallery, as were Mrs. Lyndon Johnson and her Lynda Bird. I sat with Midge Morse, who told me that the Senate doctor is always in attendance on the floor when the Senate stays in lengthy session. She remarked of her concern about the health of senators who, though already exhausted from a year of hard work, had to withstand the additional strain of being up around the clock. Even Senator Green, who was then ninety-two, stayed on the floor until dawn broke over Washington; amazingly enough, we saw him on the Capitol Hill streetcar at noon—just six hours later. He was obviously on his way to his office.

Bill snatched three hours of sleep that morning and then returned to the Senate Office Building to do a television recording. After a last-minute check at his office, he left Washington at 2:00 P.M., headed for Wisconsin and a four-month itinerary of speeches and meetings. My last prayer that morning as he drove up Ordway Street was that the old Chevy would hold up. It was approaching the 90,000-mile mark and, being that exhausted, its performance was slightly less than predictable.

Chapter IX

A MAN OF MANY HATS

Former Congressman Luther Patrick of Alabama once pointed out that the modern legislator in Washington "has became an expanded messenger boy, an employment agency, getter-out of the Navy, Army and Marines, a wardheeler, a wound healer, trouble shooter, law explainer, bill finder, issue translator, resolution interpreter, controversy-oil-pourer, glad-hand extender, business promoter, convention goer, civic good will promoter, veterans' affairs adjuster, ex-serviceman's champion, watchdog for the underdog, sympathizer for the upper dog, kisser of babies, recoverer of lost baggage, soberer of delegates, adjuster for traffic violators and voters straying into Washington and into the toils of the law, binder-up of broken hearts, financial wet nurse, a good Samaritan, contributor to good causes, cornerstone layer, public building and bridge dedicator, and ship christener. To be sure, he does get in a little flag waving, and a little Constitutional hoisting and spread eagle work, but it is getting harder every day to find time to properly study legislation, the very business they are primarily in Washington to discharge, and it must be done above all things."

Though no legislator can be all things to all men twenty-four hours a day, Congressman Patrick was not exaggerating in his long-term assessment of a Congressman's myriad duties and responsibilities. Each day contains at least a few of the activities he described.

The day begins at our house at 6:30 A.M., when the alarm goes off. Bill gets up first, does strenuous calisthenics, fixes his own breakfast (it's a simple one of fresh orange juice, whole-wheat toast, and skim milk, so I rationalize that he doesn't really need me to prepare it), and then sets off for the office, briefcase in hand. He walks a mile and a half to the bus terminal where he picks up transportation directly to the New Senate Office Building.

Bill's penchant for walking has gotten him into trouble occasionally. Once I recall a weekend trip he made to Madison. He had landed at Truax Field and decided to walk the three miles to town, since it was a beautiful Sunday.

It happens that Truax, in addition to being a commercial landing field, is a military base for jet aircraft. As Bill strode determinedly across the fields toward town he was stopped by a guard who requested his identification. Bill explained that he was Senator William Proxmire, but the guard couldn't believe that a U.S. Senator would be hiking out there on a Sunday afternoon. Officers of higher and higher rank were consulted and a phone-call was made to a friend in Madison before the base authorities were convinced of Bill's identity. Since then he has chosen his places for hiking more carefully.

Bill has discovered that the ride to the office on the bus allows him time to read the Washington *Post* and scan the *Congressional Record*. If he drove himself to work, this time would be wasted. (The only Senators whom the government provides with chauffeur-driven cars are the Majority and Minority Leaders and Whips of both parties and the President Pro Tem.)

When he arrives at the office he reads the New York *Times*, *The Wall Street Journal*, and a vast collection of Wisconsin newspapers. He tries to finish them before 9:00 A.M. when the rest of the office staff reports for work. He then has about an hour to prepare floor material, a committee presentation, or a radio show.

Committee meetings start at ten and last until the Senate convenes at noon. Bill usually gobbles a sandwich at his desk before going to the Senate floor. Floor action and committee meetings often continue simultaneously during the afternoon, and he will shuttle back and forth between the two, sometimes as often as eight times, until about 5:00. Then he returns to the office to dictate correspondence, to read and sign the mail, and to prepare for the next day. By that time it's usually 7:00 P.M. He packs a briefcase full of research, reading, and speech material and calls a cab for home.

It is truly hard to describe a Senator's "typical" day, because each one is so different in actual requirements. In addition to conducting Senate business, there are constituents to meet, news-papermen to be given interviews, phonecalls, staff meetings, groups of school children to greet, "must" receptions and usually a crisis or two that can throw all the normal activities into a mad scramble.

Bill speaks around the country twenty or thirty times a year, and these trips have to be worked somehow into his weekly schedule. Every time such a speech is accepted during a week when Congress is in session, departure time for the airport is questionable. Many is the time that it has been necessary for a police car to take him to the airport to catch the last possible flight that the speech delivery time will allow. I always feel uncomfortable when there is a wild departure, especially when I myself am the frantic driver through rush-hour traffic.

Once we just weren't making any progress, and Bill became concerned about getting to the airport on time. In the middle of Constitution Avenue we spotted a policeman on duty, and I pulled up beside him. Bill stuck his head out the window and said, "I'm Senator Bill Proxmire of Wisconsin. I'm in a hurry to catch a plane. Could you help me get to the airport?" He expected immediate sirens and swift delivery. Instead the policeman, totally unimpressed, said, "Sure, I can help you get to the airport. Go straight ahead, turn left, cross the Fourteenth Street Bridge, and you'll be there in no time." I drove a slightly chastened U.S. Senator to the airport, by that route, and I'm afraid he will never hear the end of it.

After an out-of-town speech, Bill usually arrives back in Washington in the wee hours of the morning, to snatch a brief few hours of sleep and then return to the office to start another day.

One of the ways in which I occasionally participate in Bill's career is working on his radio and television shows. Unknown to many visitors, there are complete radio and television facilities in the Capitol itself for the use of the Members of the Senate. There are a few simple props in the television room: a desk, books, a globe, a backdrop picture of the Capitol. Every two weeks Bill plans two five-minute television shows and a one-minute spot, and every week a fifteen-minute radio show. He chooses subjects that are timely, and I am his interviewer. At first I was terrified of the eye of the camera, and I am still not completely at ease or relaxed while doing these shows. But it has been an interesting experiment. At least I have proved to myself that television stardom is not for me. If I had to do this regularly, with a live audience to boot, I would be a total wreck.

But men in politics must perform constantly on radio and television, and, with the rapid growth of our population, this is often the only way to maintain contact with constituents. In the past ten years television has become, I think, the single most important aspect of political communication. The need to use it effectively has added one more burden to an already tension-filled occupation. Despite my baptism into the world of lights and cameras, I am still impressed with the skill many of our political figures have developed in their use of television. Without a script, Bill can now do a one-minute, five-minute or fifteen-minute show with substance and systematic development of material and finish, to the second, with a sensible conclusion.

Frequently, Bill has discovered three simultaneous appointments on his morning schedule—a meeting of his Small Business Committee, an Agriculture Committee session at which dairy experts are to be heard, and a television show. This means rushing through the broadcast and then dividing the rest of the morning between the committee meetings. The fact that many people don't seem to realize the importance of these meetings has resulted, I think, in a general misunderstanding of the legislative process.

When, in 1960, the Eighty-Sixth Congress received 3,500 bills in the first six months and acted on only 150 of them by the end of June, some people assumed the legislators had spent those six months twiddling their thumbs. In fact, this seems to be the standard assumption as the middle of every session approaches. Actually, hundreds of hours have been spent in committee hearings at which important witnesses have testified, in executive sessions of committee to "mark up the bill" (prepare it for final committee vote), and meetings where Majority and Minority views of the final bill are presented.

The reason for this rather shallow understanding of the procedure by which a bill becomes law is mostly, I think, the fact that there are so many bills, and the processes of preparation are so involved and so "dull" to the average citizen, that very little is written about the work that goes into each one. This apparent lack of understanding is only reinforced when a tourist visits the floor of the Senate or House and finds very few Congressmen in their seats.

Before a bill becomes law, it must be carefully prepared by the individual Senator or Congressman. He must then introduce it on the floor of the Senate or the House, after which it is referred to the proper committee. The committee invites supporters, opponents and, most important of all, competent experts who may favor or oppose the bill to testifiy at hearings. Members of the committee must study the testimony with utmost care in order to vote for or against the bill. If a majority votes against the bill, it is dead. If a bill is passed in committee, it is reported out to the full Senate or House to be put on the calendar until the party leadership "motions it up."

Once a bill has been debated and possibly amended on the floor, it is passed or defeated by a general vote. If it is passed in the Senate, it then moves over to the House (or vice versa), is referred again to committee, again reported out, debated, and passed or defeated.

If a bill differs in any respect after it emerges from the second house, a "conference committee," which includes representatives of both bodies, is appointed to iron out the differences. When agreement is reached, a "conference report" is presented to both bodies for approval.

After passage, the bill goes to the White House to be either signed or vetoed. Only the signature of the President of the United States can cause it to become law (although occasionally bills are passed over a presidential veto).

The above is merely a "civics course" sketch of the usual procedure. In reality, there are numerous pitfalls that can delay or kill a measure, many of them arising secretly. A recalcitrant committee chairman, for example, can refuse to report out legislation; a bill can be quietly dropped by committee action or talked to death (in the Senate), especially as the urge to adjourn becomes more pronounced. Or it can be so amended that it bears little relation to the original intent of the authors.

Bill has found that one of the most trying of the many responsibilities he bears is that of waiting and watching on the floor. I remember in particular his role in the fight against a water diversion bill in 1958. In previous sessions this minor bill had been the first piece of legislation introduced into the House (H.R. 1), and yet had been held over for action until the last night of the Congress. It was a bill which involved only a few states, mainly Illinois and Wisconsin, and Illinois had always had its way (at the expense of Wisconsin) just because everyone was anxious to go home. This time Bill made it clear to the leadership that he was not going to allow this to happen again, so he had to take his seat on the floor and stay there, ready to talk, for most of three days. Because of parliamentary procedure which can dispose of a bill by quick, almost unobtrusive action, it is necessary that someone interested in a bill be constantly present on the floor and wait for its "motioning up." This can be trying and tedious—almost like being a night watchman or a guard at some remote outpost who waits and listens for something to happen. It takes a lot out of a man.

The truth of the matter is that, despite the possibility of floor action, the standing commitees are the real muscle of the Congress. The fact that months of work precede the reporting out of a bill means, too, that the last weeks of any session are hectic and much too crammed for comfort.

At its best, this system focuses immense concentration and intelligence on our lawmaking. At its worst—even when legislation is stampeded in morning-to-midnight sessions—good laws sometimes result. Appropriations bills somehow manage to be passed before the deadlines; private bills go through before immigrants are deported; major legislation is handled each time —never to the satisfaction of everyone, but handled.

As in all human endeavor there are inequities, oversights and mistakes of judgment. This is democracy—inefficient, expensive, in need of improvement, but nonetheless by far the best way of lawmaking yet devised by the mind of man.

In the last months of a session when Senators appear to be drowning in a torrent of paper, when nerves and minds are getting too much exercise, it is important that we wives devise a means of seeing that our men get some sort of relaxation. I have been interested to observe how other families keep their Senators healthy. Senators Lausche, Symington and Fulbright play golf. Senator Douglas swims and hikes. But Senator Wayne Morse is the one who finds relaxation in the most unusual way. Bill and the children and I have been delighted to observe how he combines the farming he loves with the exercise he requires.

One summer day, we all drove out to the Morse farm near Poolesville in the heart of Maryland's rolling countryside—an area rich in Civil War history and famous for its Senatorial adopted son. Here Wayne works 68 acres that he owns and another 150 acres which he uses on a rental basis. The land is devoted primarily to raising enough feed—barley, corn, hay and pasture—for his prize animals.

We knew before our trip that Wayne had been brought up on a farm in Verona, Wisconsin, and had had farming in his blood all his life. But the extent of his success had not occurred to us until we saw the rows of blue ribbons and the magnificent animals they represent.

There is a Devon bull, weighing more than a ton, which has won grand championship after grand championship. There is also a fifteen-year-old American saddle horse that Wayne has trained and shown many times. There is prize poultry. There are sheep, palomino ponies, Shetland ponies and donkeys.

The hit of our visit was Rosie, a twenty-four-year-old mare on whose back all the Morse girls learned to ride and who still patiently initiates youngsters into the world of riding.

As we turned to wave goodbye to Wayne, we saw him striding toward the barn to look after an ailing bull before hurrying back to Washington. It was easy to understand how his Sundays on the farm help erase the lines from his brow and replace them with a ruddy glow and a twinkling eye.

In a sense it can be said that Wayne's political life is dependent on his rural one: the farm so completely involves him while he is there, whether it be at 5:00 A.M. (he often drives out to his farm to do chores before reporting to the Senate at nine) or on a Sunday, that his strength is renewed for political combat. It was a truly revealing experience to see this man who seems to live and breathe nothing but politics in an entirely different setting, and find there, too, a real reward.

During the warm summer months when golfing and farming can be enjoyed (if time permits, for then the legislative burden is the heaviest), thousands of young people come to Washington. They come for many reasons—to have a good time, to acquire autographs, to be photographed with their elected officials but, most importantly, to see at first hand the symbols of freedom and the monuments to the men who made their country great.

I have often wondered what these young people really see, what they learn, and what they take home with them. Bill makes a practice of visiting with as many of them as he can, to answer their questions and to encourage them to consider public life when they choose their careers. These meetings take another large chunk out of each of his days, and are a steady certainty to be considered when planning his schedules.

Bill feels very strongly that the kind of a world we live in demands well-educated men and women with inquisitive minds and creative intellects that will seek answers to the increasingly complex problems of our age.

In constant conflict with the urgent need for youthful participation in government is the often unsavory picture of politics that the young have inherited from their elders, and the fact that the rigors and uncertainty of political life seem strenuous and unremunerative when contrasted with the traditional American dream of material success.

We have found that many of the young people we have talked with envision the typical politician as a fast-talking fellow with a big black cigar in his mouth, one glad hand extended and the other in the public till. Revelations of loose practices in the expenditure of public funds on trips and exposures of influence peddling in high places don't help improve the picture. We have found, too, that not only does this picture discourage young people from choosing a life of public service, it also tends to discourage those already in office who are honest and diligent in their work.

When the hordes of young people descend on our city each spring and summer, we try to find something to show them or to tell them that will improve their opinion of their elected representatives and their impression of politics in general.

We try to bring them the message that during their lifetimes the world has passed from the stage of hot war to that of cold war; that, in essence, it has gone from the battlefields of bloody struggle to those of ideological conflict, and that the future will require the keenest mentality and the highest level of morality.

These are only a few of the things Bill and I try to register in the minds behind the bright new faces who visit our office on any typical day.

There are others who come in a steady stream: couples who wish to adopt a baby, businessmen who want a factory for their home town, others who want to arrange for a TV license, have Bill speak at a banquet or meeting, see the office or have a cozy chat with the President of the United States. Bill will come out into the reception room and greet as many as he possibly can, and if his schedule isn't too jammed, will have an extended conference with those in real need.

In his book, *Member of the House,* the late Clem Miller, unforgettable Congressman from California, described with spontaneity and wit the way things are in Congress. "Often what is of over-riding significance gives way to what is immediate. The competing interest, the endless details of Congressional routine, too often take hold. Members are called to the floor for a quorum call as the afternoon's debate begins. Soon, nearly everyone arrives to answer his name. Most stay for a while, listening and chatting. Then, inevitably, the drift begins. Pages hurry up and down the aisles with sheaves of messages, calling a Congressman or Senator to argue with an executive department on behalf of a constituent, or to tell a garden club delegation why he favors the Shasta daisy for the national flower. Or the Member goes down for lunch, or over to the other body, or downtown to a conference. Almost without volition, he finds himself back in his office trying to keep up with the mail, interviewing, and being interviewed by a stream of callers." * And so goes each day for each elected official.

For me the most difficult of all aspects of a Congressional day is the state of constant interruption. For six years I have worked in the office if there was something of a clerical nature to be done, but I am not grappling with the problems of the world and people are not coming to see me one after another. Each Senator must learn to write or draft or amend or peruse while buzzers and phones are ringing, and as staff members keep opening his office door. Even on the rare occasions when he treats himself to a sitdown lunch in the Senate Restaurant, he is usually interrupted by a quorum call or a roll-call or the need to greet someone in the dining room. I am constantly amazed that most of those who serve in Congress don't have ulcers or nervous collapses.

The proof of what I am saying can be found in the fact that, rather than attempt to write this book in such surroundings, I

* Clement Miller, *Member of the House.* Copyright © 1962, by Charles Scribner's Sons and reprinted by permission.

fled to a friend's house where I could work alone and undisturbed. I am afraid I wouldn't have the stamina to concentrate on writing under the conditions usually found in Congressional offices.

I am reminded of the story of a news correspondent who submitted his expense account after a stint of National Convention coverage. In the silent aftermath of trying to recall his expenses for the week, he included the item, "$34.00 spent that's not recalled; just say seventeen pounds of flesh, my own, at the rate of $2.00 a pound." Senators and Congressmen seem to live under this kind of hysterical pressure all the time; yet they survive and even thrive—some of them. To me these men are a special breed. At the end of these days during which there is much frustration, question-answering, and production, sleep finally steals us away. Unless you stay up and worry—which we do.

Chapter X

"DEAR SENATOR PROXMIRE..."

O NE MORNING there arrived in our mail a letter with a decidedly threatening tone: "Dear Senator Proxmire [it read]: I would like some information on the situation in Ghana. I want you to know I have a pen pal in Ghana, so I can check up on you. I don't wish a timid answer and don't tell me it's classified, for the Reds know what we are doing there, don't they? Would you please answer these questions?" There followed a series of detailed queries about American policy toward Ghana. The writer concluded: "I would like the truth, ever so harsh as it may be. Even though I am in the eighth grade, I'm no dope."

Not all the letters we get give us as much pleasure as that one.

When we first arrived in Washington, Bill and I were astonished to discover the mounds of letters already piled up in our office. Since then we have continued to be surprised how few people know of the burgeoning volume and broad scope of this mail. The bushel baskets that held our first onslaught have since been replaced with overflowing "in" baskets, but the steady stream has never abated.

Because of the two-pronged job every Senator must fulfill— legislating on a national scale and directly serving his constituents—the kind of staff required is different from that in any other profession.

At the top of the heap is the Administrative assistant, who primarily is responsible for running the office smoothly and helping with policy decisions. Below him is usually a Legislative Assistant and a legislative research person who concentrate on the drafting of bills and the preparation of material for the floor. Of course there are the Senator's personal secretary, a couple of "case workers" (more about these later), and two or more people who are responsible for answering legislative mail. Rounding out the average staff are a receptionist, three or four typists, a file clerk, and two or three people who are responsible for handling the facilities for addressing envelopes to the regular mailing list, and filling routine requests.

At first glance this seems to be a substantial array of talent—and it is. These helping hands cost the taxpayers a lot of money. But once a steady, unprejudiced look is taken at what a Senatorial office produces each year, I think it makes the efficiency requirements of other office jobs pale by comparison.

The first adjustment Bill had to make in accepting the necessary set-up of a Congressional office was that all but three of the people on the staff had to be involved in some way with mail. The average person imagines that a Senator does nothing but make speeches, study legislation, and Lead (strongly and creatively of course). This *is* the surface pattern of his job, but his staff must concentrate on other areas if the people back home are to be served and satisfied and if the Senator plans to stay in office.

The mail varies in volume at different times, but I think it's safe to say that Bill's office receives and handles at least 100,000 pieces a year. And the longer you are in Washington, the more you get—it keeps spiraling. In January, 1961, for example, when interest was running high on a particular piece of legislation, the total of letters we received and answered was 8,000; in February, 9,600; in March, 14,844; and in April, 15,200.

There are three main categories into which this mountain of paper can be classified—legislative mail, requests for information and material, and what we call "case mail."

From a human standpoint, I have found the case mail, which requires the solving of individual problems, the most interesting of all. About twenty-five percent of our mail falls into this classification. To many who would never dream of writing to their Senator for anything, this proportion must seem surprising. Into this group of letters fall such subjects as Social Security problems, veterans' claims, military service requests, adoption and immigration cases, emergency leaves, post office problems, government procurement and surplus property inquiries. We get pleas from those who are in the Army and who want to get out, from those who are *not* in the Army and want to get *in*, and from persons in prisons and mental institutions who feel they are wrongly incarcerated and want us to arrange their release.

In a high proportion of these cases our office is successful in helping the beleaguered individual. Two of the most touching I especially remember. One involved the family of a six-year-old girl who had a serious heart condition that could only be corrected by a difficult operation which could not be performed in her home town. Her grandparents wrote to us after exhausting every possibility of having her helped. It happened that the child's father was in the Air Force, stationed in Newfoundland. Through the work of our office, he was transferred to Bolling Air Force Base near Washington, and under the Army family-medical program the operation was successfully performed at Walter Reed Hospital.

A second, delightfully successful case concerned a sixty-year-old widow who lived in East Germany and wanted permission to come to Milwaukee to marry her childhood sweetheart. She had successfully crossed the border once but had had to return to East

Germany to settle some business affairs. By the time she was ready to leave the country, the Wall was up. It took our office a year to convince East German officials that she should be allowed to leave, but finally she was permitted to walk across the Wall.

Some of the cases are of an emergency nature, and their solutions are often the most rewarding. One that immediately comes to mind occurred on a Memorial Day weekend. Late the afternoon of the 29th we received a call from a small town in Wisconsin. The caller's husband had died suddenly and she wanted to reach her only son immediately. He was in the Navy, on board ship. Although it was a holiday weekend, a member of our staff stayed near the phone all day. Finally, at 9:30 that evening, a call came through from the duty officer of the ship. The boy had been reached and was on his way home—just twenty-four hours after we had been asked to help.

Another emergency case involved a Wisconsin family vacationing in Mexico. The four of them had been sight-seeing on a small boat which had somehow caught fire. All sustained only minor burns, except the mother. She had to be hospitalized in a small, poorly staffed Mexican hospital. The husband had telephoned a lawyer friend in Wisconsin, who then telephoned us to see if we couldn't arrange for her flight back to the United States. This entailed endless calls to the American consulate in Mexico, consultations with doctors about the manner in which she could be moved, and discussions with the family. Finally we arranged to have a doctor from Madison flown down to Mexico to fly back with her, since that was the only procedure the Mexican doctors would permit. The accomplishment of this mission took a twelve-hour working Sunday for Bill and me.

Other cases provide us with a few lighter moments. One man wrote and asked us to request that the Weather Bureau name the first hurricane of 1958 after his wife; another gentleman sent us all his unpaid bills to prove that it was impossible for him to live on his Social Security allotment. One woman wrote complaining that there was no pork in canned pork and beans. Another wrote enclosing the label from a can of chicken soup. Glued to the label were two tiny bits of chicken which, she said, were the only ones in the can—a fact which to her mind indicated misrepresentation of the product. An old couple explained that they had been living together for years, both receiving individual Social Security checks; would they receive a larger allotment if they got married? One city government requested a submarine, and another a battleship, both to be used as war memorials in their respective town squares. We didn't have either item in stock that week.

Requests for information and material come from every age group, every type of organization, and for every purpose under the sun. Just sample a typical day's mail; it should give some idea of the kinds of things people ask for and what they hope to find in the Pandora's box of Senatorial "treasures." In one batch, I uncovered requests for the following (reading from top to bottom of the pile in my hand): a request for a copy of a publication called *Magnetism of the Earth,* for information on Medical Care for the Aged, for Bill's monthly newsletter, for information on the manufacture of potato chips, for a copy of *Selling to NASA,* for help on a Ph.D. dissertation, for several autographed photographs, for information on Siberia or Asiatic Russia, for a pamphlet on the preparation of foreign nationals for citizenship, for the new Senate report on Cuba, for help on an American history project which would deal with Senator Proxmire (this request included all the following: picture, biography, news releases, recent speeches, magazine articles, bills and committee reports), for advice on infant care, for a copy of *Your Child from One to Six,* for Senator Thomas Kuchel's speech on "fright mail," for booklets about Wisconsin, for anything we could dig up on the population problem in this country as well as in foreign nations, for five different publications dealing with economic policies and programs, for the proceedings of the Banking and Currency Committee, for a nomination speech which would serve a candidate for the presidency taking part in a mock political convention, for Bill's test-ban speech, for a copy of the Anti-Communist Training proposal and the committee report on Un-American activities.

And so the requests flood our desks. Fortunately, we can fill most of them. Where we draw the line, however, is when students ask us to write their term papers. This, I feel, is substantially above and beyond the call of duty for us or for our staff. It is nevertheless surprising how many of our citizens (junior and otherwise) expect this kind of service, while they at the same time are often the ones who complain about the size of our staff or how much the operation of government costs the American people.

The Senator himself probably pays more attention to the legislative mail than to any of the other categories. For, after all, he is elected to legislate, and in this part of his job he hopes to reflect the interests and viewpoints of the people who voted him into office, as long as these interests do not conflict with his own conscience. Tons of mail on a particular subject would never in itself make a Senator change his mind about voting on a particular issue, but it is a consideration.

Legislative letters take many forms. Some are merely petitions from pressure groups who hope to impress us by the sheer number of those who write in. Some letters threaten; others contain hints of special favor. Much of our correspondence, however, comes from thoughtful supporters or opponents of particular bills, those with a genuine interest in the status of a piece of legislation. During the period when interest was running high on the provision for withholding the tax on dividend interest, we received 16,000 letters in the span of ten days on this one issue. It was obvious to us that people in Wisconsin who had dividend income were deeply concerned about the final form of this bill, and that ninety percent of the ones who wrote in were opposed to the provision as it was reported out of the Finance Committee.

Each of the 16,000 or more who wrote in on the subject eventually received a reply. We found that part of the problem was a basic misunderstanding of the initial proposal. Interest on dividends is presently taxable under our tax laws; but because of the kind of a campaign run by the interests who opposed the legislation, people were led to believe that this was to be a completely new tax. Hence the frantic reaction.

In cases like this the Senator's office and the Senator's position can serve to educate and inform on a subject of concern to his constituents.

Sometimes, I must admit, we wish we received a larger proportion of mail from people who have a genuine concern about the laws that govern them. Senator Kenneth Keating of New York was the recipient of a card that read: "I was given this card to urge you to support a bill I know nothing about. Since I have complete confidence in your judgment, I will use it instead to wish you a Happy Birthday."

All the letters written to a Senator are useful when they are disciplined and balanced, provocative when they are refreshing in tone and subject matter, and hard on the blood pressure when they are abusive, threatening and unreasonable. These last are hardest of all to handle. When one of them arrives we have to decide whether it should be ignored, answered in a flat, unresponsive way ("Many thanks for your recent letter. I was delighted to hear from you and to know your views. You can be certain I will take your opinion into consideration when the legislation you mention comes up for approval on the floor of the Senate"), or treated with the bluntness it deserves.

One vituperative letter we recently received fell in the "legislative" category and, we thought, demanded an answer in kind.

The threat:

"I want an immediate reply of your stand on this question because if not, I will send out a letter to all of our clients throughout Wisconsin (and we have many, many clients, having been in business for forty-two years), stating in this letter that according to our opinion you are not working for the general welfare and common good of the people of this state, but purely to perpetuate yourself in office at the public's expense, and particularly to those who can least afford to keep you there."

This was one of many instances when Bill himself undertook the reply. He wrote:

"Dear Mr. B—:

"You are a very hardhitting, direct, no-nonsense letter writer.

"Seldom in my five years in the Senate have I ever received a more insulting or brazen threat than yours.

"Apparently you don't know me very well. No man or group of men is ever going to tell me how to vote on any issue. I am happy to listen to reasoned argument, but my main job is to do all I can to arrive at an intelligent and just decision based on all the facts, and I will do so in this case as in others.

"It is very interesting that you should attach to your letter a carbon copy of the great statement by Dean Alfange entitled *I Do Not Choose to Be a Common Man*.

"My reply to you is very well stated in the last few lines in which you quote from Alfange. Here it is:

'I will never cower before any master nor bend to any threat. It is my heritage to stand erect, proud and unafraid; to think and act for myself; enjoy the benefits of my creations and to face the world boldly and say, this I have done. All this is what it means to be an American.'

"And to this, I might add, all this is what it means to be a United States Senator.

"The purpose of this letter is to serve notice on you that you should at once write to all of your clients throughout Wisconsin stating anything you want to state in your letter.

"Thanks again for a hardhitting, vigorous letter and an opportunity for me to go on record publicly, asserting once again that no threats and no manner of intimidation are going to press me into voting against my conscience."

No matter how carefully a Senator tries to explain the issues to his constituents, there are constant examples in each mail bag of extreme and unreasonable requests, accompanied by garbled bits and pieces of information that make no sense at all.

We were luckier than most in that we had a staff man who took some of the "impossible" letters and drafted "dreamworld" replies—ones we'd *like* to send out but of course never will. Here are a few of these letters and the answers he drafted. We call this collection the "Ivan Papers" (our man's name was Ivan), and turn to it whenever the doldrums set in.

One letter we received included a quotation from Thomas Jefferson, a derogatory statement about Chief Justice Earl Warren's "pro-Communist" decisions, and a suggestion that Mr. Warren be forced to copy the Jefferson quotation a hundred times after Court every day.

Our unsent reply: "Dear Mr. J—: We did have Justice Warren write that quotation from Jefferson a hundred times, but he began to get surly. So we sent him outside to chip some words in stone in the front of the Supreme Court Building. He wrote: EQUAL JUSTICE UNDER LAW. We didn't keep him after Court any more."

Another letter demanded that Bill vote against a measure that would have bestowed the title "physician" on chiropodists. The sender said it would be "ridiculous to give the title of physician to a chiropodist." Our reply (unsent): "Ridiculous, my foot!"

Another: "Dear Senator Proxmire: Most of your views are contrary to mine. I am sending them to you as a guide in your voting if you consider yourself a representative of Wisconsin, because I am from Wisconsin. I am against Federal Aid to Education, Social Security, foreign aid, President Kennedy's program, Freeman's farm bill, and any income tax revision."

The reply we wish we had sent: "Dear Sir: Most of your views are contrary to mine, but I got elected and you didn't. That's the way the old cookie crumbles, pal."

Last but not least: "Dear Senator Proxmire: In reference to the King bill. I am against it. First, dagbusted taxes are ridiculous enough. Second, we have too much socialism as it is. If you are for the King bill, I want to know why."

Reply (in fantasy): "Dear Mr. S—: By the 'dagbusted taxes,' I assume you are referring to the tax on dagbusts, and I am inclined to agree with you. There is entirely too much swearing going on nowadays. It's bad for the kids. By 'too much socialism,' I assume you mean all this cocktail party business here in Washington, and again I am inclined to agree with you. There is entirely too much socializing going on nowadays. It's bad for the kids. I am not for the King bill, or the Queen bill either, for that matter. I am no dagbusted Socialist Monarchist!"

These letters provide us with the "pause that refreshes" and make the serious handling of mail more possible.

To describe the position of file clerk in an office the words "drudgery," "routine," "tedium" and "detail" usually come first to mind. When one considers the amount of mail that pours into an office like ours, the variety of subjects covered and the necessity for keeping it in an orderly fashion, then the position of file clerk assumes a new quality. We had the best when we had Shirley Preston to oversee our fantastic files.

For four years it was Shirley's creative intellect that held the mechanics of our office together. She devised a system that made it possible to find things easily, no matter how obscure the subject matter or unreadable the signature. She not only filed, she read and digested hundreds of letters. Her interest in the material was intense, and this interest made it possible for her to truly know what was what—and where.

Time after time there would be a rush call for something that the staff member making the request could only recall in the vaguest way. Shirley would remember, because she read what she filed.

The same was true of material from the *Congressional Record*. Her interest in the stuff and substance of the Senate was profound and genuine and thus her secure knowledge of the daily procedure made it easy for her to track down a debate for which someone was searching. More important, though, was the fact that she enjoyed her work. She would shake with laughter or shudder with dismay as a passage of a letter or debate from the *Record* struck her.

She was very proud of the thoroughness of her work, but her greatest strength was the way she lived through the most painful and prolonged kind of illness. Although the inevitable certainty of death was her constant companion for years, Shirley's ringing laugh is something all of us will remember. She read everything she could get her hands on, tried new recipes, made hot food for others who were ill, and never gave up hoping.

With great effort her work continued up until two weeks before her death and even at that time, a pitifully wasted figure, she apologized to a fellow staff member that "The Senator hasn't gotten his money's worth out of me this month."

It was April, 1962, the month she died, a time of contrast and extremes. Winter had seemed to hang on in the early days of the month, but suddenly the mercury zoomed to the high eighties and we had summer. The Congress recessed around Easter time, as it usually does, but the subtraction of these few people from the Washington scene was immediately offset by the tourists who poured into town. Great issues like the future of the UN, nuclear testing, and the steel controversy dominated the newspapers, but the extraordinary volume of our mail then reflected interest in a single aspect of the proposed tax revision bill. The saddest contrast of all, though, for us, was the sudden glorious beauty of spring and the void left by Shirley's death.

We still miss the quiet efficiency and the delightful chuckle that accompanied the filing in the past. At the same time, all of us in 4327 New Senate Office Building will be better people having known Shirley Preston. She combined all the qualities that are necessary in large measure for anyone who takes on a job on the Hill: loyalty, willingness to work overtime often, interest in her work, and devotion to public service.

Though the mail occupies us most of the time, we have a monthly newsletter to get out, itineraries for home visits to plan, press releases to prepare, speeches to research, reservations to make, invitations to answer, bizarre requests to fill (for cuff links, handkerchiefs, ties, hats and such), address plates to cut, mailing lists to maintain, mimeographing to do.

On the plus side, this means that all the people who work in a Congressional office eventually get to do a variety of jobs. Things are never dull. But—on the minus side—it means that the requirements of each day are completely unpredictable. If there is a sudden emergency, or a sudden deluge of correspondence, it, too, must be handled expeditiously. This means that many of the members of our staff take work home with them in the evening or on weekends, and it often requires that Bill and I and those who work for us put in twelve- to fifteen-hour days in order to stay a little ahead of the game.

As Doris Fleeson once said: "There are no 'wonder men' or 'wonder women.' Just you and I, and others like us who believe in freedom, to tackle the job. There are only those of us with vision to see the world as it is and the courage to try to do something about it."

I believed when we arrived in Washington—and this belief has been strengthened as the years have fled—that it is a Senator's job to legislate, to help constituents when possible to obtain some government service, to thoroughly understand what is happening throughout the world and with his pen and voice educate and inform. It is the constituent's job to make himself aware of the issues at stake, of the demands on his Congressman's time, and to be fair and objective in his letters and requests. He should remember that his letter is only one of thousands, each of them important to someone, that cross a Congressional desk. He should consider the necessity of his request. Is it in the general interest? Is it plausible, courteous and legitimate?

Congressman Silvio O. Conte of Massachusetts put it very well in an article of advice called "Writing to your Congressman: The Why and the Wherefore." * He said, "Every citizen has a right to representation and his Congressman in Washington is elected to preserve and extend those rights. It is perfectly clear, then, that every citizen has (to coin a phrase) a right to write.

"The best reason for writing to your Congressman or Senator is to make sure that he is, in fact, representing you and will continue to work diligently for the best interests of both his district and his Nation. Don't forget either that an elected official represents all the people of his constituency regardless of political party. Though your views on some issues might differ, he will still be interested in hearing from you.

"A few hints may be in order. 1) Know what you are talking about; 2) tell your Congressman or Senator how the proposed legislation will affect you and your business; 3) believe in the value of a personal letter rather than a form or petition; 4) don't forget to write legibly and always include your address, even

* The article appeared originally in the Sprague Electrical Company *Log*, March, 1963.

134

on petitions. This can save both time and temper and assures an answer. Letters help the Congressman or Senator bridge the growing gap between the individual and ever-increasingly big and complex government."

The legislator's relationship with his constituents is thus a two-way street—a kinship such as was beautifully described by the English philosopher Edmund Burke, who wrote in 1774: "It ought to be the happiness and glory of a representative to live in the strictest union, the closest correspondence, and the most unreserved communication with his constituents. Their wishes ought to have great weight with him; their opinion, his high respect; their business, his unremitting attention. It is his duty to sacrifice his repose, his pleasures, his satisfactions, to theirs; and, above all, and in all cases, to prefer their interest to his own. But his unbiased opinion, his mature judgment, his enlightened conscience—these he ought never sacrifice to you, to any man, or to any group of men living. These he does not derive from your pleasure; no, nor from the law and the constitution—they are a trust from Providence, for the abuse of which he is deeply answerable. Your representative owes you not only his industry, but his judgment, and he betrays, instead of serving you, if he sacrifices it to your opinion."

Chapter XI

JUST FOR THE RECORD

THE OTHER DAY, I picked up a copy of my favorite periodical in Bill's office. I knew it well, but this issue seemed particularly interesting. It contained articles on handicapped workers, labor unions, a test ban treaty, the UN International Conference on Trade, an education plan to service industry, transatlantic fares, free enterprise, the Alliance for Progress, captive nations, the debt limit, gold, vocational agriculture, Cuba, Laos, "managed news," the University of Maryland, the remarkable apple, Northwest electric cooperatives, cultural exchange, the space program, Ronald Reagan's speeches, the Oppenheimer case, federal troops in Alabama, the World Health Organization, the general welfare, the UN's cash crisis, the wheat referendum, the federal budget, the fifteenth anniversary of Israel, the economic development of Mexico, the future of American seapower, financial support for the arts, breaking through the "cancer curtain," the REA, the VFW and the DAR—all between the first and last pages of one issue. These articles made up just the Appendix portion of the timeliest, most provocative, most up-to-date publication I know—the *Congressional Record*. The daily transcript of debate in the Senate and House takes up the remaining two-thirds of each day's issue.

Of course, nobody ever sits down and reads the *Record* word for word. It would take forever. But if one did have the time, I can't think of any other publication that offers so much varied information. In addition to the debates, there is the above-mentioned Appendix, containing the most significant editorials, speeches and articles from magazines and newspapers from all over the country.

Each issue of the *Congressional Record* is a 100,000-word book, more or less, which is written daily on the floor of the Congress. It contains the word-for-word transcript of every minute of debate, plus the insertions made for the Appendix. Some of the debates are just plain dull for the average person. But a number make exciting and often entertaining reading—a sort of real-life *Advise and Consent*.

To me the unsung heroes of the Senate are the official reporters who handle the enormous job of taking down in shorthand every one of these tens of thousands of words. Theirs is an exacting, complex job that requires the greatest of patience and accuracy.

Not long ago, I happened to talk with Mr. John Rhodes, second in command of the fifteen-man staff of Senate reporters, who told me that because there are no microphones on the floor of the Senate, the official reporters often sit in chairs of absent Senators in order to catch every word. They are so unobtrusive in their work that people in the gallery often think they are Members of the Senate.

Only six men of the fifteen actually handle the shorthand end of the *Congressional Record*. Each reporter works ten minutes out of every hour on the floor. He then dictates his notes into a machine, turns them over to a typist, who returns the triple-spaced pages to the reporter for an initial check. If the Senator whose words are being recorded wishes, he may go over his remarks to see if what he said was reported accurately. Mr. Rhodes or Mr. James Murphy makes a final inspection for grammar before the material is rushed to the Government Printing Office.

Bill and I have often made late-night trips to the Printing Office to make sure that his copy was correct. It is fascinating to see this tremendous printing operation in process. Some of the people there have held the same job for forty years, working all that time on the *Record*. My own grandfather worked there for that amount of time, and for this reason my trips to the Printing Office have a sentimental appeal.

James Murphy is really "Mr. Congressional Record." This senior reporter has been on the job for sixty-three years, having taken over in 1896 from his uncle, Dennis F. Murphy. Uncle Dennis, in turn, had been at the task since 1848 when he was picked by Senator John C. Calhoun to give verbatim reports on Senate debate instead of the brief summaries recorded before that time. So the story of the *Congressional Record* as we know it for the past hundred and eleven years is actually the story of the Murphys, Dennis and John.

Even when a session runs late into the night, we have usually found our copy of the *Record* waiting on our doorstep early the following morning. When you consider that most of the issues run well over 150 pages, it is a truly remarkable example of efficient production by a few skilled men.

I asked Mr. Rhodes why modern stenotype machines aren't used instead of relying on shorthand "by hand." There are many reasons, he said, for keeping the old-fashioned procedure: the reporters must often write while walking toward a speaker; the atmosphere of the Senate is better preserved by having the reporters do their job as silently and unobtrusively as possible; because of the acoustics in the Chamber, the reporters must often sit at a desk adjacent to that of an orating Member and a clicking machine would be an impossible distraction. I think, too, that there is a certain reluctance to cast away a tradition that has served so well all these years.

There are no statues, plaques, or citations to these diligent men in the Capitol. Very few even know the name of the greatest reporter of them all—Mr. Theodore F. Schuey, who came to the Capitol in 1868 and worked until the day of his death in 1933 without missing a day! Shorthand might be fast becoming a lost art in this age of machines, but as long as the Senate and House have Official Reporters, it will be used to bring to the public mountains of words and volumes of some of the most interesting and significant reading available—more than 13,000 pages usually by the first of June each Congressional year.

By law each Member of the Senate is allotted one hundred copies of the *Record* and each House Member is allotted sixty-eight. We can mail out these copies to those who so request and use the rest for office purposes. The run at the Printing Office each night is about 44,000.

The average citizen in Oshkosh, Sacramento, or Seattle probably has little chance to read the *Congressional Record*. So other ways must be devised to present the ideas and accomplishments of legislators to the public that elected them. A Senator communicates through press releases from his office, through newsletters, through personal correspondence, through newspaper interviews—and, more and more, through television and radio.

I am convinced that a combination of swift travel and swifter communication, both written and spoken, lies at the heart of modern politics. The former is symbolized by the modern jet airplane and the old-fashioned suitcase, the latter by the newspaperman's pen, the mimeograph machine and the mystery of the wires. Velocity and vocabulary, strato-cruisers and semantics, speed and the spoken word—all are inseparable components of the life of our politicians in the 'sixties. Sometimes this ease of communication works to the disadvantage of Congressmen, for misleading statements and vilification can travel as swiftly as the truth. Most of the time, however, it is a real boon.

Without the airplane, each week would be an impossibility for

Bill or for anyone engaged in the work of modern political communication, whether he is running for the Senate, the House, or for Governor of a State. How else would it be possible to be in Washington, then New York City, then Washington, then Rochester, then Washington again, then Milwaukee, Madison, Chicago, Washington and Boston—all in the space of two weeks?

A constant companion in this incessant coming and going is the old-fashioned but necessary suitcase. Bill's is usually hurriedly packed, but nonetheless I always attempt to see that it contains enough so my traveler can survive without too much inconvenience. Of course, the pitfalls are many in this kind of guessing game. I have packed a handsome shirt with French cuffs—and forgotten the cuff links; I have put in a razor, but no blades; I have failed to include extra shoelaces and even galoshes, forgetting that my peripatetic husband might find himself in the midst of a blizzard "at the other end." Our miscalculations have been many, even though packing has become almost second nature to us, but somehow "makeshift" and "make-do" have also become second nature in this here-today-gone-tomorrow existence, and the price of inconvenience becomes a part of the job.

Written communication is considerably more unpredictable and often harder to handle. There's nothing like putting it down in black and white. There are the piles of personal letters to be answered, quickly and judiciously. Yet even the most beautifully phrased, carefully thought-out reply goes only to one person, and has very little impact on the public as a whole.

As much as he would like to communicate with every constituent personally, the politician must resort to the "press release" in order to disseminate his views as widely as possible.

Press releases go out regularly from our office, describing in detail positions Bill has taken on the floor of the Senate or speeches he has made on a given subject. Whether or not these are subsequently used by newspapers in Wisconsin is up to the individual editor. Quite often the releases—sometimes for lack of space, more often because of policy—are not run, so we must rely more heavily than most on radio and television programs taped here in Washington to get our point of view across to the citizens of our state.

With the use of this form of communication there is no possibility of distortion or omission resulting in a mistaken understanding. We have often used the debate form on our TV shows to make them more interesting and meaningful to our listeners. One year Bill ran a series in which he invited a Republican Congressman from our state to take part with him on each show. It was a worthwhile experiment which was subsequently broadcast on all eleven stations.

We have concluded after six years in Washington that a politician can never win a fight with a newspaper. He expects, naturally, that there will be occasional editorial disagreement with his philosophy, point of view, or his vote on a particular issue. But one thing most of us will never get used to is editorial positions that mount an assault on personal motivation and honesty. I remember in particular a column in which the writer assumed, without ever checking with us, that we were out to scuttle a fund-raising effort here in Washington for the campaign of our fellow Democrat, Gaylord Nelson, now Junior Senator from Wisconsin. In truth we had cooperated in every way with the local Nelson committee, offered to have a party in our home and even provided lists of names that would be useful in an initial mailing. Though we wrote a letter explaining this to the local papers who had run the original column, no retraction was ever made and the impression still persists in the minds of a lot of people that Bill Proxmire was somehow cool to the Nelson candidacy.

There have been other more substantial examples of editorial dishonesty and unwarranted personal attack, and it is a maddening and frustrating situation. But the trials of delayed and cancelled planes, missing items in a hastily packed suitcase, or frequent misunderstanding are all part of the game for those in public service in a democratic government. Despite this, the rewards are substantial. Most planes *do* arrive on time, the sun is often shining at both ends of the road, constituents are usually thrilled beyond expression at some effort we make in their behalf, and occasionally we are the recipients of a glowing, complimentary editorial. All of which goes to show that modern communication does have its advantages and a necessary place in modern politics.

One other way in which we communicate with the folks back home has been my effort, through bi-weekly columns, to tell off-beat stories to the readers in Wisconsin. One of my most interesting assignments was tracking down some of the Wisconsin appointees in their new jobs in Washington.

My first foray took me to a makeshift headquarters on Connecticut Avenue where a brand-new federal agency was being set up—one that had and still has dramatic possibilities for our country and for the cause of world peace. For the first time since 1933, Washington was witness to the birth of an agency that has stirred the imaginations of people everywhere. It all happened so quickly that when I arrived at the headquarters I found mail piled up 13,000 pieces deep, phones jangling at empty desks, and equipment and personnel borrowed from other agencies just to handle daily problems as they arose. This was home base for the Peace Corps, which I chauvinistically regard as one of the Midwest's most promising brainchildren.

Chief Congressional sponsors of the Peace Corps were Representative Henry Reuss from Milwaukee and Senator Hubert Humphrey of Minnesota. The Director is R. Sargent Shriver of Illinois and the Director of Public Information at the time I visited was Edwin Bayley, formerly of Milwaukee and Madison.

The President's original message to the Congress on the Peace Corps called forth such an incredible response that the tiny staff that had been rounded up in Washington specifically for planning purposes was immediately drowned in office detail. Everyone, including the top people, was handling correspondence, taking messages, interviewing applicants and answering reporters' questions. Many of those who had come to apply or to ask for information found themselves a part of the organization before they had even been interviewed for a specific job. Everyone from volunteers to janitors was questioned by TV and newspaper reporters. Three publishing houses sent writers down to do a book on the Corps even though the details of the program had not even been worked out. At the time I called at the headquarters, Congress had not appropriated a cent for the program, and none of those then working knew what they were to be paid, when, or if at all.

I sampled the mail and found that those interested in participating ranged in age from ten to eighty-three. One elderly gentleman wrote to say that he had had a complete physical checkup, was found to be in perfect condition and concluded that he felt more able to serve and to stand the adverse conditions overseas than most young people. A woman in New York State even volunteered her husband for service in Siberia, indicating that she wasn't sure how it would affect world peace, but that it would certainly make for peace in her house.

Ed Bayley told me of his expectations, which have since become reality. He described the effort to train young people in special skills and in the languages and customs of the countries to which they would go; how they would be sent overseas to work side by side with people who need help. He described the intent and purpose of the Peace Corps: to add a new dimension— a human dimension—to our foreign policy. To Ed this was an effort to wage war on the *causes* of war: human misery, ignorance and lack of understanding between human beings.

I came away from our talk convinced of the wisdom of this program, really the first one in which an individual citizen could do something with his own hands, heart, and mind to serve other

143

people around the world. At a time when the fires of self-sacrifice seemed to be burning low among our people, I realized that these Peace Corps volunteers would be doing something for America that fit well with our historic tradition of boldness and individual effort.

Another man who started a new job in Washington in the winter of 1961 was Newton B. Minow, formerly of Milwaukee, and at that time the new Chairman of the Federal Communications Commission. He was the man who for two years had more to say about what we saw on television and heard on radio than any individual in America.

When he first took on his new responsibilities, Newt was astounded by the amount of paper work involved. The seven-man Commission which he supervised met every Wednesday, and the average number of votes taken in each meeting was and still is 150. Each vote encompassed decisions of great importance and involved millions of dollars.

At one point he testified three times in seven days before Congressional committees—once on educational television, once on his agency's budget and once on the equal-time bill. Naturally, every one of these appearances required substantial preparation.

For Newt Minow personally, the job had meant moving his family from Chicago, giving up his law practice, working long night hours and, until his family arrived, maintaining three separate establishments.

Whenever I talked to Newt I was aware of his deep interest in government and his desire to contribute to it. In fact, he once said that if he could have picked any job in Washington, he would have chosen this one. Since the average American spends more time watching television than in any other activity except sleeping or working, he found it an extremely challenging undertaking.

Rather than attempting to legislate the viewing and listening habits of Americans, Newt saw his job as one of leadership.

Throughout his tenure, he consistently fought for the public interest, encouraged local participation when it was time for a broadcaster's license to be renewed, and tried to put his agency on a pay-as-you-go basis.

He said to me, "I think the real job of the Commission is to examine the licensee's performance and to see whether the promises that it has made in obtaining that license have been lived up to. If they have promised to devote some time to public service programming and it turns out that they haven't, then I think it's the FCC's function to see to it that they do."

One of the first letters Newt received after taking office said, "First you should abolish daytime TV; then you should abolish nighttime TV; then you should go home."

After he had been there for a while a letter came applauding him. It said: "You have substantially improved TV. Now what can you do about TV dinners?" (These made me feel better about some of our own letter-writers.)

In the course of his two years of service, Newt, a naturally gentle and conciliatory man, developed the hide of a rhinoceros and a permanently stiffened backbone. His promise of more "wide open spaces between the Westerns and more public affairs instead of Private Eyes" has become a reality, and I think that, thanks to him, we have taken a giant step toward a better viewing future.

Another Wisconsin emigrant with a new job was Philleo Nash, the new appointee as Commissioner of the Bureau of Indian Affairs. Since I actually know very little about this particular aspect of governmental activity and since Philleo came from the cranberry bogs of central Wisconsin, I decided to do a little investigating.

The story he told me was fascinating. The first Commissioner was appointed in 1775 by the Continental Congress. He and his agents were charged with the responsibility of securing the loyalty of the Indians to the new government, in spite of British attempts to incite them to violence. The frontier years saw many later-to-be-famous names on the roster of Indian agents and Commissioners. Outstanding among them were Ben Franklin, Patrick Henry, and Kit Carson.

Since then the role of the federal government in Indian life has been concentrated in three specific areas: 1) the provision of local government services to the 380,000 Indians who live on or near reservations where these services are not supplied by the states; 2) the management of the 53,000,000 acres of Indian land that are held by the federal government in trust for beneficial use of Indian tribes and individuals; 3) the provision of special services such as vocational and educational instruction which substantially speed the process of Indian integration into everyday metropolitan American life.

The ultimate goal of federal participation in this two-hundred-year-old problem is maximum economic self-sufficiency for Indians, full participation of Indians in American life, and equal citizenship privileges and responsibilities for these forgotten Americans. The program seems slow and costly, but progress is being made. Some would dispute this progress, as one Sioux did after an Industrial Development meeting recently. He contended that the ordinary American spends fifty weeks a year doing what he hates in order to be able to spend two weeks in the lap of nature—living as Indians do.

Most of those Indians who have had the benefit of vocational instruction are now gainfully employed. Thousands have left the reservations and are now living in big cities all over the country. In case after case, training has helped even those on the reservation to become valuable producers of livestock, arts and crafts and timber products, and thus has made the reservations largely economically self-sufficient.

I was reminded that the efforts of Philleo and his Bureau extend from reservations as far north as the Arctic Circle and as far south as the Florida Everglades. Many areas are remote, unbelievably primitive, and full of natural resistance to change. English is a second language in many settlements. I could see that the Commissioner's job was a tremendous one. Like those of elected officials, his efforts are geared to finding rational solutions in fields of frequently irrational opinion.

Every man who serves the public in Washington makes a constant effort to communicate with those who elected him, with those who write *to* him and *about* him, with those who listen to him and expect him to listen to them. There is no single, sure method, so he tries them all—the *Record*, a newsletter, television, radio, columns, letters, speeches, releases and feature stories. His one hope is that understanding will eventually replace the usual quick emotional reaction to what a politician does and is.

As Nelson Polsby said in his review of Clem Miller's book, *Member of the House*, "Congressmen share certain experiences that to a degree separate them from other men—the crucible of running for office, the rigors of campaigning that bind them together. 'These people, these Congressmen,' Miller observed, 'have all been through the mill. They have returned from the indifferent cruelties of the political wars. They may have been saddened by the failure of friends to understand as much as they were outraged by the indignities suffered from their opponents. Elections are unrelenting and painful.' For Clem Miller (and for all of us who share political life) the key to politics is understanding, not moralizing. His was a mind that ruminated upon the classic questions of politics: What moves men? What prizes do they covet? When are they hesitant? When bold? What leads them to affection? To animosity?" *

* Clement Miller, *Member of the House.* Copyright © 1962, by Charles Scribner's Sons and reprinted by permission.

Chapter XII

MENDING THE FENCES

Every congressional year is peppered here and there with "recesses." Because most people remember "recess" from schooldays, they associate the word with a break in work and a fine time on the playground. The word itself implies a vacation.

Up until World War II, Congressional sessions were short, and adjournment time usually came before the middle of the calendar year. Because of this and the relative lack of speedy transportation, elected officials in Washington were not expected to return to their home districts at all during a session. Many of their wives and families did not even accompany them to Washington.

Now the reality of the jet plane and the need to serve an expanding population, all of whom want to see their leaders in the flesh, means that a "recess" represents exactly the opposite of its childhood connotations.

Bill and I decided very soon after our arrival in Washington that he should use these recesses to go back to Wisconsin, to travel throughout the state as much as possible and to regard the trips as a sort of investment in the future of his job. It was a hard decision to make, not only because travel is an expensive proposition, but because it means that the available time for family life is inevitably cut to almost nothing.

Even the holiday weekends that most families count on as family gatherings are the times when Senators and Congressmen most often have to be away from home maintaining and mending the fences. Valentine's Day falls during the February recess, Easter during the spring recess; the Fourth of July and Labor Day bring dozens of picnics, parades and rallies back home, to which political figures are invited—and in which they are almost required to participate. Thanksgiving falls during the period after adjournment when most Congressional families are separated. Only Christmas can truly be depended upon. The week between the 25th of December and New Year's Day is, fortunately, the worst possible time for politicking—so then and only then can we count on our men being home.

To be more specific, let's take a typical February recess and examine it in detail. Usually this is a ten- or twelve-day period during which the Senators are assured they can touch home plate without missing any roll-calls. There are a few *pro forma* sessions every three days or so, to comply with the Constitutional requirement that the Senate never adjourn for longer than three consecutive days. However, no legislative business that requires a vote is transacted on these occasions.

Usually when this period approaches neighbors ask us, "Where are you going for a vacation?" And each year the idea of a long rest grows more tempting. But it never seems to develop beyond the point of temptation. For most men who reach high elective office, there really isn't much difficulty in choosing between such alternatives; the drive and energy that carried them to success in the first place don't disappear once the election has been won. And the pull of the people back home usually wins the tug of war on the private battlefield of each Congressional family. As Lindy Boggs (wife of Hale Boggs, Democratic Whip in the House) once said, "All political wives must learn early in the game that their husbands will always be having a love affair. Fortunately, it is an affair with their work, not with another woman."

The February recess I recall most vividly was one in which the people of Wisconsin won out again—not only over my plans for a vacation, but over a doctor's advice about the wisdom of Bill's making a trip with a strep throat and a heavy cold.

That year Bill decided to make an intensive swing through the major dairy counties of the state. The late winter months are good times to strengthen farm contacts, because farmers' field work is less demanding, and most of them have time to attend meetings.

It turned out to be a grueling ten days, plagued with the worst weather of the year. Bill had to make the trip, had to be on time at each stop. The staff and I had to see that he had a place to speak and an audience when he got there—the bigger the better.

How did we do it? First, we scanned the Livestock, Dairy and Poultry publication of the Wisconsin Department of Agriculture, observing and recording the counties in which there was the greatest concentration of dairy cattle, and therefore, dairy farm families. This is a new twist—first finding cows and then people —but that is the way we had to go about it. With this in mind, we laid out an orderly pattern for the course of the itinerary.

Then, using a township map, we pinpointed the names and locations of town halls and wrote to each of the respective town chairmen asking for the use of their town hall for a meeting. We set our goal at seventy-nine meetings for the ten-day period, so the hourly schedule was tight and mileage had to be figured out precisely.

For the final check, our Wisconsin representative went over the route to see that such an undertaking was physically possible. Then press releases were sent to all newspapers and radio stations detailing the itinerary.

Many who knew about this particular trip asked, "Why go to all this back-breaking effort, especially at such a dismal and unpredictable time of the year?" I think the answer clearly lies in the result. My husband was able to talk to about 10,000 farmers during this one "working recess." This convinced him (as if he had needed convincing!) of the importance of going out to the people.

A political trip like this means getting constituents' views, answering their questions personally, shaking their hands, informing them about developments in Washington that affect them, and using this knowledge for future decision.

As usual, there were many mishaps and miscalculations. Some of the town halls were unheated (in below-freezing weather); some were only heated with pot-bellied stoves and bursts of hot, dry air almost wrecked forever Bill's already miserable throat; some people insisted on reading long documents during the question period, a fact which played havoc with our carefully pared time schedule; many of the roads were icy, and hair-raising rides resulted. During the middle of the week Bill was scheduled to fly to Chicago for an evening speech and then return to the tour. Calls to Senator Humphrey's office alerted the police at the Minnesota border, for there were only minutes to spare to make the only flight. After a perilous drive at high speed over icy roads, the plane left, five minutes before Bill and his driver reached the airport. This disappointment, the chances they had taken to make the flight, and the fact that Bill could scarcely speak above a whisper by this time, almost caused the cancellation of the rest of the trip. But so much had gone into its preparation and so many had turned out at the previous meetings, that Bill decided to finish it up. On the personal side, my husband will probably never be able to look another hamburger in the face—especially a cold one.

But the moments of warmth and friendship made up for everything. One farmer compared Bill's tour to the ones old Bob

La Follette used to make; the county sheriffs were marvelously cooperative in helping us keep on our tight schedule; and there was even an elderly couple who insisted that Bill drink hot milk for his deep chest cold before continuing on the road.

This February tour and those that preceded and followed it brought Bill closer to his people, the voters of Wisconsin. He learned their grievances and received their suggestions and recommendations. Those of us who were responsible for setting up the itinerary and doing the advance work were delighted when the great effort was history (we have never actually tried anything this ambitious since). But we were equally pleased that our complicated preparations paid off by making a trip that seemed "impossible" on paper an extremely productive and rewarding reality.

Spring and summer trips are of a different variety. The time allotted is usually shorter, say, a four-day weekend, so the distances Bill expects to travel are somewhat more realistic than the winter farm tour just discussed. Usually the itinerary is built around specific functions such as "Bratwurst Day" in Sheboygan, the South Side Music Festival and Parade in Milwaukee, a county fair appearance, the crowning of a Queen, or an American Legion picnic. On Memorial Day Bill can usually take part in three different programs in three different towns, providing they are close to each other.

In between the more formal appearances there are stops at plant gates each weekday morning where there are scores of hands to shake, outdoor concerts where there are hundreds of hands to shake, and, of course, the Milwaukee Braves baseball games where there are thousands of hands to shake. There are always ward meetings and union meetings, too, and the members are always pleased when their Senator drops in.

During the fall recess we plan a different kind of itinerary. This time we have three and a half months to schedule, so we concentrate on the areas of the state that are harder to reach on weekend trips. Three autumns in a row (1959, 1960, and 1961) Bill concentrated on speaking to high school assemblies. The advance planning here first involved writing letters to each of the high school principals in the state inquiring if they would be interested in having Bill speak to the students briefly while they were in assembly. As the answers were received we laid out the geographical part of the schedule. Our over-all goal was four towns a day.

This meant the first high school assembly would be set for 9:00 A.M., the next for 11:30, the next for 1:30 or 2:00 and the final one at 3:30. After each high school appearance Bill would drop by the post office to greet anyone who wanted to see him, to shake the hands of store owners on Main Street before heading on to the next town. Sometimes there would be an opportunity for an afternoon plant gate stop before some county party function took place in the evening.

It takes a great deal of stamina to survive this kind of daily routine, but my husband, like most successful politicians, seems to thrive on it. Some men, particularly Senators Humphrey, Morse, Douglas, Gore, Javits and Kuchel, even look much better after months of this kind of effort than they do after a grueling legislative session. I am not that adaptable, I'm afraid, and even after years of trying still find heavy campaigning an exhausting experience.

My own schedule for returning to Wisconsin each year goes something like this: I go back for our annual State Convention, our annual Jefferson-Jackson Day Dinner, and for a week during each of the fall months Bill is in the state. While there, I concentrate on mending other kinds of fences—mainly seeing party people and elected officials whom Bill doesn't get a chance to see as often as he would like. In addition, I try valiantly to avoid getting food poisoning, which seems to be my inevitable fate after a few days of eating at truck stops in remote areas. Bill has never had an upset stomach in his life, and this has stood him in good stead, especially on his hectic fence-mending tours. I envy him.

One of the most troublesome aspects of a Senator's job is the problem of "patronage." I have always said that politicians are so busy with each new stage in their careers that they have little time to think of what lies ahead or even remember and enjoy what has just happened. That is part of the profession's attraction, but also part of its frustration. The fresh problems and burdens of the new Administration had never occurred to us until we had to face a few of them ourselves. We had been so busy working for the success of the Kennedy-Johnson ticket, we hadn't contemplated what success would really mean. Soon after 1961 began we learned—especially about patronage.

To the average citizen the word itself has an evil meaning. But to anyone who has had anything to do with active and practical politics, it *can* have a constructive meaning—the hope and possibility of jobs for qualified supporters if your side wins. According to Webster, patronage means "the right or control of nomination to political office; also the offices, contracts, honors, etc., which a public official may bestow by favor." And there are hundreds of such jobs that change hands when a new Administration—local, state or national—comes into power.

During our 1961 trips home I think we managed to personally cross paths—and swords—with most of those who were interested in getting one of these jobs. They wanted Cabinet posts, sub-Cabinet posts, diplomatic posts, overseas assignments with government agencies, and federal judgeships. They wanted to be U.S. District Attorneys, U.S. Marshals, local postmasters, Hearing Examiners for the Civil Service Commission, heads of Savings Bond Districts, meat cutters with the Army, and elevator operators.

Thousands of letters descended on our office with pleas of need, claims of long service in behalf of the Democratic Party, professions of undying devotion to us and to the President. These letters were often accompanied by endorsements from prominent local officials. Some even threatened dire political consequences if we didn't attempt to satisfy them.

The kinds of people we saw in 1961 on trips home were different from types we had seen before. Factions began to develop within some of the county organizations, one side backing one candidate for a job, and one side backing another. We decided then and there that the consequences of the patronage system are often less than happy ones for a Senator, his party, or the individual job-seeker.

It has long been a saying among men in Congress that when there are ten applicants for a single office, the final choice creates nine enemies and one ingrate. The fact nonetheless remains that in the past many a strong and unbeatable political machine has been built on the power of appointment. I think most men in office today would prefer that only those who are eminently qualified be appointed—men not only interested in helping those who appointed them, but in doing their new jobs to the best of their abilities. This would be the ultimate ideal of good and sound government, but it is not as yet a reality.

We learned to live with the "spoils system" in 1961, and on all our trips had to battle with the problems and disappointments of job-seekers in hotel lobbies, airports, restaurants, meeting halls and stores. As Pendleton Harris says in *The Politics of Democracy*, the struggle with spoils is still the "tar baby" of American politics.

Bill finds it both embarrassing and troublesome to be confronted with persistent job-seekers. Not that this isn't a very real part of the political picture, but the fact doesn't make it any easier—especially when he gets calls for support before a deceased office-holder is even buried, or when someone who is unqualified but deserving in party terms requests help, or when his interest in a particular appointment puts him in conflict with another member of his Congressional delegation. These are the times when I dread the phone's ringing or the opening of the mail.

Bill did, however, have something to do with one appointment that was eminently appropriate. One James Dillon of Green Bay, Wisconsin, set out to get a U. S. Marshal's appointment after the Kennedy Administration set up shop. He was nominated and confirmed, so eastern Wisconsin now has its own Marshal Dillon—and a good one he is. Bill satisfied the Democrats and the fans of *Gunsmoke* simultaneously.

In addition to "mending fences" in Wisconsin, Bill travels the length and breadth of the United States working on behalf of the national Democratic Party and speaking to extraordinarily varied groups. He has participated in university debates with prominent Republican spokesmen, talked at prep schools, and lectured to groups on such subjects as education, small business, civil liberties, civil rights, the new state of Israel, banking legislation, agricultural legislation, government spending, and government waste, unemployment, peace, nuclear test ban proposals, the Communist challenge, the West German economic miracle, and dozens of other topics.

His travels have taken him into thirty-nine states in the last five years. At first I resented this additional intrusion on the little time we have for family life, but gradually learned as the years went by that this was another of those "inevitables" for people holding positions of national office.

For me personally there are three aspects of this life of constant flight that depress me occasionally. I would like to go along much of the time, but my desire to be with our children makes it impossible. (Just as well, for a great many organizations who request a speaker forget that he might have a wife who might like to go along—and make absolutely no provision for her.) Secondly, I know that when Bill is on the road he is more absent-minded than he is at home. He doesn't take care of his health, and I'm sure we have had to replace more hats, raincoats, shaving equipment and traveling alarms than any other living political family. Thirdly, and perhaps this is to be expected, a group doesn't just want a man to speak and run. They want him for hours before and hours afterwards. They insist he arrive long before the meeting begins, attend several cocktail parties, eat dinner, and then sit around for three more hours before the program gets around to him. Then there are always a few people who *must* see him privately before he is driven back to the airport for the return flight home.

Frequently such trips mean a twenty-one-hour day for a Senator who travels. Often Bill has called me from O'Hare Field in Chicago late at night (he has called me so often from O'Hare I think we should be allowed to buy a piece of it) to ask whether or not he should stay the night at the airport motel and get six solid hours of sleep, or take the late flight and get four troubled hours of sleep during the early morning hours at home.

One of the times I especially remember, he decided to come home. I had agreed to come out and meet him at Friendship Airport (forty miles from Washington) at 1:30 A.M., even though there is nothing I hate more than highway driving after midnight. As the crowd spilled from the huge jet, I spotted Bill talking animatedly with Chief Justice Earl Warren, who had obviously been his fellow passenger from Chicago. The Chief Justice had graciously offered Bill a ride in his limousine as far as the Sheraton-Park Hotel, which is only a few blocks from our house. As we drove back I pointed out, a trifle acidly I'm afraid, that I seemed to be a bit superfluous on that occasion.

In November, 1957, Bill went overseas on a kind of international fence-mending trip. He had been selected as a member of the United States delegation to the opening of the German

Bundestag (Parliament). In order to relate the trip specifically to national groups in Wisconsin, he also made brief stops in Denmark, Poland and Norway. Bill had never been abroad before, but on this ten-day trip he saw and learned a lot. In Germany he was able to get a first-hand picture of how the German economy had recovered, how the cities had been rebuilt, and how the industrial and business places were being re-vitalized.

In every country he visited he talked with officials and learned of their attitudes toward NATO and of their individual trade situations with the United States. His special interest was in the type and quality of education found in each country, how their political parties worked, and how their labor unions operated. He visited schools, factories and, through an interpreter, spoke to citizens in all four countries.

I had mixed reactions about the trip when talk of it first arose. I had never been to Europe either, so I had hoped we could go together the first time. We had just finished our first campaign for the Senate and were still in debt, so it hurt to have to spend $1,000 for such a trip. (The only paper that had ever supported Bill for office in Wisconsin looked unfavorably on most Congressional international traveling, so in order to re-assure them—and the rest of the people in Wisconsin—that we had not fallen into the Congressional globe-trotting mold, Bill decided the best thing to do was to accept the honor of being chosen, but to pay his own way.)

As a consolation prize I went to Minnesota (where I had never been either) to substitute for Bill at a State Convention to which he had been committed for two months. I was pregnant and miserable. My feeling of displeasure mounted when I read in a nationally syndicated column that Bill had "run out of money" in Germany and had had to "wire his father" for more. This proved to be untrue, but reading the story only added to my distress.

Actually it all worked out for the best. Bill returned moved and inspired by the obvious affection the people of these countries felt for America. Personally he feels that these Congressional trips can be constructive and immensely worthwhile if undertaken with sound purpose and serious intent. Nevertheless, he has found that lack of time and money makes them out of the question for the two of us as a Congressional couple. His main legislative responsibility falls in the category of domestic economic problems. If he served on the committees with emphasis on foreign relations and international trade, occasional travel would almost be a necessity.

The sum total of all this flying, running, walking and visiting around would seem to be that a working Senator must consider this part of his job as important as lawmaking. Within reason, he must place himself at the disposal of all those in his state who seek help, jobs, money, material or advice. I think it takes a special kind of a man, and a special kind of a hand, and my husband *is* one, and *has* one.

Speaking of hands brings to mind a story told by Gaylord Nelson that beautifully illustrates the importance of this kind of constant personal contact. Gaylord was visiting in Sheboygan one day and inquired how Bill's campaign for re-election was going. One person he met answered, "Why, he's in great shape! I've shaken hands twice with Bill Proxmire since I last saw my mother and father—and they only live on the other side of town!"

Chapter XIII

"THE WOMEN
THEY MARRIED..."

A FAMOUS wit once observed that Washington was a town full of brilliant, accomplished, charming men—and the women they had married when they were young. This statement was hardly complimentary to Washington wives, but fortunately it has become increasingly inaccurate.

Up until the late nineteenth century a politician's wife was rarely seen and certainly never heard. While her husband campaigned for office she stayed quietly at home taking care of the chores and the children. If her husband was elected, her official role was mainly a social one and, in many instances, she didn't even move her family to Washington.

The early 1900's saw the emergence of a new kind of political wife, typified, to me, by the amazing Belle La Follette, "old Bob's" wife. She was the first woman to be graduated from the University of Wisconsin Law School. While her husband was in Congress, Mrs. La Follette handled his correspondence, attended debates in Congress, traveled around the country with him and was a constant counsellor when important decisions were at hand. However, her role was never a public one, as we understand the word today.

When Senator La Follette died, many urged her to seek his seat. She declined the honor, saying: "For many years I have shared with Mr. La Follette the rewards and hardships of public life. At no time in my life, however, would I have chosen a public career for myself. It would be against nature for me to undertake the responsibilities of political leadership."

The wives of Presidents, whose doings are much more conspicuous and chronicled, have demonstrated the shift from wives who are demure drawing-room figures to those who are active forces in world affairs.

Eleanor Roosevelt had been bred in the gentle tradition. She was shy about her high-pitched voice and nervous laugh. But when her husband decided to resume an active political career after his crippling illness, she knew she would have to be his eyes, ears and legs. The active, vocal political wife became a reality. Even before her husband became President, Mrs. Roosevelt had begun traveling widely, taking up unpopular causes and expressing controversial opinions of her own. She was often roundly criticized for her public role; at that time many Americans felt it unbecoming for a woman to be so prominent in what heretofore had been a man's world. During World War II, however, Mrs. Roosevelt expanded her travels and after her husband's death put her own stamp on the quest for mutual understanding and lasting peace. At the time of her death in 1962 she was hailed as the First Lady of the World.

Today's men are being elected to high public office at a comparatively early age. Their wives are younger, more mobile, usually better educated than in the past, less tied to a specific place and way of life, and more at ease generally with everyone from dime-store clerks to diplomats. Because of this, modern political wives are often more than full partners of their husbands; they are frequently political personalities in their own right.

Separate itineraries are now planned for wives of some political candidates, with a special circuit of coffee hours, interviews, teas and club meetings. (Once, at the height of the 1960 Presidential Primary campaign, I heard Jacqueline Kennedy describe her own prodigious efforts and add with a smile, "This is the closest I have come to having lunch with my husband in four months.") We wives are often expected to handle platform appearances with as much skill and assurance as our spouses. We must answer questions on everything from the way we raise our children to the leading problems of the day. The voracious appetite of American news media and the current emphasis in this country on appearance and fashion mean the contemporary political wife must look well in addition to sounding informed.

In our complex world the burden of public responsibility has necessarily expanded to include all adults—men *and* women. As Congressional sessions become longer and the number of issues multiply a thousandfold, the role of the political wife has *had* to grow. She is first and always a mother, a cook, a chauffeur, a seamstress and a homemaker, but she is also an advisor, a social secretary, a campaigner and even a TV personality.

It is still a man's world and we wives are usually glad of it, but never should the world's political leaders underestimate the power of the women behind the men. With the changes that have been evident over the past fifty years in the duties of political wives, the old saw about the hand that rocks the cradle ruling the world has more of truth and less of fiction in it than ever before.

Not all political wives see themselves in the terms I have just described. Many are upset by the demanding roles their husbands play; others miss the family and lifelong friends they have left behind; almost all are slightly bitter about the long separations and impositions on their private lives.

Many dislike politics intensely and develop interests of their own which separate them almost completely from their husbands' worlds. There are even some senators' wives whom I have never met at all, and some who don't even live in Washington.

A certain number wish to take on only social obligations, and have no desire to know anything about the way their husbands' offices are run, to take part in campaigns or to hash over the ins and outs of political combat. This doesn't mean, though, that they love or respect their husbands any the less.

Many are determined to maintain their own identity and outside interests despite our modern notion that husbands and wives in politics should face the world in tandem. They feel that "togetherness" is a private matter.

Our present First Lady is a good example of a wife whose interests were, in the beginning, widely divergent from her husband's, but who has come to understand and appreciate his fervor for and total absorption in his job. (That *doesn't* mean she has become a politician!) By the same token, it is clear that she has encouraged him to relax and to take a deeper interest in the world of the arts, and has even refined his tastes in food— or so I'm told.

I am not critical of political wives who have chosen a way of life different from my own. Each husband and wife must decide this matter for themselves. Actually politicians have been getting elected for hundreds of years without the distaff side of the family lifting a finger. Sam Rayburn became Speaker of the House and Dick Russell Senator from Georgia without ever being married at all.

Other men have overcome the stigma of divorce and risen to high office in spite of their difficult position. Fortunately, prejudice against divorced persons in public office is diminishing, and even remarriage need not mean the end of the road for a politician. It can, in some cases, prove an asset. William V. Shannon, the distinguished Washington correspondent, made this point in a recent article on Presidential politics in *Commonweal* magazine (which is, incidentally, a liberal Catholic journal

163

of opinion). "Voters," wrote Mr. Shannon, "are not really worried about divorce and remarriage. . . . They want their President to have a wife and thereby be able to engage in the ceremonial and symbolic actions and gestures that befit a head of state.

"This fact was borne in on me," continued Mr. Shannon, "when I mingled with the crowds during the Eisenhower-Stevenson campaigns of 1952 and 1956. Governor Stevenson was the innocent party in his divorce, and he did not remarry, but this did not protect him from being the target of a stupid whispering campaign: 'A man who cannot keep his family together cannot keep his country together.' At Republican whistlestop appearances, many women voters were patently more interested in Mrs. Eisenhower than in anything her husband had to say about the issues. I came away from those campaigns convinced that Stevenson, politically speaking, would have been much stronger if he had married a second time and had a happy, smiling wife to present to campaign audiences." *

Yet appearances can be deceiving; to me, the greatest asset a politician can have is a loving wife whose encouragement and enlightened companionship mean more in the long run than her face, wardrobe, or public pose.

I made the decision to work closely with my husband for a number of reasons. In the first place, Bill works such long hours and is away so often that I knew I would see next to nothing of him if I didn't participate in some way in his work. Secondly, the only professional experience I have ever had is in the field of politics. I find the challenge and variety of political activity both absorbing and rewarding. Lastly, it would seem a shame to me to spend a big chunk of my life in Washington and not savor all it has to offer. I cherish the people I have met here, as well as the atmosphere of the city itself.

* William V. Shannon, *Commonweal*, June 21, 1963.

Of course this decision has entailed substantial sacrifice for me, and there are times when I yearn to escape from the stress and controversy and turn my attention to calmer pursuits. But I always come back to agreeing with Mrs. Warren G. Harding, who, when asked about her hobbies, answered, "I have only one hobby—my husband."

Other political wives I have known have had varied concepts about the best and most satisfactory role for them. These roles run the gamut from working full-time in their husbands' offices to a real and active interest that is a bit less circumscribed.

When Senator Maurine Neuberger's late husband, Richard Neuberger, was Senator from Oregon, she worked regularly in his office, edited his newsletter and collaborated closely with him on nationally published articles. Her transition from politician's wife to U.S. Senator in her own right was not as abrupt as it might seem, because of her brilliant mind, thorough understanding of the Senate, and her consistent partnership in Dick's career. She had served with him in the State Legislature, she had a penchant for public life and the intelligence and constitution to match.

Mrs. Paul Douglas is another example of a Senator's wife who has had a distinguished record of her own in government. She was a Member of Congress from Illinois in the 1940's and now works side by side with her husband, particularly on radio and television shows and research. Though she does not spend that much time in Paul's office, they have a real political partnership. She still manages to have time left to lecture all over the country as a lay leader in the Unitarian Church.

Lady Bird Johnson is often called on to speak and to lend her name and prestige to various charities. She travels a great deal with her husband, runs her own substantial business interests in Texas, is a charming hostess and an utterly feminine person. It is obvious that she sees her role as a public one, and relishes the life her husband's career has dictated for her.

Mrs. Ernest Gruening, though now in her seventies, still goes to all the meetings she can, keeps herself well-informed, and spends many hours in the Family Gallery following the debate.

Mrs. Clair Engle, Mrs. Daniel Inouye, Mrs. Frank Church, Mrs. Vance Hartke, Mrs. Birch Bayh, Mrs. John Sherman Cooper, Mrs. Daniel Brewster, Mrs. Eugene McCarthy, Mrs. Lee Metcalf, Mrs. Alan Bible, Mrs. Tom McIntyre, Mrs. Wayne Morse, Mrs. Albert Gore, Mrs. Gale McGee, Mrs. Wallace Bennett, and many others work regularly with their husbands, making speeches, helping out in the office, planning the campaigns, and filling in where and when needed. Quite often their Senatorial husbands give them the lion's share of the credit for whatever victories they have achieved. That is probably too generous an assessment, but I am convinced that an active, informed, attractive political wife is not only a delight to her husband, but a "plus" for the general appreciation of the art of politics.

Two of the women I know who have successfully combined the roles of homemaker and public political wife are Jane Freeman, whose husband is Secretary of Agriculture, and Bethine Church, wife of the young Senator from Idaho. Modern conveniences have eased the mechanical burden of keeping house for them, as they have for women all over America, but each feels deeply her responsibilities at home and at the same time the need for a specific role in connection with her husband's position.

Jane Freeman is the mother of two teenagers. Her husband was Governor of Minnesota for six years and is presently one of the busiest Cabinet members. The Freemans found that life as the First Family of Minnesota was somewhat easier than that of other Governors' families because there was no Mansion or official residence. Rather than have her home life interrupted and regimented by numerous receptions and teas, Jane Freeman went out to organizations, discovered their interests and problems, and met with the people of Minnesota in a more informal way. She says that she learned more about them and their needs in this way than if she saw them only at crowded receptions or teas at which she was the hostess. Their children continued to go to the same schools and church and were able to maintain their neighborhood friendships.

When Governor Freeman was called to Washington in 1961 to take the Cabinet post of Secretary of Agriculture, it was a wrench for them and their children. Jane found life in Washington exciting and busy, but different from the ways in Minnesota.

In the first place the role of a Cabinet wife is less clearly defined than that of a Governor's wife. There are no directives as to what she must or must not do. When a request or invitation arrives, she alone decides whether or not to participate. Secondly, their family activities are not under the constant spotlight of public scrutiny. (Washington is full of VIP's, but Cabinet members—having no specific constituency—may find that a certain anonymity is possible.) Thirdly, there are ten Cabinet wives, so the responsibilities of their position can be divided. One change that was not so pleasing to Jane Freeman was the fact that their area of activity encompasses all fifty states and often other nations of the world, so there is not quite the same satisfaction or immediate opportunity to see results.

As so many others like her have found after living in Washington, Jane commented: "It is sometimes hard to keep your feet on the ground as ordinary Americans." Because everyone you know is struggling with problems of national or international import, there is an overwhelming feeling of involvement in a moving world where crisis piles on top of crisis and concerns of ordinary people can become somewhat remote. The Freemans miss the daily grass-roots contact now that they are in the rarefied atmosphere of Washington, but if anyone can remain true to their roots, they can.

Jane Freeman's charm and common sense, which were such an asset in Minnesota, have enabled her to brighten Washington in her present role. Whether she is chairing a charity, rushing to the Department of Agriculture with a clean shirt for her husband, or substituting for him at a conference in Finland, she adds a new dimension to the ideal all of us in public life seek.

For the wives of men who hold elective office in the Congress the stresses, challenges and daily demands are of a similar but more insistent variety. Once our husbands have won elective office, we pack our children and belongings and start the long trek to Washington. We usually move in December or January —a hard time to make a change, both from the house-hunting and the school point of view. Because of the immediate need for a roof over our heads, we usually find ourselves buying or renting a home that is more expensive than we intended, and then settling down in anything but a holiday atmosphere. The children immediately and especially miss their friends because it is Christmas, and find adjustment to a new school system in the middle of the year anything but pleasant.

Before the curtains are up or the crates unpacked, the requests for pieces of our time begin to pour in. Aside from the social affairs, there are charities, political functions, visiting constituents, and Washington projects that require the participation of all the states, none of which we as new Congressional wives know whether or not to accept.

Before you can say *"Congressional Record"* all kinds of questions loom. How much time should be spent with visiting firemen? Should the family phone be listed or unlisted? How often should a wife return to the home state with her husband and, if often, how much will it cost? How can the children ever see their father when the working hours of the Congress never coincide with a 6:00 P.M. dinner hour? Should we rent our house back home, give it up, or leave it idle ten months of the year? Should we take the children out of school in Washington and return home in the fall, or live here year-round and forego going home as a family altogether? If the decision is to stay in Washington pretty much year-round, what happens during a campaign year?

We each resolve the dilemmas in the way that is best for ourselves and our children's needs. But to my mind one of the most successful juggling acts of all is the one performed by my good friend Bethine (Mrs. Frank) Church.

Bethine grew up in a political family in Idaho, worked hard for her husband's election, first in 1956 and again in 1962, and came with him to Washington when he was elected—the youngest Senator at the time. For the Churches, and for the rest of us as well, the roughest time of all is a campaign year. Idaho is 2,000 miles from Washington and the farther away the constituency, the more expensive and time-consuming is the effort to get home. While Frank was away beating the bushes, Bethine found that her children's interest and understanding were a cheering influence. Their teen-age son, Forrest, enjoys politics and follows it closely. He urges his mother to participate in his father's campaigns and tries to follow in detail the whole effort. But Chase Clark, the baby of the family, looks at all the endless coming and going with a slightly jaundiced eye, and has often stated clearly, "I want everyone to come home and *stay* home."

That will never be possible as long as this very political couple remains in the national arena. But Bethine's skill in balancing all the varied responsibilities of her days and weeks makes a happy solution possible. She will always be able to take the necessary flying trips home without completely disrupting the continuity of life for the boys; she is, of course, concerned about raising adequate money for each campaign, but she doesn't worry herself into a nervous collapse about it; like all of us she is aware of the ever-present possibility that forces beyond their control will upset the applecart, but she doesn't dwell on the fact to the point of bitterness and rejection of all that's rewarding in her hus-

169

band's chosen profession. She faces the daily uncertainty without becoming a victim of it. She recognizes that her husband's position puts an unusual strain on family life, but that many families have worse problems to face.

Despite the trials I have lived with for six years, I find that, like most political wives, I am glad my husband is doing what he most wants to do. Most of us plan our roles to be complementary ones—to see that our husbands eat a few square meals, that they sleep occasionally, that there are patches of peace in this, our frenzied world of too much to do, and that whatever contribution we can make on the political scene is done with gentleness and skill. In these days of the Madison Avenue image, I find it encouraging to rediscover that people still appreciate old-fashioned femininity, the concern for others and personal warmth that only a woman can provide.

Actually many of the problems we political wives share are matched by those of other women in this country who are married to men who lead active and demanding lives. We are not the only ones whose lives are disrupted by our husbands' obligations. Servicemen's wives sometimes spend years at a time separated from their husbands. Other men work odd hours, a fact that forces their wives constantly and completely to revamp their lives in order to see them occasionally. Women married to busy corporation executives must not only lead the kind of a hectic life that living with any ambitious man requires, but must also look well, entertain beautifully, and in some cases wear a mask of amiability.

I must confess that my life might seem more glamorous than many others, for Bill's position has enabled me to meet and come to know some of the most fascinating and important people of my time. But for every hour I have spent in the White House I have spent a thousand typing or stuffing envelopes in the office. Even though I am invited to diplomatic receptions, I am, most of the time, just a working wife who doesn't even get a paycheck.

Even though I love my life and have been able to order it according to my own talents and inclinations, the occasional hardships, sacrifices and inconveniences I have suffered have taught me how to live in peace with anxiety and to give to my children a secure home and the feeling that I am there when they need me. I have learned to appreciate more fully the problems of other women in similar circumstances, and I only hope that by reading of my experience, women everywhere will learn something about making the best of unusual situations.

There are some women, however, whose children are grown and have left home or whose situation makes it possible for them to devote a lot of time to outside pursuits.

I have read so often in recent months about the hundreds of women who have too little to do and therefore spend long, empty afternoons playing bridge, or golf, or even as a last resort, drinking or engaging in extramarital affairs in an attempt to bury their boredom, frustration and confusion. What a pity, when in reality there is enormous need for hands and heads in the field of politics, education, teaching and social work.

The first step in the achievement of fulfillment for women in a society that needs them is the realization that in home and family lies but a portion of the opportunity life holds for them. The second is the use of the education the modern woman has spent one quarter of her life acquiring as a tool—something to be used and shared, not stored and forgotten about. And thirdly, the myth must be forever exploded that men are endowed with special qualities we cannot ever hope to possess. As Esther Peterson, Under-Secretary of Labor, said in a speech at Smith College, "From the dawn of civilization, men have dominated the positions of power and decision. Leadership, good judgment, wisdom and an ability to relate to others are all individual qualities. Women are endowed with them as liberally as men are, and can bring them equally well into play in high-level, demanding jobs." Mrs. Peterson is an outstanding modern example of a woman who has been able to combine a husband, a home and a family of four with twenty-five years of the most vigorous and effective public service—without slighting any of her responsibilities.

I am convinced that women of all ages can find this desired outside activity in the field of government and politics. From county seat to Capitol Hill there are many more things to be done than there are people to do them. The first advantage a woman has in becoming involved in political activity is that she can serve on a part-time basis during the years when that is necessary. The second advantage is that by being involved and keeping informed, she has a real sense of achievement, not only personally but for her family as well. I recall a part of Belle La Follette's book on her husband in which a friend described a visit to their home in Madison.

"There was a solidarity about the La Follette family beyond that of any other I ever encountered. The children took part in every discussion and expressed their opinions freely. There was never an attempt to impose the opinion of the grown-ups upon them. Always they were treated as persons. The right government of the country was the very life of the household, and they imbibed this feeling as the warp and woof of their being." *

Government touches every woman every day in every way and at every level—through the schools her children attend, the taxes her husband pays, the roads she drives on, the money she spends on groceries, and most especially in her hopes for peace. First she must be informed. She must read, learn, study and ask questions. She has more time for self-education than her husband does, even when the children are young. She can lend her special talents for detail and her sympathetic understanding to local

* Belle Case La Follette and Fola La Follette, *Robert M. La Follette*. Copyright © 1953, The Macmillan Company.

political organizations which are always on the hunt for help. Precinct work of the door-to-door variety constantly suffers from a lack of volunteers. It has been my experience that there is no better way for a woman to get her feet wet in politics than to do some of this kind of on-the-job training.

Beyond the precinct level, a woman can make a real contribution in fund-raising, running dinners, doing research or home office work for some elected official, and even trying for some of the party offices on the county level.

Once she has solidified her position with the party organization, she's on her way! (With ability and sincere effort, it only takes a year or two to be influential in almost any political organization.) Then there is the ballot. Local office after local office goes begging or even goes to the least qualified just because there is no one else available or interested in running. Most city councils meet in the evenings and are not full-time occupations, so they are perfect jumping-off places for women who are interested in public service.

The state legislature races are the next rung on the ladder. Most of them meet only for a part of each year (some only every other year), so it is conceivable that many more women could arrange their lives to take on such a post. After the Legislature, of course, lies Congress, and today even a seat in the Senate is within the reach of a qualified woman.

If public office is not her meat, a woman can do so much behind the scenes of government. Her patience, her willingness to be useful in almost any capacity, her truly deep concern with social problems and social injustice, and her personal stake in peace fit her especially well for the needs of today. I am now inviting women everywhere to join a political party, to offer their time and talents and then to enjoy the real feeling of accomplishment that will surely follow. This is a challenge to choose between living life to the fullest or rejecting a marvelous opportunity. But whether or not a woman chooses politics, she must choose whether to remain where she is (and *as* she is), or to move through life with an adventuresome spirit.

I think of these things so often when I hear the complaints, the selfish bitterness and withdrawal that are so often evidenced by the wives of public officials. The personal role that the wife of a politician plays can be much more than being the other half of a Bachrach picture or campaign poster—the half with the hair. To be a "political asset" is to be more than photogenic, it is to be a partner. That doesn't mean being career-driven, or anxious to make speeches or aggressive or unfeminine. It doesn't even mean sitting in her husband's outer office typing letters or seeing callers. It does mean making some effort to learn of the pressures and problems her husband faces and, above all, to see that her children are happy and that her weary husband has a comfortable haven away from the fray where he can share his triumphs and nurse his wounds.

A creed I read in the *Congressional Record* in 1962 is my creed. It was spoken by Leo Rosten at the National Book Awards presentation in April, 1962.

"The purpose of life is not to be happy—but to matter, to be productive, to be useful, to have it make some difference that I lived at all.

"We must meet fanaticism with courage, and idealism with caution.

"We must learn that those we like are not always right, and those we don't like are not always wrong; for an idea has nothing to do with who is for it or who is against it.

"We must learn to seek change without violence. Always change, and never violence—not even in words, much less in deeds.

"We must be strong enough to be gentle.

"We must know that life will always have unbearable stretches of loneliness, and that we can never be truly understood—even by those who love us; and that we cannot completely understand

174

someone else, no matter how much we want to. We must moderate, therefore, our demands on others.

"We must have the courage to live without absolutes, without dogmas, the courage to seek imaginative escapes from the strait jackets of conformity, knowing—with Emerson—'Whosoever would be a man must be a non-conformist.'

"We must learn to meet life in a series of tentative and impermanent approximations, knowing that the final goals may never be reached, that the last truths may be forever unknowable, but that life holds nothing more precious than the process by which, to the fullest stretches of which man is capable, we stretch the mind and the heart."

For me—and for the man whose burdens I share—this says it all.

Date Due

The Stages of
Political Development

The
STAGES
of
POLITICAL
DEVELOPMENT

A. F. K. Organski

THE UNIVERSITY OF
MICHIGAN

19  67

Alfred · A · Knopf : New York

THIS IS A BORZOI BOOK,
PUBLISHED BY ALFRED A. KNOPF, INC.

Published August 30, 1965
Second Printing, September 1966
Third Printing, February 1967

L. C. catalog card number: 65–13462

To my wife Katherine

Preface

This book is a beginning, an attempt to chart a huge terrain, and—for me—a first approximation. My intention is to provide a new theoretical framework for the study of comparative politics. The basic ideas have jostled each other on the fringes of my consciousness for many years, but now that I try to set them forth for others I am acutely aware of the work that remains to be done. I do not shy from sharing these early ideas, but I hope in future years to elaborate them further, to refine, to correct, perhaps to alter them. I hope they will stimulate some of my readers to differ, to argue, to correct, perhaps even to agree, but primarily I hope they will help to focus the minds of others upon what seems to me a very important task: the creation of a framework within which to organize the ever more vast accumulation of factual data, reportage, and opinion which threatens to overwhelm the twentieth-century student of political development. The need for good theory was never greater.

In my own attack upon this ambitious project I have been directly and materially helped by five people to whom I wish to express my profound gratitude.

My wife Katherine was a major source of intellectual support. In the writing of this book, as in all my previous work, she participated in the weaving of the initial web of ideas, in the organization of the work, and in the endless editing and paring of the final version. Her insight, her critical bent of mind, her thoroughness, and her editorial skill have contributed much to this volume. I gladly and gratefully acknowledge my large debt to her.

In any field there are a very few men with sufficient energy and wisdom not only to do their own work but to help others as well. Professors Rupert Emerson of Harvard University, Kalman H. Silvert of Dartmouth College, Dr. Victor R. Fuchs of the National Bureau of Economic Research, and Professor Robert E. Ward of the University of Michigan are four such men. The first three read the entire manuscript and made valuable suggestions. I am grateful to Professor Emerson for wise, kind, and constructive criticism based on his own thorough knowledge of the matter at hand, and I particularly want to thank Professor Silvert for generously making available to me, both in comments and in extended discussion, his own profound insight into the problems of political development. Dr. Fuchs deserves the special gratitude that goes to those who make truly constructive criticisms even of those sections with which they disagree. Professor Ward reviewed with me the section dealing with Japan. His vast knowledge of the subtleties of Japanese political development was of great help in saving me from error, and I am very grateful to him for his advice.

In addition to these five people, others helped in various ways. I owe a special debt to Professor Walter Mais, Dean of the Faculties at Brooklyn College, who for many years encouraged my research and writing by giving me the time and the freedom essential for such endeavors. I wish to thank Mr. Peter H. Skala of Armour and Company, a longtime friend who over the years has given generously to me of his wisdom in matters treated in this book. I am

PREFACE

also grateful to Miss Marni Bard, whose grounding in Greek led her to suggest the term *syncratic* as a name for the politics of compromise which is one category in the second stage of political development. Finally, I wish to acknowledge the help extended to me by Brooklyn College's Research Center in Comparative Politics and Administration and its director, Professor Albert Gorvine, help which made it possible for me to do the things necessary to complete this work.

All of these people have aided me, and had I been capable of utilizing their help more fully, this might be a better book. None of those mentioned here, however, is to be taxed with any responsibility for the shortcomings of this work. I alone take full responsibility for what I have written.

A. F. K. ORGANSKI

CONTENTS

Contents

STAGE THREE

The Politics of National Welfare

STAGE FOUR

The Politics of Abundance

CONTENTS

The Stages of
Political Development

I
PREVIEW AND
OVERVIEW

It is no trick to see things partially, but to see them whole, to encompass their sweep, to search out the significant, to order the vast confusion of bits and pieces—this is the scholar's work and the statesman's need; this is the task I have here set myself, with the full realization that one man's view of so broad a landscape will never quite satisfy another.

This book is about the building of nations, from their beginnings in sixteenth-century dynastic Europe, in eighteenth-century America, in the colonies and new nations of Asia and Africa, through their struggles with industrialization, up to whatever point they have reached today, and then on into the future to what one supposes will be their eventual disappearance. The subject is broad, but the focus of course is much narrower. We shall deal with the role of politics, with the changing nature of government and with its changing functions as nations move from what appears to me one recognizable stage to another.

The world today is a world of nations in construction.

Beside the old nations, stately structures erected over centuries, there are rising new states thrown up in haste and built in a fury with whatever comes to hand: tribal ties, ancient tongues, common ties of hate, or simply hopes. This is certainly an age of doers.

It is also a good time for looking on. So much activity provides the grist for rich generalization, and watching the new nations cope with their problems today helps jog our memories about our own imperfectly recorded past.

The variety of nations is immense, and this too provokes comparative generalization. In one moment of time a look round the world will fall upon nations at every conceivable stage of construction. Some of the newest are little more than blueprints. In others the walls are up, the flooring down, and the outline of the roof is coming into view. A few are fully built, but even here alterations are in order to let in more light and provide more space.

The metaphor is perhaps dangerous, for it implies the old fallacy that all mankind is marching toward a single goal (represented, of course, by our own achievements). It implies that our own house is fully and properly built and that nations of differing shape represent various stages of arrested development. Methodological sophistication demands the rejection of any such idea. The world is not necessarily marching toward monogamy, Christianity, free enterprise, and two-party government. It does, however, appear to be marching toward industrial efficiency and national political organization. Within the narrow confines of political analysis it does not seem biased to focus on a world engaged in building nations. Generalization enfolding past and present is legitimate provided we remember that generalization is an intellectual exercise which selects what is common and ignores what is not, rather than a description of the whole.

One other caution is necessary. It is easy enough to select from the experience of today's new nations those elements they share with the beginnings of European nations long ago. It is even possible to take the political institutions of the industrializing nations, Communist, fascist, and democratic, and compare them across the board as possible solutions to common problems that will face the new nations in their own industrialization soon to come. It is far more dangerous to consider the political systems of the developed nations as archetypes of the future. There are few examples of the later stages of political development, and more allowance must consequently be made for variations as yet unborn. Finally, it must be recognized that there is no end to the process of political development, no haven where all the nations will finally come to rest. Change goes on. We shall follow it as far ahead as we can see and then leave it to march on out of sight.

THE IDEA OF DEVELOPMENT

Most of the growing literature about "developed" and "underdeveloped" nations is concerned at heart with technological and economic change. It is assumed that the social and political changes that accompany industrialization are also "development." To some extent this is true: one can indeed tick off a long list of changes that have everywhere followed along.

It seems useful, however, to be as specific as possible about what is meant by *national development* or *national growth* or *modernization* (the terms are used interchangeably), and to locate the areas of political development within this complex.

National development is characterized particularly (but

surely not exclusively) by increasing economic productivity, by increasing geographic and social mobility, and by increasing political efficiency in mobilizing the human and material resources of the nation for national goals. The three are closely related.

Economic productivity up to this point in time has been increased primarily through an agricultural revolution followed by industrialization, though now automation is bringing a second industrial revolution. The early stages of economic development, then, can be measured in a rough way by the percentage of workers engaged in agriculture, a nation being considered economically developed when more than 50 per cent of its economically active men have moved out of agricultural work and into other pursuits. This index will not do for the future, but it will serve for the first three stages.[1] For the future some direct measure of economic productivity is required, and *developed*, like *modern*, becomes a relative concept, not an absolute state. The higher the productivity, the more developed the economy, and as we move into the future, the present developed nations will seem very backward indeed.

By a very rough shorthand, measures of economic development can be made to stand for national development in general. Indeed, this shorthand is often used. It would be more exact, however, to realize that political and social development, though obviously related to economic modernization, may differ in pace and in priority. At present, for example, it is becoming increasingly the

---

[1] The ingenious suggestion has been made that the economic development of more advanced countries may be measured by using as a yardstick the percentage of the labor force employed in the provision of services. It is interesting to note that the United States is the only country where more than half of the labor force is so employed. *See* Victor R. Fuchs, "The Growing Importance of the Service Sector," a paper delivered at the American Statistical Association Meetings, December, 1964.

pattern for a certain degree of political modernization to precede rather than follow economic modernization.

Political development can be defined as *increasing governmental efficiency in utilizing the human and material resources of the nation for national goals.* Such efficiency has increased and will increase further, but there is another aspect to political development. The primary function of national government also changes as a nation moves from one stage to another, and at each stage the national government, if it is to qualify as "developed," must fill the new function as well as consolidate the gains of the past. At a time when no nation had progressed beyond a primitive stage, a politically developed nation was one that was politically unified. In the next stage of advancement a "developed" political system governed not only a unified nation but also one that was successfully industrializing. Today political development requires national unification, economic modernization, and also a welfare state. Tomorrow it will require all of these functions as well as an automated economy that is in addition politically responsible. Political development, then, is a very specific idea. The rest of this book is devoted to spelling it out.

THE STAGES OF DEVELOPMENT

The stages of political development as set forth in this book are: (1) the politics of primitive unification, (2) the politics of industrialization, (3) the politics of national welfare, and (4) the politics of abundance. A word about each is in order here.

The Politics of Primitive Unification

The politics of primitive unification is that which attends the birth and the childhood of nations. It begins at a point which is often difficult to locate exactly in time, for the roots of human development always lie far in the past. By the sixteenth century much of Western Europe had reached this primitive stage. In much of the rest of the world the beginnings of the nation-state came with the creation of European colonies. The end of the stage of primitive unification is far easier to place, for it comes as the country begins to industrialize in earnest or roughly at that point W. W. Rostow refers to in economic terms as "the take-off."[2]

The path of each nation through this first stage is unique, but our interest here is in the conditions, the problems, and the solutions which the travelers hold in common. All were, or are, as our age puts it, "economically underdeveloped" nations, that is to say, preindustrial. All have had governments we would call inefficient and undemocratic. And all have had to struggle with the problems of unification.

At this stage as in others, the aims and the conscious concerns of those who govern are many—personal aggrandizement, national power—some even talk of economic development. But the primary function of government is one: the creation of national unity. Whatever their various intentions, rulers at this stage find themselves preoccupied with problems of national unification, for the countries they rule are deeply divided and these divisions constantly frustrate the plans of the national government.

There is, first of all, the elementary problem of establishing central political rule over all the territories and peoples to be included within the national boundaries, a problem which is generally solved brutally and unimaginatively through military conquest.

There is then the problem of maintaining this rule in the face of ethnic divisions, dissident minorities, and separatist

[2] W. W. Rostow, *The Stages of Economic Growth* (Cambridge: Cambridge University Press, 1961), p. 36.

movements, not to mention the problem of dealing with regional and provincial authorities, both military and civilian, who seek for themselves a high degree of independence from central control.

There is the problem of bringing some pattern of national economic unification to a patchwork of local economies based largely on subsistence farming. There is the problem of extending political control to the villages through the creation of a new national bureaucracy and political parties. And there is the problem, largely postponed till the future, of expanding the meaning of nationhood to engage the efforts and the loyalty of the mass of the citizenry.

The politics of primitive unification struggle with all of these problems and achieve a measure of success, but at the end of the period great tasks remain. The nation may be viable but still is far from full-grown. Indeed, a *nation* in the modern sense does not yet exist. The fabric of political and economic unity is thin and torn. A vast chasm separates the rulers from the ruled, for though the common people are politically subject they participate little in the life of the nation. The national government offers them little or nothing in services, and they for their part cannot be mobilized to contribute wealth, time, effort, or concern to national purposes. Unification, in short, is "primitive." Nevertheless, it exists and forms a necessary base for the developments that follow.

The Politics of Industrialization

With the coming of industrialization the shape and the work of the nation change. The second stage of political development occurs at this time of transition during which a new class takes power, a new economy is built, and the mass of the citizenry is finally incorporated into the nation.

Up to the present, developing nations have been shepherded through this difficult transition by three different types of government: bourgeois (or Western democratic), stalinist (the term I prefer for Communist government at this stage), and fascist. Nations approaching industrialization today face a choice, with the possibility of selecting a modern variant of one of these three systems (the third of which should not be ruled out) or of devising new forms still unknown.

The primary function of government in this second stage of political development is to permit and aid economic modernization. All three varieties of government—bourgeois, stalinist, and fascist—have done this, and though the differences in the three systems are large and significant, all are alike in performing three important tasks which help the nation industrialize.

First, they make possible a shift of political power from the hands of the traditional elite to the industrial managers who wish to modernize the economy. The stalinist system acts swiftly, by eliminating the old aristocracy in its initial revolution. The bourgeois system shifted more gradually, with the bourgeoisie slowly gaining the upper hand over the traditional aristocracy and then sharing its power with the masses. Under fascism the old landed gentry held on most tenaciously, ruling jointly with the new industrial elite throughout the fascist period but losing out in the end.

Second, all three forms of government permit and assist the accumulation of capital, so essential for industrial development. This is done primarily by holding down mass consumption while permitting capital to accumulate in the hands of those who will reinvest at least a portion of it in capital goods.

Here again the stalinist system proceeds most drastically,

pinching its workers and peasants to the bone and depriving them of both political power and the power of economic bargaining. Wages are low, capital investment high, particularly in heavy industry. The result is extremely rapid industrialization at a high price of human suffering and repression.

The bourgeois system also encouraged the accumulation of capital at the expense of mass living standards. Here too the masses were deprived of political power, in this case through a limited franchise, and unions were outlawed (rather than controlled). In consequence wages were low, working conditions poor, and capital investment relatively high. Industrialization proceeded somewhat more slowly than stalinism could propel it, in part because of the nature of bourgeois democracy and in part because the bourgeois nations were the first to industrialize.

The fascist system proceeded the most hesitantly, accumulating capital from a limited base, since the agricultural sector of the economy was exempted from paying the price for industrialization and left relatively untouched. Here too, however, industrialization advanced, though presumably at a slower pace than would have occurred under bourgeois or stalinist institutions.

Third, all three forms of government have presided over a large-scale migration of people from country to city. This migration provides the labor for burgeoning industry and at the same time helps speed the destruction of the old peasant world. English enclosures and Russian collectivization both speeded the departure of peasants from the land. Fascist governments provided little help and some hindrance to urban migration, but migration nevertheless proceeded.

It is in this second stage of political development that the nation is enlarged, first to include the industrial elite and then—slowly, progressively—to include the masses. Ordinary working people become dependent upon a nationwide economy. The masses are awakened to political interest and participation, and—in the bourgeois democracies—they begin to demand real political power.

The Politics of National Welfare

The politics of national welfare is the politics of fully industrial nations. Throughout stage two the mutual dependence of people and government has grown; in stage three it is complete. The power of the state has come to rest upon the ability of common people to work and to fight, and the common people, along with the lords of industry, have come to depend upon the national government to protect them from destitution in depression and from destruction in war.

The primary function of government is reversed from that of the preceding period. In stage two it is the task of government to protect capital from the people and their demands for a higher standard of living. In stage three it is the task of government to protect the people from the hardships of industrial life: to keep the economy running smoothly, to provide the higher living standards so long sought, and to aid the disadvantaged.

In the mass democracies the common people begin to exercise their new economic power (achieved through unionization) and their new political power (gained through an expanded franchise). They use their new power to win protection by the national government, and it is their demands which bring the government to exercise its new function.

However, mass democracy is not required to create the welfare state. The Germany of Hitler and the Russia of

Khrushchev and his successors both qualify as examples of the politics of national welfare. It would appear that all governments of economically developed countries must intervene to keep the economy running smoothly, must adopt welfare measures—must, in short, assume a prime responsibility for the economic and social welfare of ordinary citizens—if they are to continue to increase the nation's productivity and power.

The Politics of Abundance

We are stirred today by the beginnings of a new industrial revolution—the revolution of automation. Its consequences promise to be as shattering as those of the original industrial revolution, and new political forms and functions will be required both to smooth its entrance and to deal with its consequences. I call this new stage of political development *the politics of abundance*. No nation has gone far into this stage, but the United States and the most advanced nations of Western Europe and the Commonwealth are standing at the threshold.

Abundance is the promise of the new technology, a promise that seems likely of fulfillment if present-day computers and automated, self-regulating machinery (and their improved descendants) are used to anything approaching their capacity. Unemployment is its threat, and many fear that a sizable proportion of the working population, perhaps even the majority, will be displaced by machines from paid employment. It is hard to imagine the consequences of such a revolution.

The period of transition that lies just ahead will be extremely difficult, for while automation is extending its scope and producing vast social dislocation, powerful interests will be exerting their full influence to block or at least to control the spread of automation, much as the old agricultural system resisted the spread of industrialism. The opposing forces will probably suffer the same fate.

If one can look ahead, however, and imagine a more or less fully automated society, it is interesting to speculate what its political and social structure will be. The range of possibilities is broad, but the probability is high that the abundant society will have these features:

Great concentration of economic power. The use of highly expensive machinery and the need for planned production to keep it running efficiently should favor the growth of giant monopolies, and within these monopolies the power of management will tower over that of labor.

Great concentration of political power. Immense concentrations of economic power would almost certainly lead to close government regulation and perhaps to direction of the economy. In the Western democracies this would probably not take the form of government ownership but rather of a close identification and exchange of personnel between big business and big government.

A new class structure headed by a small elite of planners who run the economy and the government, supported by a minority of highly skilled workers and technicians. These groups, as well as other professionals and employed workers, would be sharply set apart from the large leisured minority, or perhaps even majority, who do no work at all and who would probably constitute the "lower classes" of the new society.

The primary functions of government in this new age will be to cushion the adjustments of social reorganization in order to make automation possible and to make an automated economy politically responsible.

The coming of automation will injure many—small businessmen, small farmers, union labor, clerks, to name a few—and it will be the job of government to ease the injury done them and to help them readjust. More crucially, the government will have to provide some means of support for the large number of permanently unemployed, not only for humanitarian reasons, but to assure, first, that they do not overturn the government and, second, that they help consume the vastly increased production of an automated economy. We can probably assume expanded welfare measures by the national government.

The second function of government will be equally needed and perhaps even more difficult to fulfill, for the whole trend of automation will probably be to push the political system away from democratic responsibility to the people. Mass democracy as it exists today is based upon the mutual dependence of people and state, but with automation the state will no longer depend upon the bulk of the people to produce economic wealth or to fight its mechanized wars. The people, on the other hand, will be more dependent upon government than ever before. Such one-sided dependence will not be conducive to popular control.

Nevertheless, the national governments of stage four must find some way to make the highly centralized economy politically responsible, if not to the people at least to the state, for such concentrated power cannot be permitted to be exercised for private purposes alone.

It may well be that national governments will not prove the best vehicles for carrying out these tasks. Automated industries may require guaranteed international markets and guaranteed international peace, and automation may in the end bring the death of the nation-state. If so, regional or continental blocs will probably be the next form of political organization. In that case, however, we pass beyond the development of nations, which is the topic of this book.

CHOICES AND SHIFTS

There is nothing inevitable about the stages here set forth, but it is striking that in all the world's many nations development has been in the same direction: toward industrialization, higher productivity, and higher living standards; toward political complexity, political efficiency, and increased dependence upon the state. To this point there is no single case of a nation's sliding back to an earlier stage.

There has, however, been some shifting and stirring within each stage of development. In stage one dynastic states have fallen under colonial rule, colonies have won their independence, and monarchies have become republics. In stage two some of the bourgeois states have shifted to stalinism and fascism, and some of the fascist states have turned back to the democratic form. In stage three there is the example of Nazi Germany deserting mass democracy of her own volition, then falling in battle and turning half to democracy and half to communism. However, voluntary shifts are rare thus far in stage three.

In general, the likelihood of changes from one form of government to another appears greatest in those stretches of time when one stage is coming to a close and another beginning, for these are the times when stages overlap and contradictory currents run within the changing nation.

Such shifts, far from trivial, are obviously of great importance to the survival of all we value. Granted that all the underdeveloped areas are struggling toward national unity and economic development, it makes a great difference whether they choose the path of fascism, stalinism, bourgeois democracy, or some new way. And granted that all the developed nations are welfare states moving toward automation, we care deeply whether they turn to totalitarianism. In the final chapter we shall examine some of the factors which determine these momentous choices.

STAGE ONE

The Politics of
Primitive Unification

II

THE POLITICS OF
PRIMITIVE
UNIFICATION

No modern manual of politics can touch the renown of
Machiavelli's *Prince*. His frankness, his scientific spirit,
his cynicism are all well known. The timeliness of his topic
is not so often appreciated. Political unification—the first
and most uncertain step in nation-building—has been a
live political problem from Machiavelli's day to ours.

The problem of unity is crucial today in the underdeveloped countries—more critical, in truth, than the
problem of economic development which attracts so much
attention, for without that stability of rule, effectiveness
of government, and unity of purpose developed nations
take for granted, economic advance is sure to be a halting
matter, especially in an age when government does so
much to push and guide the course of economic change.

Some foundation for national unification is necessary before economic modernization can proceed very far, and though the new governments of the underdeveloped world may talk economic development *ad nauseam,* many of their actions can best be understood if they are seen as steps toward the creation of national unity.

Most of the countries in the world today are struggling with the problems of what I choose to call *primitive unification,* and the rest have won their struggle at some time in the past. The stage of primitive unification thus covers a lot of ground and includes a wide variety of experience. Some generalizations, however, can be made—more handily if we consider four types of political experience:

1. Dynastic politics, by which is meant primarily the nation-building process in Western Europe, where it was carried on by absolute monarchs. The form still exists in such states as Saudi Arabia and Ethiopia.

2. Colonial politics, where primitive unification takes place (though usually is not completed) while the country is under colonial domination by a foreign power. This form is typical of the present and former European colonies in Africa and Asia and probably in the Americas as well.

3. The politics of newly independent underdeveloped countries in which former colonies continue their unification under their own governments. India and Indonesia provide good examples.

4. The politics of old and established countries that have remained economically underdeveloped and are still less than fully unified. Iran and some of the Latin American states are examples.

The first two types, dynastic politics and colonial politics, are almost extinct; the third and fourth are still the most common varieties of politics today.

BEGINNINGS: DYNASTIC AND COLONIAL

It would seem natural to emphasize the differences between political life in Western Europe in the sixteenth, seventeenth, and eighteenth centuries and that in the colonies on other continents in the nineteenth and twentieth, but in one respect at least there are striking similarities. Both periods in question were times of primitive national unification in which rulers struggled with common problems, and though the intentions of early modern monarchs and later colonial administrators varied widely, the end results of their labors were not so different as one might expect. Perhaps the major lasting political contribution of both was to bring to the countries they ruled a thin surface layer of unification, like the shell of an egg, within which a nation might grow.

Both sets of rulers sought power for themselves; both imposed their rule upon communities of peasants who were poor, economically inefficient, politically divided, and local in their loyalties and interests. In the process both conquered and absorbed the former local lords and chieftains. Both won their initial victories through military conquest and drew new boundary lines around their conquered lands, marking out domains that were unified in little but name. Both solidified their rule and deepened the unity of the country by creating a national bureaucracy of administrators and by encouraging the beginnings of a national economy. And for all their accomplishments, both built states that were far from being nations in the modern sense, for a great gap separated the rulers from the ruled. Nevertheless, both took the first steps essential in the building of modern nations, and without their work the world today would be unrecognizable to our eyes.

The Search for Power

Let us trace these steps in somewhat more detail. A quest for greater power was probably the major conscious motive that led the absolute monarchs of Europe to unify their kingdoms. They sought to increase the internal power of the monarchy in order to make the reigning dynasty secure against the ambitions of domestic rivals, and through greater internal power they sought advantage in their competition with the rulers of other lands. This constant struggle required unprecedented contributions in men and wealth, for the cost of keeping the nobility as courtiers was immense and the cost of waging war even greater. The feudal methods of raising men and wealth did not meet the new needs, and the crown was forced to meddle with the traditional organization of society to make it yield the wherewithal to rule and to fight. The European monarchs built on a feudal base, but in the process they ruthlessly destroyed the traditions of feudal times and hastened the destruction of a system that had prevented effective control by the crown.

So too with the great colonial powers, whose interest lay not so much in the domination of foreign lands for domination's sake as in the conquest of properties that might enhance the power and the reputation of the nation in its struggles with other European powers. The race for colonies that occupied the major European nations in the nineteenth century, like the race for arms and the race for allies, was part of a general contest for power among themselves. And the extension of European rule throughout the conquered colonies—the building of roads, the sending of administrators—were designed primarily to facilitate the extraction from the colonies of minerals, cash crops, taxes, and manpower that could be converted into power on the European scales. In the process, incidentally and unintentionally, the bases of the old native social structures were destroyed, clearing the way for the growth of new and modern nations.

New Armies

The first step in both dynastic and colonial nation-building was to place under one centralized political rule the extensive territories and the divided people to be included. With few exceptions this was done through military conquest, and in the old monarchies of Europe this necessitated the creation of a new institution—a professional army responsible to the national government alone.

Europe's emerging monarchs were originally little more than major feudal lords whose power depended in important measure upon the shifting loyalties of semi-independent vassals. Quite obviously an ambitious ruler could hardly use a feudal army to guarantee his own superiority over other lords, for a feudal army was not one force but composed of many, each responsible not to the king himself but to the vassal who raised it. To destroy the power of the lords, the king had need of an army of his own, an army of professionals paid from his own treasury and responsible only to him. Moreover, a vastly expanded military force was thought necessary to defend each monarch against the ambitions of his fellow monarchs, who were also arming.

Henry VIII, for example, poured coffers of gold into building the English navy while the kings of France expanded French might on land and sea. The preoccupation of European rulers with increasing their military strength during the sixteenth, seventeenth, and eighteenth centuries makes clear that the arms race is no recent innovation.

In their colonies, too, the Europeans generally found a variety of local units, each with its independent military force. In their early conquests, the Europeans were aided by local forces whose rivalries they exploited to set one group of natives against another. Ultimately these forces were disarmed or absorbed into the army of the conqueror. Indeed, *pacification,* by which was meant the substitution of European military force for native military force, was the first important job of every colonizer.

The difference here, compared with Europe, was that the professional army came from the outside. When the Europeans left, the core of the central government's professional army often, though not always, departed with them, leaving the government of the newly independent nation without efficient, unified military forces to guarantee internal unity and external defense. Thus the military unification the European monarchs bequeathed to their successors was considerably greater than that provided by the later European rulers of the colonies.

New Bureaucracies

Professional armies conquered and held the territories of European dynasts and colonial powers, but more was needed to solidify these holdings into nations. Perhaps even more important than military unity in the long run was the creation of a professional national bureaucracy.

In Europe this development, although it took place gradually, was of great significance. Feudal monarchs held their kingdoms as their own personal property, and nothing transcended their personal rule. The development of a bureaucracy to administer the state brought about important changes. At the top level of government, many of the functions of the crown were bureaucratized; that is, they were performed by career officials who had had some rudimentary training and whose jobs were specialized, whose powers and responsibilities were defined and limited, and whose official behavior tended to be more impersonal and more predictable than in the past. This freed the execution of governmental policy from dependence on the personal qualities of the king, though the ruler remained the mainspring of action. It also increased the efficiency and continuity of governmental action.

Equally important, bureaucratization spread below the top layers of government. A group of representatives of the crown developed, dependent directly upon the king and strategically located to assist with the execution of the policies of the crown. The intendents in France and the justices of the peace in England are examples of such officials.

Similarly, in the colonies bureaucracies of colonial administrators helped the process of unification. The colonial powers were represented on the spot by resident governors or commissioners who, with a small number of aides, magistrates, district officers, and the like, imposed a thin network of centralized control and uniformity over the colony.

As in Europe, the number of government administrators was small. The apex of the administrative pyramid was always in European hands, but the base was necessarily in the hands of the native inhabitants. Just as the European nobility left the peasants pretty much to their own customs and problems as long as they paid their taxes, so too the colonial rulers left the natives to their own affairs as long as native life did not interfere with colonial aims. Europeans sought to avoid the burden and, more important, the expense of becoming involved in native problems.

How far down the administrative ladder the European

could be found and how far up the native rose to meet him varied from colony to colony and from time to time. In some cases the entire native governmental hierarchy continued to function under colonial rule, with the result that the European and native administrative hierarchies overlapped. In practice this meant that rule was indirect. Local conditions and other factors dictated at what point the power flowing down the European stalagtite crossed over to the native stalagmite and continued down to the base. At certain times the lower portions of the European structure were effectively bypassed. At others, the native pyramid was in effect truncated because decisions and execution of policy remained almost entirely in European hands almost to the local level.

It should be made clear, however, that the essence of the difference between direct and indirect rule lay in the degree to which natives were used *to carry out* colonial policy. Decision and control always remained in European hands. Control over the use of force, taxation, tribal boundaries, agricultural policy, mineral policy, and labor questions as well as the settlement of major disputes and the judgment of major crimes rested with the European administrators, who were responsible ultimately to their home governments and not to their colonial subjects. Moreover, the Europeans reserved to themselves veto power over the acts of native authorities and participated in selecting the members of the native governmental hierarchy.

In general, it can be said that the control of European colonial powers over their colonial subjects was more complete than that of the early European national monarchs over their subjects. However, it does not follow that the unifying effect of the colonial bureaucracies was also greater. The European bureaucracies grew up gradually over a long period of time and found their practices accepted and imbedded in local tradition. The colonial bureaucracies were imposed suddenly from outside and staffed by outsiders, and their rule was resisted from beginning to end. The whole notion of impersonal rule by trained specialists was generally foreign to native experience and the principles of such rule were seldom widely accepted. As a result, the maintenance of an efficient bureaucracy has been one of the most acute problems experienced by the governments of newly independent former colonies.

Economic Unification

Economic policies have also been an important unifying force in both Europe and the colonies. Mercantilism, generally noted as an economic system, had political consequences of the first importance. From a political point of view, mercantilism can be viewed as a method of national unification with the towns its major targets. As strongholds of modern life, the towns were generally outside the feudal framework; to build a modern *national* life it was essential to integrate them into the national economy and bring them back under the control of the crown. Mercantilist policies helped accomplish this. In addition, mercantilist monarchs stimulated manufacturing and commerce and built networks of roads and canals, all of which increased the economic interdependence of the nation's population and laid the foundations for a deeper national unity.

It is of course true that the architects of mercantilism were not thinking primarily of national unification, or even of the economic welfare of the population. The most important reason—perhaps the only reason—for the mercantilist desire for a national economy was the generation of greater wealth which might be used to increase the power of the ruler and of the state. The result was nonetheless important to future unification.

In the colonies the economic policies of the European rulers are reminiscent of mercantilist policies both in aim and in effect. Though roads and railways were built primarily for military purposes or to permit the export of minerals and cash crops, they also permitted the native inhabitants to travel, meet, and mingle for the first time. This helped begin to break down the local particularism typical of precolonial days.

Even more important was the unifying effect of the modern economic enterprises introduced by the Europeans. European mines and plantations, with their demand for native wage labor, were undoubtedly the most important factor in detribalizing and urbanizing important segments of the native population and in enmeshing the bulk of the population, at least to a limited extent, in a national, money economy. Here again, the aim was to extract wealth from the colony for the benefit of the rulers, and the general population was largely excluded from the benefits of greater national wealth, but it certainly shared the consequences of the new national economic activity.

Remaining Tasks

The dynastic state with its national army, national administration, and beginnings of a national economy was truly something novel. So too was the European colony, so different in its organization from the tribes and kingdoms it succeeded. But neither was yet a "nation" in the full sense of the term. In considering the important steps toward nationhood that had been taken, it is easy to overlook the tasks that remained unfinished.

In colony and dynastic state alike, the newly achieved national unity formed only the thinnest layer stretched across the top of a varied and divided society. This unity was almost entirely political. It had as yet shallow roots in the economy and no roots at all in the hearts and minds of the people. Nationwide trade and industry occupied only a tiny fraction of the population; the overwhelming majority were peasants with the provincialism native to their class. As we know today, not until the peasant world with its static institutions and its nonsecular, particularistic ethos is destroyed can national unity in the modern sense begin.

It is startling today to realize what a chasm separated the rulers from the ruled in the old dynastic states of Europe. The modern conception of nation as including all the people living within the boundaries of the state was totally absent. The state was the province of the king, and the nation extended only to include the king and the nobility. The people were subjects in every sense of the word, to be traded and taxed and ruled for the advantage of the crown. A French, Prussian, or Polish nobleman would have considered his horse a member of his nation sooner than include the peasants living and working on his estates.

Nor did the people themselves have such aspirations. Hard-pressed, hard-worked, immobile, and ignorant of the wider world, they lived their daily lives with little concern for or interest in the state and its perennial dynastic quarrels. Wars and taxes afflicted them like disease and drought, manifestations of powers they did not understand, but otherwise their lives were little touched by the changes occurring in the organization of the state. They did not contribute to the military power of the monarchy, for fighting was done by nobles or by mercenaries. They did not deal with the growing bureaucracy, which lived and worked in the towns, not in the countryside. They did not benefit from the new organization of economic life, nor were they intended to. And they felt no national identity with those who ruled the realm. Rulers and ruled lived in two different worlds.

The dynastic state laid the groundwork for the nation as we know it today, but its unification remained at a primitive level, for it did not include the population as a whole. Their inclusion, and with it the creation of the modern nation, remained for the future.

The gulf between ruler and ruled was even greater in the colonies, for here differences in power and wealth were underlined by differences in race, language, and culture, resulting in greater prejudice and discrimination on the part of the rulers, greater resentment and hatred on the part of the ruled, and, on occasion, greater violence when the relationship was ended.

Colonial peasants, like European peasants before them, have felt their lives remote not only from their European rulers but also from the native rulers who, with independence, succeeded them. Their lives, however, have probably been more drastically affected than those of the earlier European peasants, for their colonial rulers have been more powerful, more efficient, and more ruthless in disregard for their subjects. The situation has varied greatly from one colony to another, but where they have chosen to do so, European rulers have possessed the power to uproot native life completely, chasing the peasants from their land, conscripting them for labor, and destroying their social system almost completely.

Contrasts

A major contrast between the unification of European nations and that of the colonies lies in the European trend toward democratization which is absent in the colonies.

Here the outside rule of the colonies has been an important factor.

Europe's rising monarchs required vast resources to conquer and to hold their domains. In order to pay their growing armies and bureaucracies they found themselves relying more and more heavily upon the wealth of the burghers, with obvious consequences for the growth of bourgeois democracy. Colonial governments, on the other hand, had less need to rely upon any part of the native world for financial support, for they drew their major military and financial power from home. There, indeed, they were forced to account to their parliaments, but this did not increase democracy in the colonies.

The lack of any democratic tradition or experience has been extremely important in the development of the former colonies after independence. New national governments have inherited centralized and autocratic regimes and foreign-controlled economies. It is perhaps surprising that they have clung to the forms of democracy as much as they have.

Colonial rule also produced a smaller degree of national unification than the comparable dynastic period in Europe. In some cases, notably in most of the African colonies, this can be attributed to the short time these countries were under unified rule before they achieved their independence, a scant sixty or eighty years—not long enough for all the young tribal warriors who fought European conquest to have died of old age, certainly not long enough for tribal loyalties to have died with them. In Spanish America and in India and Indonesia, however, colonial rule lasted for hundreds of years, presumably long enough to have achieved a higher degree of unity than in fact was achieved.

Colonial unity has generally been fragile because it

was imposed from the outside. Indeed, there was no aspect of colonial life that was not affected by this crucial fact. "National" identification was imposed by foreign conquest in which existing military forces were destroyed or absorbed. The new national armies that replaced them were unified at the top by European officers but had a tendency to break down into rival factions when the Europeans left, as in the Congo, in Algeria, and in the abortive struggle in Indonesia.

National bureaucracies were also imported from outside, the whole top of the administrative system operating in opposition to the traditional rulers around whom traditional loyalties clustered. Replacing these bureaucrats after independence with native personnel who were competent and would act as *national* representatives has been extremely difficult.

Economic unity has also been tenuous; the national sector of the colonial economy revolved heavily around European interests while the subsistence agriculture that occupied the bulk of the population remained as backward and as local as ever. Colonial rulers made no efforts comparable to those of the mercantilists to stimulate native commerce and industry, and efforts by newly independent governments to take over and run European-controlled mines and wells and plantations without European partnership have run into many difficulties.

Most important of all, the European rulers of the colonies, despite illusions to the contrary, never succeeded in generating any popular loyalty for their new nationwide government. The native population remained in hidden or open opposition. So long as the Europeans remained in full control, this opposition tended to concentrate around the traditional regional rulers. Only with the beginning of the final liberation movement did native loyalties begin to gather around new national leaders. Indeed, it would seem that the greatest unifying act of the European rulers was to unite the population of the colonies against them in its fight for independence.

Liberation from Colonial Rule

Under colonial rule the native population played a passive part in moves toward national unification. The boundaries were drawn by the conqueror and the natives found them artificial. The army, the bureaucracy, the economy were all imposed upon the natives, who bore them but did not believe in them. In the fight for independence the natives began to play an active part in unification, for the fight was of necessity a voluntary and cooperative venture where goals and actions transcended the traditional divisions within the colony.

A new nation is conceived the moment a colony begins to struggle for liberation. This struggle is different from the original, traditional resistance to European encroachment and different from early traditional revolts against the colonizer. In seeking liberation, the natives fight the Europeans on European terms, with European weapons and forms of organization, and, ironically, for European values of liberty, independence, and nationalism.

The degree of unification provided by the fight for liberation depends upon the length and violence of the conflict. It seems plausible to argue, although the empirical evidence is not conclusive, that the longer and bloodier the conflict, the greater the unity of the new nation, for it is this fight that has given the new nations practically the only cohesive strength they possess when they finally become sovereign. It is this struggle that has produced the leaders who rule the new nations, the martyrs and the symbols of national unity that fire their nationalism, and the military organization that enforces unity and order within the new states. The movements of rebel armies across the land and the flight of refugees from one area to another have provided another layer of painful but unifying experience.

That the fight for liberation is important for unity is underlined by the lack of cohesion in some of the nations that have won freedom from colonial rule without a fight. Consider for example the Belgian Congo. When the international community intervenes early in behalf of a colony struggling for independence, in one sense it does it no favor. Similarly the colonizer who leaves gracefully before he is forced to leave does not act as beneficially as he imagines, for nations born of Caesarean birth are weaker.

Common ties of hate as well as common action help unify a nation; these, of course, have been present in all the colonies whether they fought for their freedom or not. The rejection of an outsider is, unfortunately, a step in finding one's own national identity, and the colonizer has provided a natural target. Indeed, the nationalism displayed by colonial peoples in their struggles for independence is little more than anticolonial feeling, and deep divisions reappear the moment the colonizer leaves.

The fight for liberation never involves the entire colonial population. Anticolonial rebels assert that the entire population of the colony is in revolt against colonial rule, while colonial rulers generally insist that, except for a few malcontents, the population supports their rule. Both claims are false. The error of the colonizers is made evident by the mass jubilation that greets their departure. The error of rebel leaders is more subtle, but their claims are also misleading in what they leave unsaid. The colonial masses hate the colonizer, but not for the same reasons that inspire the revolutionary leaders.

Let us be clear. The Europeans present particularly good targets for native hatred because they are foreign, wealthy, and different in race, color, and culture, and the native mass is frightened by and hostile to all that is foreign and strange. In addition, the Europeans have often given them good reason to hate. But hatred toward the colonizer is only part of the hostility, conscious and unconscious, that ignorant peasants living in abject poverty harbor toward *all* who rule them—dark or white, native or foreign.

The aims of the revolt of the populace are not the same as those of the revolutionary leaders. The leaders seek to eject and to replace the Europeans who rule the country, but the native masses are flailing out against their own misery, and the Europeans, who are to be sure partly responsible for it, are a convenient target for more general hostility.

The Liberators

In spite of widespread popular hatred of foreign rule, colonial revolutions have rarely been true mass uprisings. They have been the work of small, dedicated groups of leaders, often not unified themselves in their ultimate aims, but united at least in opposition to their European rulers.

Over the years, the nature of this opposition has shifted. One must be cautious in making generalizations from the muddled history of colonial conflict, but in the case of the European colonies in Asia and Africa, there seem to have been three distinct "generations" of colonial leaders who have opposed the Europeans in different ways.[1] Quite frequently the first resistance to colonial rule has sprung from the traditional elite who were trying to stop Western

[1] Edward Shils, "The Intellectuals in the Political Development of New States," *World Politics,* XII (April 1960), 329–68.

erosion of the traditional culture. In one form or another they asked for a return to the purity of old ways. Often the resistance was religious in orientation, as in Egypt, where the call was to return to the principles of the Koran and the solidarity of Moslem against infidel. Such traditional leaders failed in the end because they rejected the European ways which gave the Europeans power to rule.

The second group of colonial leaders were more modern in outlook and more limited in aim. They were the constitutional liberals clamoring for reform, not freedom, who appear so frequently in the colonial setting. Educated in Europe, usually, and enamored of European ways, these Europeanized colonials had little love for the traditional native way of life. Coming from the top of native society, as they so often did, they had no wish to put a complete end to European rule, which underwrote and protected their own social and economic position. What the constitutional liberals really sought was to share the rule of the colonizing power. In this their hopes were naïve, for although European rulers might grant them some of the forms of constitutional participation, they had no intention of parting with any of the essential elements of control.

The third group of leaders was made of sterner stuff. This is the group that has become dominant in the recent successful struggles for independence. Europe-trained like their predecessors, these men have turned against the arbitrary rules of the old society, the unreasoned way of life, the suffocating blanket of tradition. But at the same time they have been deeply alienated from many of the values of Western life. Unlike the constitutionalists, who sojourned among the upper classes of Europe, these later pilgrims to Europe experienced more bruising racial discrimination and also came into contact with new currents of socialist thought that challenged Western constitutionalism.

Thus many of these new revolutionaries have helped to create a new nationalism, strongly anti-European and at the same time antitraditional. They have, in effect, created a new tradition and invented a new past. Opposed to old-fashioned backwardness and humiliated by colonial subservience, they found the real world depressing. One way to escape it was to invest the masses of their own people with virtues and wisdom which never existed and to dig back for the kind of past that would make them proud. Armed with such a past, they would lead their people into a Utopian future.

This new nationalism is proving an important ingredient in the national unification now taking place in the newly independent nations of Asia and Africa. It did not play as large a part in the fight for independence as one might think. That fight was waged and won by surprisingly small groups of men who plotted, negotiated, and fought their way to victory with enthusiastic but generally passive support from the bulk of their countrymen. They owed their victory more to the weakening of their rulers in two world wars than to any strength they themselves possessed, and the "nations" they created were still a long way from being national in anything but government. Nevertheless, the nationalism fostered by the revolutionary leaders in their fight for independence will be an important tool as these leaders now begin the long hard task of creating substance to stuff the forms of nationhood.

NEW NATIONS

The genuine unification of the nation in social, economic, and cultural terms—indeed, even the maintenance of political unity—remains the main job of political leaders in the new nations even after they are free of their old colonial rulers. Thus the politics of primitive unification continue, and many of the institutions in the new nations bear the stamp of this continuing struggle.

The amount of national cohesiveness in the underdeveloped countries is related at least in part to the length of time they have been independent states. Most of the new nations that have become independent since World War II face great unification problems, and this includes nearly all the countries of Africa, most of those of Southeast Asia, and some of the countries of the Middle East. In many cases the boundaries of these states include people who do not share the same culture or the same history, people whose only common experience has been a common colonial overlord. Colonial boundaries were generally drawn by Europeans with little regard for the people within them. Indeed, the initial boundaries were not intended for the colonials at all, but merely advertised to other colonial powers the extent of the colonizer's claim.

Thus it is common for new nations to enclose traditional enemies within their borders and to be troubled by dissident minorities. Often they exclude people with stronger ties who live across the border. Separatist tendencies are strong, and the central government must wage a continuing battle to keep the country from breaking down into its precolonial parts.

Divided Elites

With the colonizer gone, the most important unifying force in the new state becomes the native elite now in power, the Western-trained intellectuals who guided the revolution. Their situation, however, is far from happy. In the first place, the members of the native elite are split among themselves. Differences and disagreements held in check during the fight for liberation erupt with violence the moment the fight is won, and in the struggle for power that follows, opposition to those in control quite often ends in house arrest, exile, or death.

Even more important is the tug of war after liberation between the Westernized intelligentsia in power and the traditional leaders who represent the past way of life. The breach here is deep and can end only with the defeat of one side by the other. At stake is the whole process of modernization, for the Western elements in power are committed to political unification through reorganization of the population along more modern lines. If they succeed, the traditional leaders will witness not only the abolition of their own power but also the destruction of the way of life they value and represent. It is probable that this will be the most frequent outcome, for economic and social change are gradually weakening the position of the traditional elite.

In the immediate present, however, the position of the Westernized political leaders is not an enviable one, for in many ways they are unable to reach beyond the traditional leaders to the masses of peasants who make up the bulk of the population. The political leaders themselves are urban people who have spent their lives abroad, in jail, or in the cities of their own countries plotting revolt. Alienated from the traditional society, they have few ties with the rural population. The organizations they head— revolutionary groups, political parties, labor unions—are essentially urban groups; to unify their countries they must reach the entire population. Usually, for the sake of even minimum effective political control over the population, they are forced to compromise with the traditional regional rulers, though such compromise greatly impedes their progress in modernizing the nation.

Finally, the Western-trained intellectual in power in the new nation is divided within himself. He is alienated both from his own culture and from the West, but he is also part of both. His contact with the traditional life which he abandoned is constantly renewed through family and friends. The shrillness of his rejection may well be a measure of the difficulty he suffers in repressing his own feelings.[2]

Not only are there profound divisions among the elite, there is also a lack of the political tools necessary to unify the rest of the country. To make up for this lack, the rulers of newly independent underdeveloped countries fan the anticolonial and nationalistic sentiments that exist among their people. Anticolonial feeling is certainly a strong unifying force during the fight for liberation, but its potency as a rallying cry wanes after a relatively short period unless new crises conveniently occur—or are manufactured. However, a course of calculated friction with the former colonial rulers is not always a wise policy for a new national government. It may help unify the people, but it endangers the economic viability of the nation, which usually remains, at least for a time, an economic dependency of its former European rulers. For this reason, the generation of nationalistic sentiments based upon something other than sheer anticolonialism is more advantageous.

No amount of rallies, parades, slogans, and speeches, however, can make up for the fact that the existing political institutions in the new nations are defective and function in a primitive fashion. This is usually true of the two major political institutions without which modern government cannot function: the political party and the political bureaucracy.

---

[2] *Ibid.*, p. 350.

Elections and Parties

An interesting reversal of Western experience is taking place in new nations beginning their national existence today. In the advanced Western nations, expansion of the franchise and growth of political parties followed modernization, while the reverse is true of the new nations. The franchise does not expand in response to the increase of political consciousness, as in the West, but precedes and helps expand that consciousness. The universal suffrage that marks the end of a long political development in the West marks the beginning of such a development in the new nations. Thus the meaning and the effects of the political institutions in new nations are not the same as in the old.

The primary effect of the franchise and of the political party in the new nations is not representation but unification of the country. The franchise is an important step in creating a national political identity. The act of voting on national issues is an experience shared with fellow citizens. It helps also to focus attention upon the national government and its policies and actions, for the clamor of an election reaches nearly everyone, even in nations where communication with the back country is poor.

The political party also has primarily a unifying function. In the Western context, political parties are a channel for representation of the popular will and a tool through which political leaders can shepherd the general populace into common thought and action. In the new nations, however, the functions of representation and manipulation take second place to the function of unification.

Because unity is their main preoccupation the new nations have tended to be one-party states. The situation varies from countries with one overwhelmingly large party dwarfing all others to those which have outlawed all opposition. In most cases, however, the fear of organized opposition appears to stem not only from the usual desire of those in power to protect their own interests but also from deep and well-founded beliefs that if organized opposition were permitted, major ethnic and geographical groups within the country would frustrate any hope of incorporating them into the greater community. In other words, to permit opposition would be tantamount to permitting the strong centrifugal forces present to tear the diaphanous unity of the nation.

Even a single-party structure faces problems in containing these centrifugal forces. The Westernized intellectuals in power desire a strong, united party—but at the same time they wish to reach the masses of the country. As urban men whose strength lies largely in urban groups, these leaders find that they can reach the tradition-oriented peasants of the countryside only by compromising with their traditional leaders. The compromise at its most extreme takes the form of the patron party, in which membership in the party is limited to political leaders. These leaders, including the heads of the traditional groups, form a federation in which the groups themselves remain untouched. Only the elite is unified, and even this unity is highly unstable, for if a leader decides to leave the party he takes all his followers with him.

At the other extreme is the mass party, which is organized more along Western lines and reaches down to individual citizens. In such parties the amount of central control is far greater and the erosion of the power position of the traditional elite proceeds much more rapidly. Ruth Schachter has described the creeping extension of the mass parties in West Africa:

> . . . the leaders of mass parties . . . tried to use their party organization in order to awaken a wider, national sense of community. They appealed to particular cate-

gories existing within or cutting across ethnic groups . . . in many villages mass party organizers went to rivals of official "chiefs"; from these they discovered local grievances. They often appealed to rural underprivileged groups . . . to rural scribes, whose modern skills set them apart, and to those who had travelled, often "strangers" who were among the most recent immigrants. . . . In some areas they went to veterans. . . . They sought out religious dissidents. . . . They found camel drivers, chauffeurs, transporters, and peddlers. . . . Finally they appealed to those who earned money income for growing coffee, cocoa, peanuts or bananas, and become [*sic*] restless with tradition; to young men who no longer listened to the old; and to women who made money trading in the market place. People responded to the mass party organizers' appeals against established authorities.[3]

Such people, however, are in the minority. To reach the masses, a party must also take implicit and explicit cognizance of the traditional social structure. Ethnic, tribal, and geographic divisions must be well represented. As they are represented, they are put in the position of fighting a rear-guard action to protect their privileged position from any governmental attempts at more fundamental unification.

Governmental Bureaucracies

The second major governmental tool is the bureaucracy. In the newest nations, governmental administration is in many respects as rudimentary and even more defective than the party system. Political parties, after all, benefited from vigorous growth during the fight for liberation from colonial rule. Administration, on the other hand, remained until the very last moment in the hands of the colonizer.

---

[3] Ruth Schachter, "Single-Party Systems in West Africa," *American Political Science Review*, LV (June 1961), 301.

In some colonies, where the rulers were reconciled to the necessity of ending colonial rule, an attempt was made to hand over the state administration in good order. For at least a few last years, natives were trained to fill top positions in the bureaucracy and were given a working apprenticeship. In some cases, where colonizer and colony parted on friendly terms, it has been possible for Europeans to stay on and help the government bureaucracy function during the early years of independence. In India, Ghana, and the Sudan, for example, the British left relatively well-functioning bureaucracies.

But even in such fortunate colonies, deaths and retirements soon create gaps that cannot be filled because of the general illiteracy level and the almost complete lack of higher education. In addition, colonial administration was based on the assumption that most native life was to be run traditionally. Outside of maintaining order, collecting taxes, and supervising traditional native organizations, the central government generally had little to do with native life. The need for a bureaucracy was therefore restricted. The new governments, however, come to power with programs of economic expansion and desire to provide a long list of essential services for the population—and such expansion and such servicing are necessary if the population is to be weaned away from the traditional way of life and reorganized in more modern forms. The need for men to staff the new government offices increases many fold and cannot be met. In consequence, the ability of the central government to reach the population, especially in the countryside, is greatly weakened.

In some cases, the situation is much worse. Often, where the colonial rulers have been forced out after a period of bitter native rebellion, there existed only the barest administrative structure, and even that structure was sometimes ripped up by its foundations. Native administration has developed only with difficulty, and the structure hastily thrown together after independence is defective not only in numbers but also in organization and the quality of its personnel.

Economic Development

The problems of the new nations are greatly increased by the urgency with which almost all pursue economic modernization. With divided elites, locally oriented citizens, primitive political parties, and inadequate bureaucracies, the governments of these countries are nevertheless determined to modernize their economies as rapidly as possible and often have grandiose plans to this end.

Here again their experience differs from that of most European states, where primitive unification proceeded slowly for several centuries preceding the industrial revolution. Even when industrialization in Europe did begin, it proceeded slowly—creating problems for the central government, to be sure, but generated and directed by private sources outside the responsibility of the national government. In Europe the problems of industrialization arose for the most part after the problems of primitive unification had been solved; the problems of industrialization, when they did arise, were not primarily governmental problems.

In today's newly independent underdeveloped nations, on the contrary, the politics of primitive unification and the politics of industrialization overlap and both tasks are considered governmental responsibilities. This places an enormous strain on the young governments.

OLD NATIONS

The same problems are found, in less acute degree, in underdeveloped countries that have existed for a longer period as independent states. There are in the world today a number of old, established nations that have remained economically underdeveloped, among them the former colonies of Latin America, which won their independence long ago. Some of the Latin American countries have modernized, but most have not. Also included in this category would be countries that had a long history as independent states before falling under colonial rule, for instance Egypt. Finally there are such states as Iran and Thailand, which escaped colonial status altogether, although they became economic dependencies of the West.

Compared with the more recent nations to emerge, some of these established underdeveloped countries have a higher degree of national unity. They appear to have overcome more of their ethnic divisions and to be less troubled by regional and provincial independence from central control. They have also had more time in which to develop symbols and sentiments of national identity.

Certainly the traditional elites that run such countries are more united, but it is difficult to be certain how much cohesion exists below the top levels of society. The bulk of the population are peasants, tied to the land of their own localities by poverty, tradition, and ignorance of alternatives. Their views have no influence and are not known, but it is probable that once their countries start to modernize and they begin to stream into the cities, they will make up the mobs so easily mobilized by modern leaders to express the excesses of modern nationalism.

At present, the old underdeveloped nations are not as sharply divided into a small governing elite and a large mass of peasants as formerly, for new strata are growing between the two groups. Nevertheless, rulers and ruled still live in two different worlds. This is not a division which threatens national existence, as do some of the splits within the newer nations, but it is a division which greatly impedes national efficiency. The "nation," in terms of those whose energies can be mobilized for national purposes, includes in reality only the ruling elite. The rest of the citizens are more or less docile subjects who can do little to help their nation and whose nations do little for them.

The Elite

The major cohesive force in traditional states is the elite, which forms a unit and sees itself as such in its relations with other groups within and without the nation. The elite is small, and its wealth, education, mobility, and self-awareness make it powerful. It is, on the whole, to be distinguished from the ruling elites of the new nations, for in the older states the traditional elite controls the national government, not the Western-trained intelligentsia. The core of the native elite, as one would expect, is the landed aristocracy; typically, the politics, economy, and social system of such countries are centered upon the land and its control. Land ownership is highly concentrated, and the national government is controlled by large land-owners.

A second element within the traditional elite is the religious leaders. Religious organizations may or may not be large landowners, but religious leaders and landowners are generally united in upholding the existing social order.

A third element is the military, of which more in a moment. This is a small group, of little use in protecting the nation against outside danger, charged primarily with keeping internal order. As such it forms an important group within the traditional elite.

Finally, there is one portion of the elite of the traditional state that is not native but is nevertheless extremely important. This is the small group of foreigners who represent the interests of foreign economic enterprises. Their influence is great since the modern sector of the economy is in their hands, although they share its profits with some of the notables in the native elite. Unlike the other elite groups, these foreigners represent a modernizing force and the effect of their presence is highly disruptive to the traditional society. However, as individuals they generally cooperate closely with the ruling native elite and help to protect it against potential domestic competitors, for not only is it the group with which they have struck their bargain and made their contracts, but it is to the favor of the elite that the foreign enterprises owe their privileged position.

The Military

The role of the military is particularly interesting in traditional states, for the military segment of the elite fulfills three somewhat contradictory functions: (1) it helps maintain the established order; (2) it provides an important channel for upward mobility; and (3) it is often a spearhead for revolutionary modernization. Let us examine each function in turn.

Underdeveloped nations in most cases possess only Lilliputian armies of a few thousand poorly trained men armed with a small amount of equipment purchased abroad. Even in the long-established underdeveloped nations, military forces are so small and weak as to be virtually useless for prolonged foreign conflict.

The military are, however, of great importance at home, where they leave their barracks and take to the streets at any sign of domestic unrest. It is the fundamental job of the military to protect the established order, an economic and social system run by a landed aristocracy. Beneath the surface of a stagnant and poor society always runs a current of pent-up dissatisfaction, and the army is there to ward off any fundamental attack upon the existing system.

It may at first glance appear strange to credit the military with maintaining order in countries where so often it is the military which disrupts the political life of the country with violence and *coups d'état,* as it has done in Egypt, Iran, Guatemala, Peru, Bolivia, and Ecuador. (By one count there were thirty-one revolutions in Latin America in the decade following World War II.)

Yet there is no contradiction in the fact that the army keeps order and at the same time causes most of the violence. In states run by traditional elites, violence is frequent but rarely disturbs the fundamental order. First of all, the violence is generally brief and claims few victims. The revolutions and attempted revolutions are palace revolts that scarcely touch people outside high government circles except to provide them topics of conversation. The president and his closest supporters may be exiled or assassinated. The situation becomes tense and citizens of the capital may even stay indoors for an afternoon, but the next day the shops reopen, the inhabitants take their evening stroll, and calm is restored.

Second, such palace revolutions may change the personnel without changing the complexion of the group in power. The grip of the landed artistocracy generally remains unshaken, and officials often play musical chairs in a manner distressing to a population which may briefly have hoped for some genuine change or reform.

The change in ruling personnel may even help protect the existing system, for it allows integration into the ruling group of ruthless and potentially dangerous persons who otherwise might become totally disaffected and turn against the system. In a stagnant society dominated by a landed aristocracy, the paths of upward mobility are few. Military careers provide the surest opening for the ambitious and disadvantaged, and palace revolts give access to more permanent sources of wealth and power to those who have shouldered or shot their way into high government office. They offer a means of acquiring land, the most stable source of wealth and power in underdeveloped countries, and they give access to control of mineral riches, which may be leased to or withheld from foreign companies—for a price. In view of all this, it seems appropriate to regard the violence as a safety valve protecting the integrity of the underdeveloped system.

The third role of the military, however, is genuinely the reverse of the other two. Not only in those underdeveloped countries that have long been independent but also in some of the newly independent states run by traditional elites (as in the Middle East), the military in recent times has become a spearhead in movements to unseat the traditional elite and move toward genuine modernization.

The currents of modernization are sweeping the world. It would be a mistake to credit the military with their origin, but it does appear that, in underdeveloped countries ruled by traditional elites, military leaders are often the first men of power to desire economic and social modernization. The cases of Egypt, Japan, and Iraq come to mind immediately, as well as that of Ethiopia, where a revolt of the palace guard was put down ruthlessly but may presage things to come, and China, where the army led the revolution of Sun Yat-sen.

In underdeveloped countries, the armed forces are relatively modern and therefore potentially a most revolutionary institution. Military leaders are often in contact with, sometimes even trained by, the military establishments of powerful modern countries. They are aware of the worth of modern weapons and modern military techniques, and they possess a common yardstick for measuring military success: victory in battle. One may argue fruitlessly about differing sets of values, differing religions, and different types of societies, for in these areas there may exist no commonly held standards of judgment. But armies are supposed to win battles, and military leaders who have been defeated by the superior power of Europeans have become rapid converts to European military methods.

It may take longer in underdeveloped countries than elsewhere for military leaders to realize that modernization of the army is possible only if the society modernizes as well, but when this realization comes the army often tries to topple the old system and impose a new one more to its liking.

This modernizing role of the military in countries still dominated by a traditional elite is in some ways parallel to the role played by Westernized intellectuals in the countries recently freed from colonialism. In most of the latter countries, the military does not initially play an important part in politics. Under colonialism, military forces were foreign-led, and in the fight for liberation revolutionary activity was more intellectual and political than military. What rebel forces existed were paramilitary, and only now—after independence—are genuine military forces, traditions, and a military class beginning to develop. Yet we must guard against the error of thinking that this state of affairs is permanent. In these countries, too, the military may come to constitute an important segment of the elite in years to come.

Political Institutions

In the older underdeveloped nations, as in the new, political institutions are stunted and do not extend down to the masses of the population. In some of the least-developed countries still ruled by absolute monarchs, such as Afghanistan and Ethiopia, political parties are non-existent, and in the past one-party governments, some outright dictatorships, have been common (as in the Dominican Republic, Venezuela, Paraguay, and Mexico). In recent years, multiple-party systems have become more usual, but one party is often heavily dominant. Even where two or more parties compete effectively, party membership is often drawn from relatively restricted groups near the top of the social scale while the bulk of the population is not admitted.

Equally defective is the development of the governmental bureaucracy. In traditional societies the government performs few if any services for the people, and its functioning, except for the collection of taxes, rarely extends into the countryside. Bureaucratic standards are not modern. Public administration is part-time, inadequate, and corrupt. A recommendation from the powerful is a *sine qua non* for a public job or for any governmental attendance to one's needs, and underpaid public employees stretch their salaries by selling favors and by moonlighting.

The leaders of traditional governments claim to speak for their countries, and it is a convenient fiction to think they do. In reality, however, they generally have little knowledge of or interest in the desires of the ruled, and they lack the political tools to reach the masses and band them together for any national purpose.

When it comes to economic modernization, the old underdeveloped countries are not so pressed as the newer nations. Even though their economies are in some cases more advanced, they are not ruled by elites who seek so rapid a rate of change. When they do turn to industrialization in earnest, they will find their relatively greater unity an advantage compared to the situation in the nations only recently freed from colonialism, where the problems of national unification and economic modernization must be solved simultaneously. They will also find that their own political unification is far from complete.

CONCLUSION

To summarize, the main function of politics in the first stage of national political development is to unify a group of people who have few ties. In all the cases we have examined—in the dynastic states, in the colonies, in the new underdeveloped nations and in the old—this is a period of nation-building in which political parties and bureaucracies develop and grow.

During this period the groundwork is laid for the economic advance which is to follow, but even at the end of the period national unification is only partial and does not include the entire population. Politics without economic modernization does a very imperfect job of unifying the country, and *primitive unification* seems a fair name for its accomplishments.

In all countries, though to differing extents and at different rates of speed, destruction of the old agricultural, social and economic system begins in the period of primitive unification and proceeds as the period progresses. It is this economic and social change, as well as the political developments themselves, which shift the focus of political life during the second stage of political growth from unity to economic development. The experience of countries in stage two is the subject of the three chapters that follow.

STAGE TWO

The Politics of
Industrialization

III

BOURGEOIS
POLITICS

Industrialization, the pride of powerful and wealthy nations and the hope of the poor and the backward, presents an immense challenge to the political system of any nation. New rulers, new rules, new distributions of wealth and power, new habits, and new ideologies are not produced without a strain. Industrialization, where it has occurred, has been accompanied by great political upheaval, and it seems safe to predict that new upheavals will take place as the rest of the world races into economic modernization.

The primary function of politics in the second stage of national growth is to deal with economic modernization. No other period in a nation's history gives as clear a picture of the way in which economic change shapes political institutions and political policies in turn direct the path and the pace of economic change. It is this relationship between politics and economic modernization that we shall explore in dealing with the politics of industrialization.

To date, industrial nations have achieved their status through three quite different systems: bourgeois politics, stalinist politics, and fascist politics. Each has solved the problems of economic development in its own fashion. Nations industrializing today have at least these three choices before them, and although the contest is usually put in terms of democracy versus communism, neofascist solutions should by no means be ruled out. Which path to progress will today's industrializing nations choose? Upon the answer hangs not only their own future but that of the rest of the world as well.

To understand why nations make the choices they do, it will be helpful to view these three systems not simply as competing ideologies but as three alternative ways of dealing with industrialization. They differ in their response to common problems. Specifically, they differ in who holds the reins of government, who provides the capital for economic development, and how fast this development is allowed to progress. We shall examine each system in some detail, but let us begin with the oldest and most widespread of the three: bourgeois politics.

THE ROLE OF GOVERNMENT

It is a common error to confuse the bourgeois politics of the nineteenth century with the mass democracies of the twentieth. It is true that the two are intimately related, that bourgeois politics were in a certain sense democratic, and that almost universally bourgeois democracy has in time turned into mass democracy. Yet the two are distinct, and the distinction is important. Bourgeois politics were characteristic of industrializing nations; mass democracy is a political system of fully industrial nations. Although one system laid the groundwork for the other, they differ in fundamentals.

The most important difference lies in the fact that under the political rule of the bourgeoisie, the vast majority of the population was prevented, in large part through restrictions on the franchise, from exercising any significant influence upon government. This difference in popular control should not be passed over lightly, for unless proper weight is given it, the course of economic development and the contribution of government to industrialization cannot be clearly understood. Nor will one understand the effect of industrialization on political development and the birth of the mass democracies, which we shall examine later.

The popular version of the role of bourgeois politics in guiding the national economy is one of almost complete governmental inaction. Compared to the governments wrestling in our day with the problems of industrializing their countries, bourgeois politics do indeed appear to have followed the maxim of governing best by governing least. The early bourgeois governments of the United States and Western Europe did not plan; they did not carry the major burden of saving; they did not map the strategy of modernization; and they did not direct the major economic efforts. Private initiative created the savings, invested them in capital goods, modernized production and distribution, and created the wealth that eventually made the citizenry rich and the nation powerful. Private actions brought about the changes that flung up the cities, filled them with migrants from the countryside, and changed the work, home, and leisure lives of entire populations. The government looked on. Or so the story goes.

There is both truth and distortion in this version of events. First, let us dispose of a crucial exaggeration. Government was not totally inactive. In important ways it extended positive help to those who industrialized the nation, and where private action was not forthcoming, the government did the job itself. It is true that in many key areas the government was merely an interested bystander, but government inaction should also be properly evaluated. Neutrality aids the stronger party in a dispute; so it was with the bourgeois governments. By remaining inactive, they gave a free hand and a clear field to the budding capitalists who reorganized the national economy. Thus government inaction was also an important form of aid.

If one accepts this view and counts both direct and indirect government assistance, the total contribution of bourgeois politics to industrialization is impressive:

1. Bourgeois politics gave the deciding voice in governmental councils to those who wished to modernize the economy and industrialize the nation and at the same time kept out of power those whose interests conflicted with major elements of the industrialization process.

2. Bourgeois politics were crucial in the creation of savings for investment. Government helped decisively in increasing production and in holding down consumption to a level where it did not consume the savings destined for reinvestment.

3. Bourgeois politics encouraged and aided the rural-to-city migration which was absolutely necessary for economic development. By doing this, the government speeded the breakup of the old preindustrial peasant system, helped usher in a modern social structure, and provided a pool of labor for the new manufacturing in-

dustries which formed the backbone of the industrial system.

Let us examine briefly each of these important contributions.

NEW RULERS

It is difficult to see how a nation could industrialize if the national government remained firmly in the hands of groups who opposed such change. Not surprisingly, the major political development of the period of industrialization—bourgeois, stalinist, or fascist—is the shift of predominant political power from the landed aristocracy to the new industrialists, be they private capitalists or government bureaucrats.

In the bourgeois democracies from the last quarter of the eighteenth century to the last quarter of the nineteenth, in country after country—in England, France, Germany, the United States—the bourgeoisie took over political power and control.

The bourgeois claim for greater voice and power was well founded. On the whole, the middle classes were better educated than the old aristocrats and possessed greater managerial skills. Certainly the experience of the new-rich in running their farflung affairs gave them greater competence in mastering the business of government, which had ceased to deal with dynastic considerations. The success of the new economy was becoming a matter of life and death to a larger and larger portion of the population, and the policies and actions of government were crucial to the new economy. Most important was the growing economic power of the new industrialists. The state itself was becoming dependent upon their wealth, both to run its concerns at home and to provide a major source of its power in international affairs. Inevitably, those who directed the new economy insisted upon being heard, and their demands were granted.

The Nation Is Enlarged

The shift from aristocratic to bourgeois control of the machinery of the state meant a tremendous change in the national participation of the nation's citizenry. Not only were a greater number of people included in national, as distinct from local, life; their involvement was deeper than that of the past.

The contrast with dynastic times was striking. As noted earlier, the dynastic "nation" was the king and his court. The rest of the population was less part of the nation than part of the estate of the crown and of the nobility. Moreover, the aristocrats had many more ties with one another across national lines than they had with their subjects at home. With the accession of the bourgeoisie to power, fundamental changes took place. The nation was enlarged to include the new middle classes; and the bourgeoisie, in contrast to the aristocracy, was highly nationalistic. In addition, the population at large, though still excluded from political participation, was drawn much more closely into the national unit. With the agricultural and industrial revolutions, the masses lost their social isolation and their economic self-sufficiency. They became, in short, dependent upon the national economy and upon the national state, and their final integration into the national unit was begun, though its conclusion was to be the major achievement of the third stage of political development.

The manner in which the bourgeoisie came to power varied from one country to another. So did the amount of strife produced by the shift in the power position of the two elites. In no case was the transition entirely peaceful, but there were great differences in the amount of violence. England suffered riots and disorders, and Germany experienced the revolutionary shocks of 1848, but in the United States and in France the aristocracy in control could not and would not share governmental power until a major revolution had shaken loose its grip.

The French nobility's rigid defiance of the demands of the French middle classes is legendary. Nor was the demand of the American middle classes that they be represented in the British parliament acceptable to the aristocracy then ruling Britain. How could it have been? How could the demands of a colonial bourgeoisie be granted when similar demands were denied at home? Thwarted and hemmed in by a colonizer that regarded the colonies its estate to plunder as it saw fit, the American middle classes revolted. In a way their opportunity was greater than that of their European brothers. Although they had to fight free of the mother country before they could rule, once free they were under far less pressure to share their power with an aristocracy.

In Europe, no matter how radical the revolution, the hold of the aristocracy could not be fully eliminated. Attempts to extirpate aristocratic privilege and power resulted only in weakening the hold of the landed gentry. After each major advance by the bourgeoisie—after the French Revolution, even after the English Reform Bill of 1832—the aristocracy regained much of the ground it had lost; the bourgeoisie in Europe had to lay siege to the citadels of governmental power again and again before its victory was complete.

Shared Power

Indeed, there was virtually no time when the bourgeoisie ruled entirely alone. During its long and bitterly contested climb to power, the bourgeoisie was the junior partner of the aristocracy. The aristocracy continued to hold the major governmental posts and used the power of government to resist the expansion of the new economy and to hinder the rise of the new-rich to political control. Gradually, however, the bourgeoisie gained the upper hand, and by the middle of the nineteenth century the bourgeoisie was supreme everywhere in industrializing Europe.

Even after the middle classes had gained power, they did not rule alone but shared their power with the aristocracy, which now in its turn assumed the role of junior partner, but still had interests to be protected and a voice to be heard. Later, when the movement that was to transform bourgeois politics into mass democracy began to gather momentum, the bourgeoisie began to share control of the machinery of the state with the mass of the population. Although the beginnings of historical periods are always difficult to locate precisely, the mass movements had started by the last third of the nineteenth century—in Germany with the unification of the country, in the United States after the Civil War, in England by 1860 or 1870, and in France with the fall of Napoleon III.

The bourgeois period is a bridge between the dynastic state and the mass state and overlaps both. The rise of the bourgeoisie to political power closed the gap that had developed when political power remained in the hands of the aristocracy while economic power had shifted into the hands of the merchants, moneylenders, and the new breed of industrial magnates. The closing years of the bourgeois period saw the masses beginning to rise in political power. The roots of the next stage of political development, indeed, can be traced to the success of the bourgeoisie in mobilizing the masses in their own battle for recognition.

Popular Participation

The masses played an important part in bringing the bourgeoisie to power. Whatever the form of the battle, whether parliamentary negotiation or bloody revolution, it is doubtful that the bourgeoisie could have won without popular support that was both wide and deep. In Germany, France, the United States, and England, it was the active support of a majority of the population that tipped the balance in favor of the bourgeoisie.

Certainly this was the case in France, where the Revolution mobilized the vast majority of the people in favor of violent change, and certainly popular support of the American Revolution was wide. But popular participation was also important in England, where no revolution took place. It should not be forgotten that the parliamentary maneuvering that led eventually to the Reform Bill of 1832 transpired in a country shaken by turmoil and strife. The Bristol riots, the burning of Nottingham Castle, the mutinous crowds in the streets of London forced the hand of the king and the nobles, and Parliament was changed from an instrument of aristocratic rule to one where the old and the new rich shared power. Thus it seems justified to say that the victories of the middle classes should be considered popular victories as well, because the masses had much to do with bringing them about.

Popular Exclusion

On the other hand, they were not popular victories so far as sharing the spoils was concerned. The population at large was not included in the democratization of the state, which extended only to the bourgeoisie. The mass of the population, which had propelled the new-rich into a position of power, was left out in the cold.

G. D. H. Cole, writing about England, sums up well the difference between the attitude of the new middle classes toward the old aristocracy and their attitude toward the working population:

> The 1832 revolution . . . had handed political power over to the middle classes from the aristocracy. The new rulers indeed contrived for many years to act through members of the upper class. Scarcely a member of the Grey cabinet was not either a peer or an heir to an old or recent peerage. But these Whigs, and in due course the Tories who succeeded them in office, were directly responsive to middle-class opinion and needs. They were even less than the old Government responsive to working-class opinion, for they had no fear of it. The working class had been kept outside, and the exclusion was entirely successful.[1]

Everywhere, with the bourgeoisie firmly in the saddle, control of government was related to the possession of property. The franchise, later to become the major formal means of popular control, was restricted to a tiny fraction of the potential electorate. Between fifty and a hundred years had still to elapse before the masses gained a full political voice and were finally integrated fully into the nation. At the height of middle-class rule, the common people were shut out from any role in government.

The importance of this exclusion cannot be overstressed. It was as crucial an aspect of bourgeois politics as the placing of the bourgeoisie in control of the national government, for the function of the middle classes to create capital for industrialization could not have been carried out under existing conditions if the working class had been given governmental protection against economic expansion at its expense.

---

[1] G. D. H. Cole and Raymond Postgate, *The British Common People* (London: Methuen, University Paperbacks, 1961), p. 258.

GOVERNMENT AID TO INDUSTRIALIZATION

The bourgeois governments of Europe and America aided industrialization in many ways, direct and indirect. Direct assistance included, first of all, actions helping to uproot the old order, whose ethos was by nature hostile to rapid economic development. Aristocratic privileges, feudal obligations, guild regulations, peasant rights—all found their legal basis undermined by the new governments.

Recognition of property rights and hostility to privilege were the new principles of government, and at an accelerating pace the web of economic arrangements woven over hundreds of years was torn beyond repair. The fabric of hierarchic rights, duties, and privileges that governed life in the countryside and in the cities was cast aside. The laborious arrangements through which the guilds controlled production and producers, limiting the one and protecting the other, were increasingly disregarded and rendered inoperative. The old ties that kept the peasant on the land and guaranteed his rights there were destroyed.

The new principles of economic organization were freedom of work and freedom of contract, and everywhere the strong, the aggressive, the experimenters were freed of legal restraints and allowed to use their property to increase production and maximize profits.

At a later date, the bourgeois governments took another important step in providing the legal framework for capital investment when they sanctioned the joint stock company, a financial practice that had evolved in advance of governmental sanction but which required legal recognition before it could operate effectively.

In addition to providing a framework for capital investment, national governments themselves took a hand in economic production. In Prussia, where tradition and circumstances favored governmental intervention in the economy, the government established mines and ran them, created factories, and imported machines and technical personnel from England. The French government also was more active in its direct economic activities than is generally recognized. It too built factories and imported machinery, opened technical schools, and advertised the new machinery and the new techniques at fairs.

In general, governmental initiative existed in proportion to the availability of private energy and will. When private initiative failed, government often stepped in. In England, government initiative was at a minimum and private initiative was greatest. In Germany, the reverse was true.

All the bourgeois governments were active in providing the communications network required by an industrial society. The French engineering corps built roads and canals and supervised and aided others in building them. Nor should we forget the direct contribution of the American Army engineers to American communications, particularly waterways, and the massive aid and enormous gifts in land and in cash awarded by the federal government and by the states to those who built roads, canals, and railroads.

Another way in which governmental action aided industrial expansion was by enlarging the amount of currency and credit. One can only be amazed today at the ingenuity early industrial leaders exercised to pay their workers. In England and elsewhere, private money was resorted to or workers were paid in shifts so that the money expended by the first shift was again available to pay the second. Each of the bourgeois governments set up banks which increased the flow of currency and expanded credit. The Bank of England enjoyed quasi-official status; the French government set up banks in Paris and pushed banking into the provinces; and no student of American politics can forget the early government's vigorous stand in favor of manufactures and, in particular, the creation of a national bank as a major source of capital.

Finally, governmental legislation was important in the protection of industrial growth from foreign competition. The long and complex history of tariffs in the Western world need not be recapitulated here, but it should be noted that government protection of industry often extended beyond tariffs. Bourgeois governments, no less than governments today, were aware that much of their power rested upon the industrial advantages they had gained, and bourgeois governments no less than the mercantilist governments before them tried to prevent the emigration of skilled technicians and the export of industrial secrets. England in particular sought to protect the lead she had gained in industrial development, but this policy did not succeed and was abandoned.

Indirect Assistance

Great as was the contribution of the bourgeois governments to expanding the facilities for production, their contribution to lowering consumption was equally great—perhaps even greater. Let us understand fully that if the increased production of early industrialization were applied immediately to improving living standards, there would be insufficient capital accumulation to increase industrialization further. It is the task of the political institutions of an industrializing society to help keep consumption sufficiently in check to permit the accumulation of capital.

Theoretically this could be achieved by permitting consumption to rise slightly, so long as the rise did not eat up all of the increase in production. In fact, it is probable that living standards were actually reduced for substantial segments of the population during the early years of industrialization, though this is difficult to measure.

To reduce consumption—or even to hold the line—at a time when production is still little above the peasant level is to insure severe want and anguish for a majority of the population. Given a choice, no people would long endure such want and such anguish to make industrialists rich, the state more powerful, or future generations happier. The people of industrializing America and Western Europe were not given a choice. Their sacrifices were not granted but extracted from them, in part without their knowledge and for the rest against their will. The importance of bourgeois control and mass exclusion from political decision-making is clear.

The way in which savings were created was not pretty. Generations of poor were overworked, underpaid, left to live in crowded filth—were, in short, fed into the machines of the industrializing West as a sort of industrial cannon fodder. Small wonder that later generations who benefited from their sacrifices and could now afford more humane values were not proud of the past and often tried to deny or disregard its misery and undemocratic foundations. Yet denied or disregarded they must not be, not for the purpose of passing judgment or finding fault (a futile pastime) but because without an appreciation of these realities, the relationship of politics to eighteenth- and nineteenth-century Western industrialization cannot be understood.

Two things should be underscored before we confront more directly the relationship between bourgeois politics and industrialization. First, government acted well within the harsh values of the times. This is an important distinction from governments helping their nations industrialize at a later date. In eighteenth- and nineteenth-century England, for example, even reformers struggling to improve the conditions of child labor believed firmly that it was good for children to work a full day. And it was the reformers who made the workhouse the hell it was. Think of the values caught by keen literary figures of the time. Remember the housekeeper in *Jane Eyre* talking to a ten-year-old girl: "You ought not to think yourself on an equality with the Misses Reed and Master Reed. . . . They will have a great deal of money, and you will have none: it is your place to be humble, and to try to make yourself agreeable to them."[2]

Second, government was relieved of accepting the responsibility for holding down mass consumption, since this was accomplished through private arrangements between employers and their workers. However, bourgeois governments gave private initiative a clear field to do as it chose and rarely if ever intervened to protect the disadvantaged. On the contrary, these governments, responsive to the needs and views of the middle classes, made the protection of the rights of property far more important than other human values, more important even than human lives.

Specifically, the bourgeois governments helped in three ways to reduce mass consumption: (1) through policies that helped keep wages low; (2) through a lack of governmental welfare measures; and (3) through the use of government machinery to repress popular protest or action against existing arrangements.

---

[2] Charlotte Brontë, *Jane Eyre* (New York: Modern Library, 1950 [first printed 1847]), p. 9.

Cheap Labor

The major way in which the governments of Western Europe and the United States contributed to keeping labor cheap was by opposition to labor unions. Because unions were outlawed and union leaders persecuted, wages were lower than they would otherwise have been. It is no accident that the major steps in the industrialization of country after country were taken in the period between the death of the guilds and the official recognition of labor unions. Very roughly, this period lasted from the end of the eighteenth century to the last quarter of the nineteenth. Throughout this period the guiding principles of government in its policies toward labor were the maintenance of freedom of work and freedom of contract.

It is significant that governmental repugnance in the face of economic combinations did not extend to combinations of employers. One or two examples will illustrate the point. In France in 1791 the Chapellier Law outlawed strikes and unions of workers and imposed heavy fines and penalties for its breach. Chapellier commented in parliamentary debate: "None of us intend to prevent the merchants from discussing their common interests."[3] The law remained in force until 1884, when it was finally repealed and full associational rights were granted workers.

In England, too, unions and strikes were forbidden. The courts handed out severe punishments to offenders, at times even harsher than the already savage laws, and appeals were beyond the reach of workers. As industrialization proceeded, Parliament struck down the laws which had regulated employer-employee relations in an earlier era, and soon enough even the pretense of protecting the

---

[3] Charles W. Pipkin, *Social Politics and Modern Democracies* (New York: Macmillan, 1931), II, 8.

interests of workers was abandoned. As in France, the laws of industrializing England spoke against all economic combinations, but laws are enforced by men, and employer groups flourished unmolested.[4] And as in France, in spite of persecution and though seriously impaired, unions continued to exist—as did political agitation for reform.

Much the same was true in the United States. Worker combinations were treated as conspiracies up to almost the middle of the nineteenth century, and antiunion activity was carried on with vigor by the state governments for decades following.

In a general way, though in differing contexts, this outline can be applied to country after country caught up in the industrial revolution between 1750 and 1900.

Two major effects of government action against unions can be noted. First, wages were held down by the use of state machinery to harass union organization and to break strikes. Second, repression and its counterpart of agitation were the beginning of the involvement of the masses with the state and therefore helped prepare the way for the next stage of political development. However, it is primarily with the economic consequences that we are concerned for the moment.

In the absence of effective unionization, wages were low and hours long. Dawn and dusk limited the workday. The twelve- to fourteen-hour day and the six-day week were common, and even longer workweeks were not unheard of, especially in the industries that had pioneered in the process of industrialization (such as mining and textiles). The victory of the ten-hour day marked a real milestone of reform and as a rule did not come until the

[4] G. D. H. Cole and Raymond Postgate, *The British Common People, 1746–1946* (London: Methuen, University Paperbacks, 1961), chap. xiv.

latter half of the nineteenth century, when the initial problems of squeezing capital out of a subsistence economy were long past.

Wages were almost unbelievably low during the early years of industrialization. Even in the relatively rich United States, Horace Greeley estimated the average earnings of simple laborers in New York City in the early 1850s —at least two thirds of the city's population—as one dollar per week "for each person subsisting thereon." Yet he estimated eleven dollars a week as the absolute minimum family budget necessary for rent, food, fuel, and clothing.[5]

A direct consequence of the low wage level were the living conditions in the towns that constituted the major reservoirs of labor for the new economy. Here is a description given by eyewitnesses of worker housing in Britain at the height of the industrial revolution:

> [Manchester] . . . A whole [Irish] family is often accommodated on a single bed, and sometimes a heap of filthy straw and a covering of old sacking hide them in one undistinguished heap . . . often more than one family lived in a damp cellar, containing only one room, in whose pestilential atmosphere from twelve to sixteen persons were crowded.[6]

> [Edinburgh] . . . the houses . . . are often so close together, that persons may step from the window of one house to that of the house opposite . . . neither sewers nor any private conveniences whatever belonging to the dwellings; and hence the excrementitious and other refuse of at least 50,000 persons is, during the night, thrown into the gutters, causing . . . an amount of solid filth and

---

[5] Foster Rhea Dulles, *Labor in America* (New York: Crowell, 1949), pp. 78–79.
[6] Friedrich Engels, *The Conditions of the Working Class in England*, W. O. Henderson and W. H. Chaloner (eds.) (Oxford: Blackwell, 1958), p. 77.

foetid exhalation. . . . The dwellings of the poorer classes . . . consisting, in most cases, of a single room, ill ventilated and yet cold, owing to broken, ill fitting windows, sometimes damp and partially underground.[7]

Such conditions were found in town after town, in Sheffield and Derby, in London and Leicester. It should be appreciated, of course, that conditions were not much better in the countryside. The reason they did not seem so bad in the country hamlets was that the impression of one or two houses in the open fields was quite different from that when thousands of such dwellings were massed in the towns.

Similar conditions were found in the United States:

There was in New York a cellar population, estimated to total over 18,000, crowded into damp, unlighted, ill-ventilated dens with anywhere from six to twenty persons—men, women and children—living in a single room.[8]

And in Boston a Committee on Internal Health reported in 1849:

This whole district is a perfect hive of human beings without comforts and mostly without common necessaries: in many cases huddled together like brutes without regard to sex, age or a sense of decency, grown men and women sleeping together in the same apartment, and sometimes wife, husband, brothers and sisters in the same bed.[9]

A second result of the extremely low wages was that the earning power of every member of the family was necessary to meet the needs of subsistence. Child and female labor were widespread among the lower classes. Parents had no choice but to work themselves and to push their

---

[7] *Ibid.*, p. 43.
[8] Dulles, *op. cit.*, p. 79.
[9] *Ibid.*

children into the mines and into the mills. From the point of view of the employers in many industries, female and child labor were the best because they were by far the cheapest, and the abundance of cheap labor helped keep all wages low.

Though wages were lower for women and children, little allowance was made for differences in age and sex when it came to workloads and working conditions. Children particularly were not spared by either parents or employers. Labor conditions in the industrialization period are so well known that only one or two examples will suffice to refresh the memory. Children sat in the mines for twelve or more hours a day opening and closing ventilation doors, and women and children, stripped to the waist or naked, pulled carts of coal on their hands and knees along the low tunnels. This was true in the English mines for decades after 1800, and these were still the conditions in the Belgian mines of the Bolinage at the end of the nineteenth century.

Child labor offers a telling example of government aid to industrialists in the provision of indentured labor for manufacturers. English and French governments turned pauper children over to the textile mills, and the appalling conditions under which such children worked and lived attest the cheapness of their labor. So bad were these conditions that the first recognition in principle that government might regulate employer-employee relations came in the case of pauper apprentices, but the initial legislation protecting them contained wholly inadequate provisions for inspection and thus was not effective.[10]

The cost of labor to employers was further reduced by the lack of safety measures in mines and factories. It is

---

[10] J. H. Clapham, *An Economic History of Modern Britain* (Cambridge: Cambridge University Press, 1938), p. 372. *See also* Pipkin, *op. cit.*, I, 9.

probably unavoidable that in a primitive stage of industrialization the toll of industrial accidents will be heavier
than at a later period, but even the few precautions possible were not taken. In the mines explosion after explosion
was caused by the accumulation of gases that could have
been avoided by ventilating shafts. Countless workers
would have been spared accidents and deformities if the
tunnels had not been so low. There is no question that the
mine owners were largely responsible and that the governments of the day did little to ameliorate conditions for
decades. Similarly, in the factories early machinery was
often needlessly dangerous—even simple guard rails were
generally lacking. Fatigue caused by the long hours contributed greatly to the toll of accidents, and the injured
worker had no claim against his employer.

Low wages, long hours, child labor, and a lack of safety
had the combined effect of greatly reducing labor costs
and of keeping a large share of the national income out of
the hands of workers who would necessarily have spent it
on their own subsistence needs. This income was channeled instead into the hands of employers who, after providing for their own subsistence rather handsomely, did
reinvest substantially in capital goods.

Welfare Measures

The general trend in income distribution was reinforced
by the almost total absence of any government investment
in welfare. Isolated employers took some pains for the
welfare of their labor force. Krupp, for example, built
houses for his workers, but in general employers did not
consider the plight of the workers any responsibility of
theirs.

The simple fact was that the welfare of the population
was not a major concern of the government or of the di-

recting classes. The health and housing of the masses was not a governmental responsibility. Charity was given those who would otherwise have starved to death, but even here the system of welfare dated from a previous era. During the early years of industrialization welfare was cut whenever opportunity permitted. The needy were defined as improvident and responsibility for their misfortune thrown on their own shoulders.

Poor laws were rewritten and harshly applied, and relief was extended only on conditions that made the applicant regret he had ever asked for help. In England, for example, the New Poor Law of 1834 granted relief in accordance with the following principles: (1) No relief to the able-bodied except within a workhouse; (2) Such relief to be less attractive than the most unpleasant means of earning a living outside; (3) Separation of man and wife to prevent childbearing.[11] The poor soon called the workhouse "the Bastille."

Repression

A third way in which bourgeois governments helped maintain low wages and low living standards for the mass of the population while permitting the accumulation of capital by employers lay in what can only properly be called political repression. This was a task in which legislatures, executives, and courts at all levels of government were deeply involved.

Legislatures passed laws that confirmed the harsh conditions of life for the working population (enclosure acts, poor laws, antiunion legislation, and the like), and when they did pass remedial legislation against industrial evils, it was ineffective. (Child labor, for example, was protected

---

[11] Cole and Postgate, *op. cit.*, p. 276.

in law in England, France, and Germany for forty to sixty years before it was protected in fact, because no inspection system and no enforcement were provided in the initial legislation.)

The executive officers of government not only enforced the antilabor laws and called out soldiers to repress attempts to agitate against them but also ferreted out potential agitators with spies and provocateurs.

The courts awarded fines, lashings, jail sentences, transportation to the colonies, and even death to those convicted of rebelling or agitating against the inhumanity of social and economic life.

How harsh repression was and which political institutions carried the main burden of repression varied with time and region. In England, local magistrates carried out a large share of the task. In France, Napoleon put the working population under the supervision of the police by issuing workbooks in which every employer had to record satisfactory performance of the employee before he could obtain new employment. (We shall meet workbooks again in Stalin's Russia.) In the United States the states, not the central government, had the major burden of keeping labor under control.

To summarize, it is a major thesis of this work that an important contribution of bourgeois politics to industrialization was the protection of the scarce savings created by the new economy at the expense of the standard of living of the population. It is impossible to measure the human costs of such a policy, but the industrialization of the West bears witness to its success. Finally, it must be emphasized that the bourgeois governments were able to shelter capital precisely because they were not representative of the popular will and were not responsive to popular anguish.

THE MOVE TO THE CITIES

There is still another area in which governmental policy aided industrialization: the encouragement of rural–urban migration. Such migration was vital to the success of industrialization, first, because it provided a labor force for the new steam-powered industrial installations, which tended to be centralized in a few locations. Even more important was the part rural–urban migration played in breaking up the peasant world and destroying its preindustrial values and customs, many of which were so inimical to economic modernization.

At the beginning of the industrial era many forces were at work tearing down the old peasant ways of life. Large-scale migration to the cities greatly speeded the process. By coming to the city, the former peasant removed himself from the influence of his fellow peasants and placed himself in an isolated position where the values he brought with him were daily exposed to erosion and destruction. Strong ties with a large family group were stretched and broken, and respect for the traditional ways began to shrivel and die. Totally dependent upon the new economy for his livelihood, the migrant became amenable to the new and different demands of his work. The discipline of industrial work seeped into his being. With his old ties severed, the migrant began to fit himself into the new, wider national community, and the social base of industrialization came into being.

Bourgeois politics contributed to rural–urban migration by protecting, aiding, and encouraging those who wished to push or to pull the peasants off the land. The natural "push" of poor living conditions in the countryside was supplemented by evictions, in which the governments of

the time assisted—particularly in England, where the enclosures were of such importance, but also in Denmark
and in some sections of France and Sweden. The "pull,"
which operated more effectively in later years, after industrialization had passed through its initial difficulties,
consisted of the higher industrial wages and the greater
excitement and variation of city life.

England is the classic example of the rural population's
expulsion from the land. The immediate causes were the
enclosures and the death of the cottage industries. High-
handed landlords had enclosed common land for their
own use before, but in the eighteenth century the number
of enclosures increased greatly and the motivation was
different. Enclosure was coming to be desired by landlords
who wished to experiment with more modern agricultural
methods and who found themselves blocked by the necessity of gaining the consent of a tradition-bound community.

Most of the enclosures were worked out through common agreement in which the peasants who had rights to
the land were paid off in some fashion, although it must be
noted that no provision was made for the majority of
peasants who used the land by custom but could demonstrate no clear-cut legal rights.

Where common agreement could not be worked out,
the landlord might petition Parliament to enclose the land,
and such petitions were virtually always granted. During
the decade from 1740 to 1750 there were 38 parliamentary
acts enforcing enclosure, in the 1750s 158 acts, in the
1760s 480, and after that the floodgates opened.

Where the land was enclosed for sheep runs, which required very little agricultural labor, the result was rapid
depopulation of the countryside. Where the enclosure
was for the purpose of raising crops, much of the rural

population was able to hang on by combining cottage industries with agricultural labor in the new agricultural enterprises. However, the later death of the cottage industries that came with the rise of the factories drove these peasants into the cities also, for they could not live by agricultural labor alone.

It is interesting to note that the landed aristocracy, not the bourgeoisie, was primarily responsible for severing the connection of the peasantry to the land in England. In so doing, the old aristocracy inadvertently gave the greatest possible stimulus to industrialization and the eventual loss of its own monopoly of power.

The experience of continental Europe with rural–urban migration differed from the English pattern, but here again government played a role. Throughout most of Western Europe landlords did not wish to be rid of their peasants but preferred to continue the old arrangements. The liberation of the serfs did not come on their initiative but was imposed by government, largely as a result of the French Revolution and the Napoleonic conquest.

This "liberation" did not always benefit the peasantry or cause it to move. Particularly in the East, where servile relations were at their worst, the villagers often lost their land altogether in the process of emancipation. To compensate for feudal rights given up the lords took large portions of land, leaving peasant holdings too small to be viable. Thus the peasants were forced to work the lords' land as hired labor to make ends meet and often lost their own small plots for unpaid debts.

The process of cutting the legal ties between land and peasantry was complete, yet the European peasant did not move. Clapham explains why this was so in Prussia, but the statement has wider application than to Prussia alone.

. . . men whose fathers had lived and died time out of mind in the old village and who, generally speaking, were not wanted anywhere else, seldom thought of moving and would probably have failed to move had they tried, especially as the lords, who still had great administrative powers, wanted to keep them. So they mostly stayed to work on the domain for what they could get. It was not until after 1848 that German villagers began to migrate in appreciable numbers; and the small folk of the east were the last to learn how to do it.[12]

Safer and easier travel, conscription with its chance to see some of the world beyond the village, and finally the higher wages of a quickening industrial system eventually led these peasants to the cities, too. Once they had found their way, the tramp of peasant feet fleeing the countryside shook the European continent in the latter part of the nineteenth century.

THE CASE OF JAPAN

There remains to be examined one interesting case of a nation that industrialized in roughly the bourgeois pattern, although it is more often considered a unique example of non-European industrialization: Japan. There were significant differences from the Western European experience, particularly in the structure of government and in political ideology; nevertheless, fundamental similarities can be seen.

In the light of the foregoing discussion of bourgeois politics, the three major differences would appear to be: first, that Japan successfully adapted a much greater part of her traditional social structure to industrial needs. Only in recent times, after defeat in war and military occupa-

---

12 J. H. Clapham, *The Economic Development of France and Germany, 1815–1914* (Cambridge: Cambridge University Press, 1921), p. 46.

tion, has the old social system really been overturned. This adaptation of the traditional system to industrial requirements proved at a later stage of development a tremendous drag on the further modernization of the economy, but at the beginning the adaptation of the old social system greatly facilitated rapid industrialization. Second, the Japanese government was far more active in promoting and directing economic development than governments in the other cases of bourgeois industrialization. Third, Japanese industrialization was extremely rapid and proceeded very smoothly compared to that of the other bourgeois nations.

The similarities and differences between the Japanese and the European experience become apparent when one considers who the industrializers were and how they came to power, how political power was used to increase production and to decrease consumption in order to further capital formation, and how the government facilitated rural–urban migration.

The Industrializers Come to Power

The men who industrialized Japan came to power in 1868 in the famous Meiji Restoration, which brought the shogunate down and restored the Emperor to the center of the political stage. In a rough way, therefore, the centuries of rule of the shogunate represent the stage of primitive unification in Japan. The end of this stage and the beginning of the politics of industrialization followed closely the coming of European traders and gunboats, but the visit of Perry was not the "cause" of the change in Japan. The tightly controlled system that the shoguns had created in an effort to freeze Japanese life into immobility had been disturbed for a century by strong currents of economic and social change that had spread discontent and rebellion throughout the land. With the destruction of the shogunate the way was free for change, and the political revolt that brought down the old order also brought the industrializers to power.

In Japan, those who gained control of the national government were not themselves members of the bourgeoisie. They were members of the lower ranks of the old aristocracy—young *samurai* who saw a chance for themselves and for their nation to rise in wealth and power, and who understood correctly that industrial wealth was at the heart of the national power needed to fend off the encroachments of Europeans. They were, of course, supported by the old merchant-traders who might more properly be called bourgeoisie, and they created the conditions for the emergence of a modern bourgeoisie as industry expanded. After the bureaucrats began industrializing, the ruling bureaucrats and the new big industrialists formed an extremely close alliance, and together they industrialized Japan.

An important difference from the European pattern is to be found in the fact that the new rulers of Japan consolidated their power without a major struggle with the agricultural elite. The power of the old elite was quickly and easily pulverized, and the feudal lords were pensioned off with government bonds to compensate them for the loss of their lands and feudal rights. The industrializers of Japan did not need to share power with a hostile landed elite.

Nor did they share their power with those below. The industrializers of Japan did not come to power in the name of the masses. Liberty, equality, and fraternity were not the political symbols of Japanese modernization, a fact which contributed to the preservation of much of the old system that was not incompatible with the new industrial needs. The Japanese masses were totally cut off from representation in government and from any control of or even voice in national decisions.

Once in power, the new governmental elite pushed the development of an industrial economy. Government and private industry were closely allied, and throughout Japanese industrialization government bureaucrats maintained enough direction and regulation of industry to assure that the interests of the government were not forgotten in the development of the economy.

Nevertheless, contrary to certain impressions, the overwhelming majority of industrial enterprises were never controlled by government. The vast bulk of the industrial activity of the country—even during the brief initial period when government was directly involved in the ownership and management of crucial industrial facilities—was in private hands. From the 1870s on, the middle classes grew rapidly in power and wealth, and the views of the bourgeoisie were soon represented in the councils that made decisions for the nation. Decisions nevertheless continued to be made by a small elite.

Government and Capital Formation

It was government that spearheaded the industrialization of Japan and, so far as capital formation was concerned, governmental action was essential in increasing production and limiting consumption. Perhaps the greatest help the government gave to Japanese industrialization lay in the destruction of the portion of the old social order that constituted an obstacle to industrial change, and in the establishment of the framework of law and order essential for industrial growth.

More specifically, the Japanese government stimulated industrial production, especially those branches important for national power, by financing new activities, patronizing private ventures, shouldering early risks, and in many cases building and managing its own production facilities. In many areas of heavy industry and communications essential for future economic growth, government was directly involved. It owned and managed shipyards, machine shops, iron foundries, and coal mines. It established cement, paper, and glass factories. It built and operated railway and telegraph lines. And until the end of World War II, the Japanese government dominated the iron and steel industry, which was so important both for national power and for the future of industrialization itself.

Two things should be kept in mind about the direct involvement of the Japanese government in the industrializing economy. First, the influence of governmental investment on economic growth depended far more on the fact that it was concentrated in crucial areas of the economy than on its total size. In fact, none of the government's investments in industry (with the exception of iron and steel) ever went beyond the stage of pilot projects. Thus the total investment of the government in the economy was never large. Second, most of the investments made were liquidated after a brief period. Government holdings were sold to private enterprise at prices extremely advantageous to the purchasers; the only major exception was the steel industry. Thus bourgeois government in Japan—as elsewhere—was bent upon having private interests carry out the industrialization of the country.

The government, however, assisted private industry by importing modern machinery and foreign experts in order to modernize traditional industries. It also propagandized the new knowledge and spurred both general and technical education as well as the adaptation of Western knowledge to Japanese use.

Much of the government's most important aid to economic growth was indirect. As in other bourgeois countries, the core of governmental help was provided through a series of policies favorable to business. Fiscal policies were important, and the bias toward industrial growth can be clearly seen. Government stimulated the growth of new industries by a wide assortment of grants in aid, dividend guarantees, low interest loans, and other measures. The Japanese could not use tariffs in their initial drive for industrialization because they were bound by treaties imposed upon them by European power in 1858 and 1866, but they became strongly protectionist after 1922. Other taxes were however used as a powerful tool to stimulate rapid economic development. The whole structure of taxation was extremely favorable to business, and in the initial stages of industrialization the needs of government were financed by heavy taxes on land and consumer goods while profits were allowed to accumulate for reinvestment in capital goods. As in other countries, the savings came largely from those least able both to resist and to afford the sacrifice.

Political power also played an important role in holding down consumption. The story here follows familiar lines, differing from European experience little except that possibly Japanese policies were even more successful in keeping the living standard of the working population low.

It is only necessary to sketch the outlines. Labor unions were forbidden; strikes brought heavy fines and jail sentences. Freedom of contract was the principle of economic life. In consequence wages were low and hours long. The fourteen-hour day, for example, was common. Child and female labor was widespread, and children and girls in their teens worked under deplorable conditions.

The study of the struggle for the amelioration of labor conditions in Japan will look monotonously familiar to those acquainted with labor conditions in the West during industrialization. Demands for relief from the acute suffering imposed upon the working population were made early, but no action was taken in the first half-century of industrialization, when conditions were at their worst. Labor had virtually no representation in the Diet. No major labor legislation was passed until 1905 and none enforced until 1916. This first labor legislation provided for a twelve-hour workday for women and children under fifteen. The ten-hour day did not come until ten years later and in some industries (such as textiles) later still. Night work was not forbidden for children until 1920.

Nor were low pay, long hours, bad working conditions, and child labor the only ways in which the masses of Japan bore the brunt of the difficulties in allowing the economy to accumulate capital. There were other familiar problems. The cities were overcrowded, housing conditions particularly bad, and health conditions hazardous. It hardly need be pointed out that in the case of Japan, technical knowledge and skills were available to ameliorate such conditions, had the government chosen to give a higher priority to improving mass living standards, but the emphasis was on accumulating capital.

There can be no doubt that capital formation was particularly rapid in Japan. There can also be no doubt that the industrial workers and peasants of Japan paid a major portion of the price for the speed and success of Japanese industrialization.

Rural–Urban Migration

The Japanese government also played a role in facilitating rural–urban migration, so important in providing the manpower for Japan's growing industries, and again the picture is well within the bourgeois pattern, although it differs in details.

As on the European continent, government cleared away the obstacles to migration, but the motive force was to be found elsewhere—in the "push" of poverty in the countryside and the "pull" of the attractions of city life. An important difference lay in the fact that the Japanese were successful in industrializing without ripping up a major portion of the old agricultural system.

The Japanese government, interested in drawing Japanese agriculture into a money economy so that it could be taxed for government revenue, and interested also in exercising more control over this sector of the economy, cleared away the old feudal superstructure, abolishing the *han*, pensioning off the aristocracy, eliminating serfdom, establishing private ownership of the land, and imposing heavy money taxes on the land. These sound like major changes, but their main effect was, as indicated, to eliminate the superstructure—to replace the feudal rent collector with the government tax collector. The daily life of the peasants changed little. Land in Japan was already very intensively cultivated, and the peasant family traditionally had taken care of its own needs in many ways. Thus the elimination of serfdom and the establishment of private ownership of the land were far easier to achieve in Japan than in Europe.

The reform did mean that the peasant's hold on his land became more tenuous, for often he went into debt to meet his cash obligations, and many lost land and were reduced to tenantry.

The whole process has been summarized by William Lockwood:

> . . . the Meiji "Restoration" wrought remarkably little change in the life of the average peasant, or his system of cultivation. This did not deprive Japanese industry, as it

subsequently developed, of a steady flow of labor from the villages. The crescendo of population growth took care of that. Nor did it prevent at least a doubling in agricultural output over the next half century. But it barred the road to any revolutionary advance in farm productivity, which would have required a sharp reduction of population on the land. It thus prolonged the poverty and self-sufficiency of rural life, and applied a persistent drag on industrial advance.[13]

Japanese agriculture did improve, both in production and in productivity, but this was achieved by a very modest contribution on the part of government and with no siphoning off of savings from the industrial sector of the economy. On the contrary, agriculture was taxed to aid industrialization.

Second, Japanese agricultural production was raised without drastic modernization which would have forced a mass migration from the countryside, as in England. It was population pressure (as well as the small size of farms), not the reform of agriculture, that drove Japanese peasants into the cities. Throughout the period of industrialization, the number of peasants on the land remained virtually constant, with the increase in population providing a steady overflow of labor for the cities.

There are, then, several major differences between the role of politics in Japanese industrialization and in the other bourgeois nations we have examined: (1) The ruling elite who directed industrialization were government bureaucrats, not private capitalists. (2) The government took a more active part in stimulating industrialization. (3) Those in control removed the old agricultural aristocracy from power and therefore did not have to share power

---

[13] William Lockwood, *The Economic Development of Japan* (Princeton: Princeton University Press, 1954), p. 553.

with them. (4) The masses were even more completely removed from political participation than in the West and did not gain in power as industrialization proceeded until after Japan's defeat in World War II. (5) More of the old system—political, economic, and social—was adapted to the needs of industrialization and more of the old forms were preserved. (6) Japanese industrialization was more rapid than in the West.

On the other hand, there were fundamental similarities with bourgeois industrialization in the West: (1) Though the government acted as a stimulant and a catalyst, private industrialists owned and directed the major industrial enterprises. (2) The masses were excluded from political and economic power, thus making it possible to hold mass consumption to a minimum while accumulating capital for industrial development. (3) The national government gave substantial assistance, much of it indirect, to increasing industrial production and to reducing mass consumption. (4) Having helped sever the ties between the peasants and their land, the government stood aside and left the overflow of villagers to find its own way into the cities and industrial centers. (5) Bourgeois politics in Japan were as elsewhere succeeded by mass democracy, although in the case of Japan this was imposed from outside after military conquest.

There is no doubt that Japanese industrialization resembled Western industrialization in many respects, both because of its own internal needs and impulses and because of its conscious imitation of the West. There is also no doubt that in over-all terms Japanese industrialization belongs to the bourgeois tradition. Perhaps we should call it *bourgeois totalitarianism* instead of *bourgeois democracy*, but it is surely an example of bourgeois industrialization.

FEATURES OF BOURGEOIS INDUSTRIALIZATION

The countries that industrialized under bourgeois governments had certain unique characteristics that set them apart from countries industrializing today. First, they were all relatively advanced countries in terms of economic development, with more capital and higher standards of living than the countries of present-day underdeveloped areas. Perhaps even more important, their preindustrial social systems and the prevailing ethos were more compatible with an industrial economic system.

Second, with the exception of Japan, the process of economic development was relatively slow compared to the tempo of change in countries that have industrialized more recently. The countries that modernized within a bourgeois framework were the first to industrialize and they took their time feeling their way from one way of life to another. Differences in tempo can be noted even within the group itself—as between England, which was the first to industrialize, and the United States, which followed about a hundred years later. This slowness of economic development probably had a direct effect upon the eventual development of mass democracy, for a slower rate of capital accumulation permits greater governmental responsiveness to popular demands for an improved standard of living.

Third, the political leaders, the businessmen, and certainly the common people of the bourgeois democracies (though not of Japan) did not have in mind the end results of the process of industrialization when they embarked upon it, for no one had ever made the trip before. For this reason, their aspirations were perhaps much more in keeping with what could actually be achieved in a relatively short span of time. This too was beneficial to the prospects for democracy, for it meant that popular demands were not so great as to stop industrialization in its tracks if they were not met at least part-way, and it meant that government officials were not hell-bent on having their countries catch up with more advanced nations, whatever the cost.

It is hardly to be expected that other countries lacking these characteristics will go about their industrialization in precisely the same way as the bourgeois democracies. On the other hand, there are certain basic problems that must be solved by any industrializing society, whatever its system of government: the placing in power of those who wish to modernize the economy, the accumulation of capital, and rural–urban migration. In the next two chapters we shall examine the ways in which two other types of political system have handled these problems.

IV

STALINIST POLITICS

As it is an error to confuse nineteenth-century bourgeois politics with twentieth-century mass democracy, so it would be misleading to equate stalinist politics with the politics of Khrushchev and his successors or to attribute the obvious differences to matters of temperament and personality. Stalinism, like bourgeois politics, represents a form of the politics of industrialization. With Khrushchev and his successors, however, Russia is leaving the second stage of political growth and entering the third, and her political system is altering itself accordingly. For this reason I prefer to use the term *stalinist* rather than the more general *Communist* to describe the period of industrialization in Russian politics. The term can also be applied to the present regime in Communist China.

There are, it should be noted, some unexpected parallels between bourgeois and stalinist politics: both occurred in industrializing nations; both gave preponderant political power to industrial managers and their supporters; both were relatively repressive compared to the systems which followed them; and the governments of both encouraged high production, low consumption, capital accumulation, and rural–urban migration.

The differences are almost too obvious to mention. Where bourgeois governments permitted and encouraged, stalinist governments performed and enforced. And of course the whole pace of industrialization differed. Finally, the savagery of stalinist repression is legendary.

THE INDUSTRIALIZERS GAIN CONTROL

In Russia and in China, the Communist revolution brought to power a new elite committed to rapid industrialization. This should not obscure the fact that in Russia economic modernization had been proceeding quietly and slowly since the middle of the nineteenth century in much the way that in Western countries had led to the eventual political victory of the bourgeoisie. China had sniffed the scent of modernization in the revolution of Sun Yat-sen. It was the Communists in both China and Russia, however, who slammed the door on the past and shoved their peoples into full-scale industrialization.

The way in which the new industrializers came to power reveals some similarities to and some fundamental differences from the pattern established by the bourgeois democracies. In the first place, there was a complete eradication of the landed aristocracy which had ruled almost to the eve of the Communist revolutions. Thus there was no period in which the new and the old elites shared governmental power. Second, after the revolution, the working class was eliminated from any influence and control of governmental machinery. Third, the original revolutionaries, who were intellectuals, were replaced in Russia (not yet in China) by new rulers who were primarily administrators, and in Russia at least it was this latter group who, a decade after the revolution, began the dizzying climb to full industrial status.

The New Elite Rules Alone

The swift and sudden elimination of the old aristocracy in Russia and China had important consequences. It produced vast dislocations in the government and raised severe problems of governmental continuity and efficiency, but at the same time it freed the new elite from the necessity of sharing power with the old. This was a sharp departure from the pattern in the bourgeois countries, where the bourgeoisie and the aristocracy had shared power for decades. Even the French Revolution was followed by a period in which the aristocracy regained considerable power.

Such a solution appeared a possibility for Russia for a brief period when both the bourgeoisie and the aristocracy were represented in the short-lived Kerensky government, but the October Revolution overtook and crushed them both. Chiang Kai-shek too achieved a brief compromise between his country's businessmen and landlords before he and they were removed from power.

Because the Russian revolutionaries were in hiding or abroad (and the Chinese in open revolt) before the revolution, and because they exterminated or drove out the old elite almost immediately after they themselves gained control of the government, the new rulers never shared power with the old. The amount of continuity was very small and the shock of the transition intense.

Both the Bolsheviks and the Chinese Communists, having crushed the aristocracy and the bourgeoisie, nevertheless made use of a number of individual members of the old elite who possessed needed skills: army officers, professionals, administrators, and diplomats. But they compelled these individuals to change their roles and to fit completely into the new system. The British lord who sat in Parliament with the newly powerful bourgeoisie remained a peer, held onto his land and his privileges, and spoke and voted for his traditional views. But the Tsarist officer who served in the Red Army changed his uniform and his manner of treating his men, followed orders, and cooperated with the commissar sent in beside him. At the first hint of an action in support of the old regime he was out—and perhaps dead. Even with such control, the new government never trusted employees drawn from the old elite. It kept them for the most part in minor posts and watched them closely.

Proletariat Excluded

The stalinist industrializers also refused to share their power with the masses—the proletariat in whose name they ruled. Like the bourgeoisie, they rode to power on a crest of popular support, but once in power they excluded the masses from governmental control far more thoroughly than the bourgeoisie ever did. After the Russian Revolution, popular influence and control in government barely existed; they were extinguished completely when the push toward industrialization began.

Some similarity with bourgeois experience can be found. The British and French bourgeoisie, for example, ascended to power with popular support and then turned their backs on their supporters. But here the similarity ends. In the Western bourgeois countries the working classes were shut out from control of the government at the beginning of the period—when the bourgeoisie was itself fighting for recognition and for control of governmental power—and in the years immediately after it had achieved control. As the economy progressed and the number of urban dwellers and industrial workers grew the franchise spread, and with the franchise popular control increased as well.

In the stalinist countries, however, the Western experience appears to have been reversed. In the Soviet Union, what little popular control there was was at its greatest during and immediately after the revolution. Throughout the period of industrialization the common people were excluded from the political process, and even now, when Russia is an urban and industrial country and the worst rigors of industrialization are past, popular control has still not appeared. The same can be said for the Chinese case, so far as it goes. The highly propagandized dictatorship of the proletariat has meant in effect that the party dictated to the proletariat and that the party leadership dictated to the party.

Popular *participation*, unlike popular *control*, increased through the stalinist period in Russia, and here again experience differed from that of the bourgeois democracies, where participation and control grew hand in hand. Stalinist politics separated the two. It placed the individual at the mercy of the national economy and deprived him of any control over the economy or over the government, but at the same time it sought to involve him heavily in the new national life, not only through his economic dependence but also by compelling him to perform a large amount of passive political action. Citizens were deluged with information and propaganda, forced to attend an endless round of rallies and speeches, and urged to the polls to vote in elections in which there was no choice.

Widespread popular participation in politics is an essential ingredient of a modern nation, democratic or totalitarian, and the stalinist countries achieved this earlier in their development than had the bourgeois nations. In Russia and China, universal suffrage preceded the creation of a national economy instead of following it, as in the West. It is obvious, however, that voting has a different function in the stalinist countries. As in the underdeveloped countries still in the stage of primitive unification, national elections in Russia and China serve as a time to review accomplishments, belabor enemies, list hopes, and relate the personal life of each citizen to the broader national goals. They serve, in short, as a means of cementing national unity, not as a means of effecting popular control.

Intellectuals and Administrators

The Soviet Union seems to have witnessed a steady narrowing and focusing of power. First the new elite eliminated the old aristocracy. Next it removed all power from the hands of the working classes. Then it thinned its own ranks and removed from power most of the original revolutionaries. This was not merely a struggle for power among ambitious men, but a fundamental shift in the nature of the Soviet ruling class: it placed political power exclusively in the hands of those most dedicated to rapid and ruthless industrialization.

In Russia the industrializers came to power in two steps (three, if one includes the abortive attempt of the bourgeois industrialists to govern as part of the Kerensky government). First came the original Bolsheviks, deeply committed to economic and social modernization. It was not they, however, who industrialized Russia. The politics of Lenin were not those of industrialization. Lenin's main preoccupations were to keep the Bolsheviks in power, for their rule was challenged from every side, and to prevent Russia from being dismembered. The politics that industrialized Russia were those of Stalin.

The first step was made by those who revolted and acquired power, the second by those who used it to industrialize Russia. The second group emerged out of the Party, of which they were members (though not leading members), liquidated the old leaders, and pushed through modernization of the country. The differences in the two groups were reflected not only in their policies but also in the men who carried them out.

The Bolsheviks who led the revolution were theorists and intellectuals. This should not be surprising. Intellectuals have the emotional and critical faculties to stand aside and view their own social system and see its faults. As Crane Brinton suggested in his classic *The Anatomy of Revolution,* one of the signs of coming revolution is the desertion of the existing order by the intellectuals. Equally important, intellectuals are able to picture a new order of things and can invent means to make the transition from one social order to another.

The Communists who pushed through rapid industrialization in the 1930s and the 1940s were, on the other hand, political and economic administrators: *apparatchiki,* party bureaucrats, who ran the Communist Party in Stalin's time and who still do—men with a bent for execution rather than revolution, for practical affairs rather than theory.

The bureaucrats exterminated the intellectuals with a venom they had not shown even for anti-Communists. The bitterness of the struggle cannot be ascribed completely to the personality of the leaders of the dispute or to the immediate circumstances of the quarrel. Stalin's ruthlessness was important in the elimination of the old guard, but the conflict was more profound. The seeds of the conflict were planted deep in the revolution and in the party of the men who made it. It was a conflict between men who fight authority and those who exercise it.

One must not oversimplify. Some intellectuals were bureaucrats and some bureaucrats intellectuals, though the difference in emphasis between the two periods is fairly clear. Moreover, many an *apparatchik* died in the cellars of Lubianka Prison, and more than one theoretician came out unscathed from the liquidation of the old guard. Nevertheless, the distinction is useful.

Loss of power by the intellectuals is not unique to Soviet experience. In bourgeois revolutions too, the intellectuals who led the revolt against old privileges tended to lose power; it was the bourgeoisie who carried out the program for which the revolution took place.

Much has been written about the debilitating effect of the Russian purges on the Party, the government, and the country, and much of what has been written is true. Yet the purges also served two useful functions for the totalitarian Party. Brzezinski observed that the purges provided an escape valve for popular discontent by allowing the tormented population the pleasure of seeing some of its tormentors get their comeuppance. At the same time, the purges provided openings for upward mobility within the Party and thus gave increased opportunity to lowly but ambitious Party members.[1]

China provides what may be an interesting variant of the Russian pattern of a changing elite. Here too the revolution was led by intellectuals, but these same leaders have already started on the industrial reorganization and expansion that was carried out by the administrators in the Soviet Union. It seems highly likely that the next generation of Chinese leaders will be more of the bureaucrat-administrator type, but it is difficult to predict what this will mean in terms of Chinese policy: perhaps greater ideological flexibility and a rapprochement with the Soviet Union in the interests of hastening China's industrialization.

---

[1] Zbigniew K. Brzezinski, *The Permanent Purge* (Cambridge, Mass.: Harvard University Press, 1956).

INCREASED PRODUCTION

Once in power, Russia's stalinist industrializers threw every ounce of energy into industrialization, pushing their people and their plant to the limits of endurance to produce more and more and always more. Their efforts to increase production can be summarized under three headings: first, the expansion of capital investment; second, the provision of the labor necessary to man the new facilities; and third, the disciplining of raw peasant labor for industrial work.

Russia's new industrializers had three fundamental choices to make in the allocation of scarce capital: the choice between consumption and investment, the choice between industry and agriculture, and the choice between heavy and light industry. Determination of the proper course to follow had been a matter of bitter dispute within the Party and within the economic community in the years preceding the first five-year plan. At that time, Trotsky had headed the "super-industrializers," as Stalin called them in derision.[2]

Stalin, however, soon outdid his opponents: once he began to lash Russia through industrialization, his efforts were far in excess of any of Trotsky's proposals. Partly of his own choice and partly pushed by circumstances, Stalin and his lieutenants saw to it that all the savings that could be scraped together beyond the absolute minimum needs of agriculture were poured into investment in industry, primarily heavy industry.

Investment in industry as a whole was twice as large as that in agriculture, despite the fact that Russia was a predominantly agricultural country, and heavy industry

---

[2] Alexander Erlich, *The Soviet Industrialization Debate, 1924–28* (Cambridge, Mass.: Harvard University Press, 1960), pp. 165, 169.

was favored over light industry at a ratio of two to one. In the first five-year plan industry received 41 per cent of the total investment while agriculture received 19 per cent, and later plans maintained similar ratios.[3] One can see vividly the stress on heavy industry in the simple fact that metal and metal-products industries received more than half the investment in all manufacturing in the years from 1928 to 1938.[4]

In China, the mania for heavy industry was even greater than in the Soviet Union. In the first five-year plan and in the "Great Leap Forward" which followed (1958–61), the entire country was mobilized into a frenzy to increase industrial production, while agricultural production barely maintained the minimum living standards of the rapidly increasing Chinese population. During the first five-year plan the proportion of investment in heavy industry to light industry reached ratios of seven to one.[5]

This emphasis on capital investment in heavy industry brought results. Although the Chinese heavy industry drive overextended itself and was followed by a period of sharp retrenchment and renewed attention to agriculture, there is still no doubt that industrial production was expanded greatly. China's rate of economic growth in the early years of her stalinist period was probably in excess of Russian growth.

For the Soviet Union more reliable figures are available. The average rate of increase in large-scale industrial output in the years 1928 to 1937 was probably around 15 to

---

[3] Norman Kaplan, "Capital Formation and Allocation" in Abraham Bergson (ed.), *Soviet Economic Growth* (Evanston, Ill.: Row, Peterson, 1953), p. 52, Table 2.7.

[4] *Ibid.*, p. 63, Table 2.13.

[5] T. J. Hughes and D. E. T. Luard, *The Economic Development of Communist China, 1949–1960* (London: Oxford University Press; 2nd ed. 1961), p. 53.

16 per cent each year,[6] and the Soviet national product apparently rose about 6.5 to 7 per cent each year during the same period.[7]

These figures are high. If one uses American experience as a yardstick and compares U.S. investment during a comparable period of economic history (the years between the Civil War and World War I), it appears that the rates of capital investment were about the same in both countries but that the Russians invested much more heavily in industry and particularly in heavy industry. In consequence, their industrial production rose much more rapidly, as did their over-all production.[8] The Soviet annual rate of growth of 6.5 to 7 per cent can be compared with an estimated 4.5 per cent for the United States and 2.8 per cent for Germany.[9] The figures suggest that speed of economic growth is an important difference between the experience of the stalinist countries and that of the bourgeois nations.

Rural–Urban Migration

The expansion of capital facilities was only one line of attack by the stalinist industrializers. Another was the provision of the manpower necessary to run the new facilities. The new industrial labor force was drawn from the countryside through massive rural–urban migration and through rapid shifting of agricultural workers into industrial work. Indeed, one of the most significant achievements of Stalin's regime was its brutal success in

---

[6] Norman Kaplan, *loc. cit.*, p. 72.

[7] Gregory Grossman, "National Income" in Bergson, *op. cit.*, p. 8.

[8] Norman Kaplan, "Capital Formation and Allocation," in *ibid.*, pp. 69–87.

[9] The U.S. figure is the annual average rate of growth for the decades from 1869–78 to 1904–13; the German figure is for 1876–1913. Gregory Grossman, "National Income" in Bergson, *op. cit.*, p. 12, note 16.

getting Russian peasants off the land and remolding them into an industrial labor force.

Stalinist politics did not, of course, initiate the parallel movements into the cities and into industrial work, but what had been a trickle now became a tidal wave. How deeply peasant Russia was before the revolution can be gauged by the fact that in 1913 there were fewer than two industrial factory workers per hundred persons in the total population. One must go back before 1820 to find such a low figure in the United States.[10] Even as late as 1926, four fifths of Russia's workers were engaged in agriculture.[11]

In the next thirteen years, some twenty-five million persons moved from rural to urban areas, and the number of people working in nonagricultural pursuits at least doubled.[12] This shift from agricultural to nonagricultural work is an important element (and indicator) of over-all industrialization.

The growth of Soviet cities during these years is truly impressive. In 1926 there were only twelve cities in the Soviet Union with populations larger than 200,000; in 1939 there were thirty-nine. The major administrative centers doubled in population, Moscow reaching four million and Leningrad three million. All in all, the urban population of the U.S.S.R. doubled in the period of a little more than twelve years between the two censuses of 1926 and 1939.[13]

This mass migration to the cities came about in response to both push and pull exerted by the Soviet authorities and

---

[10] Frank Lorimer, *The Population of the Soviet Union: History and Prospects* (Geneva: League of Nations, 1946), p. 21.

[11] 80.8 per cent of the employed males of known occupation.

[12] Warren Eason, "Population and Labor Force" in Bergson, *op. cit.*, pp. 114–15.

[13] Lorimer, *op. cit.*, pp. 146–52.

by the industrial system. The push was collectivization. The cohorts of the Communist Party stormed the country-side and took the peasants on; the war between them soon took on the characteristics of a fight to the finish. The *kulaks* dug in. They hid the grain. They refused to join the collectives. Worst of all, they slaughtered their animals rather than let them be collectivized. The severity of the battle for collectivization was recognized by the authorities. When Winston Churchill visited Russia in 1943, he asked Stalin whether the stresses of the war had been as bad for Stalin personally as the collectivization drive, and Stalin replied: "Oh no, the collective farm policy was a terrible struggle."[14]

In one respect the stalinist drive to collectivize the land was similar to the English enclosures and dissimilar from the experience of the rest of Europe, for the English enclosures not only broke the bonds of the peasantry but also expelled the villagers from the land. In Russia too the collectivization of the land during the first five-year plan severed the tie between peasants and land, pushed large numbers of peasants into the manufacturing centers, and broke up forever the old peasant society.

The pull in the great migration was exerted by the expansion of industrial facilities with its promise of jobs and a higher standard of wages and living. Over the years the push became less important and the pull more significant. Together they uprooted Russia's vast, backward peasantry.

Chinese experience with rural–urban migration appears to be different, primarily because of China's different population problem. In China the early years of industrialization were accompanied by large-scale movements to the cities, as peasants started moving from the country-

---

[14] Winston Churchill, *The Second World War*, Vol. IV, *The Hinge of Fate* (London: Cassell, 1951), p. 447.

side, in flight from the rigors of country life and in search of the higher standards of living that prevailed in the urban centers, but the government fought this human wave back and forced many of the migrants to return to their villages.

The reasons for this policy are fairly plain. China's population was increasing by twelve to fifteen million people each year, while urban employment was increasing about one million. So long as industrial employment could not keep up with the rate of natural increase, the bulk of the burgeoning population had to be kept on the land where it would not upset the workings of the small but crucial modern sector of the economy.

Rural–urban migration is taking place in industrializing China and will continue to take place, but so far as inadequate information reveals, it seems that the role of the national government at this point is to limit and control the movement rather than to encourage it.

New Values

Physical movement is not enough to create a modern labor force. Probably the most difficult part of the entire industrialization process is creation of the values and attitudes that transform peasant villagers into urban dwellers and disciplined industrial workers. These values and attitudes are the social underpinnings of any successful industrial system. They are the social capital of an industrial society, more difficult to create than any other capital, for capital goods can be purchased from abroad and the ability to make them and run them can be learned from books and from foreign technicians, but changes in values and attitudes must be home-grown. There is no more difficult, slow, or painful process.

Ordinarily such a change requires at least three generations. Nations seeking to industrialize rapidly therefore
find themselves confronted with a serious bottleneck.
Stalinist politics hastened the process and squeezed the
population through the bottleneck.

The essence of the problem of transforming the peasant
into an industrial worker and the stalinist solution to the
problem are beautifully presented by Arthur Koestler in
his novel *Darkness at Noon*. This dialogue takes place between Gletkin, the NKVD interrogator who personifies the
new administrators, and Rubashov, an old guard Bol-
shevik whom Gletkin wants to confess to sabotage so that
his confession can be used in the Moscow treason trials of
1938.

> Gletkin: "Industrial sabotage is, according to experience,
> the most effective means for the opposition to create dif-
> ficulties for the Government, and to produce discontent
> amongst the workers. Why do you so stubbornly maintain
> that you did not use—or intend to use—just this method?"
>
> "Because it is a technical absurdity," said Rubashov.
> "And this perpetual harping on the *saboteur* as a bogyman
> produces an epidemic of denunciation which revolts me."
>
> The long-missed sensation of triumph caused Rubashov
> to feel fresher and speak louder than usual.
>
> "If you hold sabotage for a mere fiction, what, in your
> opinion, are the real causes of the unsatisfactory state of
> our industries?"
>
> "Too low piece-work tariffs, slave-driving and barbaric
> disciplinary measures," said Rubashov. "I know of several
> cases in my Trust in which workers were shot as *saboteurs*
> because of some trifling negligence caused by over-tired-
> ness. If a man is two minutes late at clocking-in, he is
> fired, and a stamp is put in his identity-papers which
> makes it impossible for him to find work elsewhere."

Gletkin looked at Rubashov with his usual expressionless gaze, and asked him, in his usual expressionless voice:

"Were you given a watch as a boy?"

Rubashov looked at him in astonishment. The most conspicuous trait of the Neanderthal character was its absolute humorlessness or, more exactly, its lack of frivolity.

"Don't you want to answer my question?" asked Gletkin.

"Certainly," said Rubashov, more and more astonished.

"How old were you when the watch was given you?"

"I don't quite know," said Rubashov; "eight or nine probably."

"I," said Gletkin in his usual correct voice, "was sixteen years old when I learnt that the hour was divided into minutes. In my village, when the peasants had to travel to town, they would go to the railway station at sunrise and lie down to sleep in the waiting-room until the train came, which was usually at about midday; sometimes it only came in the evening or next morning. These are the peasants who now work in our factories. For example, in my village is now the biggest steel-rail factory in the world. In the first year, the foremen would lie down to sleep between two emptyings of the blast furnace, until they were shot. In all other countries, the peasants had one or two hundred years to develop the habit of industrial precision and of the handling of machines. Here they only had ten years. If we did not sack them and shoot them for every trifle, the whole country would come to a standstill and the peasants would lie down to sleep in the factory yards until grass grew out of the chimneys and everything became as it was before. Last year a women's delegation came to us from Manchester in England. They were shown everything, and afterwards they wrote indignant articles, saying that the textile workers in Manchester would never stand such treatment. I have read that the cotton industry in Manchester is two hundred years old. I have also read, what the treatment of the workers there was like two hundred years ago, when it started. You, Comrade

Rubashov, have just used the same arguments as this women's delegation from Manchester. You, of course, know better than these women. So one may wonder at your using the same arguments. But then, you have something in common with them: you were given a watch as a child. . . ."[15]

Repression

Repression permeated the stalinist system from top to bottom and was heavily relied upon to bring about changes in the behavior and attitudes of Soviet workers and management. For management, there was the constant fear of losing one's job, one's status, sometimes one's freedom, possibly one's life. Failure to meet production quotas could and often did mean dismissal, and when the stalinist executive lost his job, he lost everything. Unlike his bourgeois counterpart, who quite likely found employment elsewhere, the stalinist executive who was fired could only accept whatever lesser post he was assigned by the same employer, like a general "busted" to the ranks. Furthermore, with the loss of his job, his entire standard of living disappeared in an instant. For the Russian executive, gone was the car that went with his job, gone the apartment in town and the country house, gone the vacation trip—gone were all the luxuries, comforts, and decencies that money buys in a capitalist society but which were perquisites of rank in stalinist Russia. Small wonder managers ran scared and lashed their enterprises to meet the production quotas.

Ordinary workers, too, faced punishment for failure to meet the new standards. Tardiness and absenteeism could be punished with dismissal—a law appeared on Soviet

---

[15] Arthur Koestler, *Darkness at Noon* (New York: Macmillan, 1941), pp. 224–25. Copyright 1941 by the Macmillan Company. Reprinted by permission of Macmillan and of Jonathan Cape Limited.

books allowing the dismissal of workers for a single day of unexplained absence. The excessive fluidity of undisciplined industrial labor was fought by requiring internal passports and the granting of visas by the police before workers could travel or change residence. People were not permitted to stay in the cities without employment. Thus dismissal could mean exile to Siberia or to the northern regions where workers would not go voluntarily.[16]

In China the industrialization drive brought similar measures to frighten labor and management into modern behavior. Special courts were set up to handle "economic offenses," and supervisory bodies were created in each factory to maintain labor discipline. Workers were sent to prison for economic "sabotage," absenteeism, mismanagement of materials, and so on. As in Russia, the authorities often adopted a scapegoat technique, blaming "capitalist" ideas, "decadent" outlook, and even "counter-revolutionaries" for the chaos, low quality, and high accident rate that characterized much of the crash program of industrialization.

In both Russia and China the stalinists have used forced labor as an important tool in building the industrial system. This has been one of the greatest differences between stalinist politics and other political systems that have achieved economic modernization.

Under Stalin, the Soviet police were given increased power and a large amount of economic activity was placed under their direct control. No one knows for certain how many people were sentenced to penal labor, but the number ran into the millions. Nor is the composition of that labor force known for certain, although it is safe to say that it included common criminals, political prisoners,

---

[16] Leonard E. Hubbard, *Soviet Labour and Industry* (London: Macmillan, 1942), pp. 61–62, 96–100.

and peasants who ran afoul of the authorities during the collectivization drive. There have even been suggestions that the police co-opted people whose skills were needed for their enterprises, whether those seized had committed any offense or not. By and large, forced labor was widely used for those unattractive tasks for which free labor could not be obtained in sufficient quantities, such as building roads, railroads, and canals or lumbering in bad climatic conditions.

Forced labor has also been widely used in China, where by official admission the great majority of "criminals" (including "feudal landlords" and "bureaucrat-capitalists") were allowed to "reform through labor." Firm figures are obviously lacking, but the Chinese Nationalist government estimated in 1952 that there were more than eight million forced laborers in mainland China. They have been used in both agricultural and industrial work, and particularly for lumbering and building roads, railroads, conservation works, and military installations.[17] The Chinese have also used military labor extensively for such projects.

There is good evidence that forced labor is extremely inefficient, but this has not been economically important to Soviet or Chinese authorities, since the investment in forced labor was very low, and capital was in scarce supply and simply not available for this kind of enterprise. In addition, forced labor served the political function of ruthlessly destroying political opposition by removing politically "dangerous" elements from circulation and by striking terror into the hearts of those who remained. The Chinese also apparently hoped to achieve some genuine political conversions through political-education programs at the labor camps.

---

[17] Peter S. H. Tang, *Communist China Today* (Washington, D.C.: Research Institute on the Sino-Soviet Bloc, 2nd ed. 1961), I, 276ff.

Incentives

No political system can rely primarily upon repression to govern and change its people. In the stalinist drive to create a modern labor force, the carrot as well as the stick was used. In Russia, the egalitarian strain in Soviet life was all but abandoned in an immense program of graduated rewards for different kinds and quantities of work. China too early recognized the practical need for increasing the wage differential for skill.

Differentials in wages were only part of the story. They were, to be sure, a crucial element in the new inequality, but wage incentives were supplemented by rewards in kind. In an economy of acute scarcity it is equally important to have access to commodities that are generally unavailable, and in Russia favored workers were allowed the right to such important goods as worker housing where empty apartments for others were simply not available.

Material rewards were tied to increasing productivity by putting most Russian production (and a large amount of Chinese production) on a piecework basis. Norms were laboriously worked out, and every increase over the assigned output was recompensed. In Russia, shock workers —*Stakhanovites, Oudarniki, Subbotniki*—were singled out as models for other workers to emulate, their main function being that in effect of Judas goats to lead their fellow workers to higher productivity and better industrial habits. China had her "labor heroes." The message they preached by example was clear and simple: Learn more than others know, take better care of your tools, stay in your job, produce more than others do, and you will live better than your fellows.

Shock workers also had other functions. The accomplishments of the Stakhanovites, for example, were used as rough indicators of what could be done and therefore pointed up the lowness of existing productivity standards and sometimes resulted in higher norms for all. For this they were heartily disliked.

The Stakhanovites also served as an important link between the elite and the mass of workers. They did the same work as other workers, but they had the values and sampled the life of the elite. Their wages were many times higher than their fellows'; they received the best worker housing available, shopped in special shops, vacationed in special resorts, were elected to important political posts where worker representation was thought important, and generally rubbed shoulders with the national elite. Thus incentives for workers as well as for management played a large and important role in persuading labor to meet the demands of a stalinist industrial system.

Education

In addition to repression and rewards, the stalinist system relied upon widespread education as a long-range measure to create a modern labor force. Well aware that rapid industrialization is impossible without a literate population and a broad stream of highly trained professionals, the Soviet and Chinese governments placed great emphasis on education. Stalin's regime is noted for its massive and successful attack on illiteracy and for the rapidity with which peasant Russia began turning out highly trained personnel. China has also mounted a major drive against illiteracy, though she faces special difficulties as a result of the complexities of the Chinese language, and has reformed and expanded her education system.

Here the stalinist countries have benefited by bourgeois experience and have tailored it to fit their needs. In the stalinist countries, mass education has preceded, not followed, industrialization, and from the very beginning the governments have concentrated on turning out the specialized scientists and technicians required by a highly industrialized economy. By knowing from bourgeois experience where they were headed, the stalinists have been able to skip many intermediate steps in the training of top industrial personnel. The result has been somewhat anomalous. In Russia, where education has proceeded furthest, the usual occupational pyramid has been replaced in many industries by an odd distribution of training: the pyramid still has a broad base and a high peak, but the middle layers of supporting personnel are often lacking. Nevertheless, the emphasis on education has greatly speeded Soviet industrialization and promises to do the same for the Chinese.

In addition, stalinist governments have created through their education programs an important source of support for the regime. Education provides a major ladder for upward mobility, particularly in the early years of stalinist rule when schooling is offered to large numbers of peasants and workers from uneducated families (Premier Khrushchev is a famous example), and it is usual for those who rise to become strong supporters of the system that has improved their lot.

These, then, are the means by which the stalinist governments have sought to increase production: heavy capital investment, particularly in heavy industry, and the creation of a modern labor force through pushing peasants into industry and retraining them for new work and new attitudes toward work.

LOW CONSUMPTION

Stalinist politics are also noteworthy for their success in holding down consumption during the early years of industrialization. Indeed, the most significant indication that Russia is now passing out of the second stage of political growth and entering the third lies in the relaxation of the government's iron grip on the standard of living.

During the stalinist era, low consumption was simply the other, less attractive side of the coin marked heavy capital investment. Russians have boasted of the speed with which they industrialized the Soviet economy and increased the national income. In the long run this has meant higher living standards, but in the early years such rapid increases in production were possible only if much of the meager output was plowed right back into capital investment instead of flowing into consumer goods. The figures tell the story: from 1928 to 1937 net capital investment more than quadrupled, while consumption rose somewhere on the order of 10 per cent.[18] The population increase for the same period was very roughly about 11 or 12 per cent,[19] so per capita consumption apparently declined on the whole, though of course there were increases for some groups and decreases for others as well as shifts in the nature of goods consumed.

Thus, despite all promises of higher living standards, Russia's new rulers held consumption down to the old subsistence levels. And promises had indeed been made. Voluntary sacrifices and major efforts were asked of the Russian people with the promise that in a few years the Soviet Union would enjoy the highest standard of living in the world, but the reward was slow in coming, and in the end the sacrifices were greater than anyone could have believed a people would make.

---

[18] Gregory Grossman, "National Income," in Bergson, *op. cit.*, p. 7, Table 1.1.

[19] The population increased 16 per cent in the period of a little more than twelve years, between the censuses of 1926 and 1939.

In China, industrial workers in the early stalinist years apparently experienced some rise in wages and in living standards,[20] but the great mass of the peasantry experienced little if any improvement. Distribution of food and clothing was equalized considerably and the outright starvation of the past due to famines was largely eliminated, but the Communist regime has continued to struggle with problems of famine and flood, low agricultural production, and peasant hoarding. In general, the government has apparently succeeded in maintaining living standards just high enough to avoid mass peasant resistance while at the same time gathering the maximum possible amount of produce for consumption by city workers, for reserves in case of famine, and for export to the Soviet Union in return for imports of capital equipment.

The stalinist governments have used some means to keep down mass consumption which parallel those employed in bourgeois politics, although of course the role of the government has been much more direct. Like the bourgeoisie in its day, the stalinists denied the ordinary workers any voice in defense of their own interests. Where the bourgeoisie had denied them the franchise, the stalinists insisted they vote but gave them no choice in elections. And in more immediate economic concerns, where the bourgeoisie had prohibited all trade unions, the stalinists encouraged union organization but perverted the unions into instruments of production. Trade unions in the Soviet Union and in China were closely controlled by government and were given the principal responsibility for disciplining labor and for encouraging higher productivity as well as for running a large welfare program.

Wages were government-controlled, with a large percentage of the population working in government-owned

---

[20] Hughes and Luard, *op. cit.*, p. 126.

enterprises, and low (nonexistent for forced labor); hours were long. Moreover, the already slim wages of the working population were further reduced in Russia by compulsory subscriptions to state loans and dues so that another 10 per cent of wages was siphoned off from mass consumption. In China, the organization of cooperatives and then of communes increased the government's control over wage levels and standards of consumption.

As in bourgeois industrialization, the use of female labor (but not child labor) in difficult tasks was widespread. Both Soviets and Chinese boast that there is no discrimination in jobs on the basis of sex, but there can be little doubt that one of the reasons many women went into the labor market was less the relaxation of discrimination than the more important fact that one breadwinner was not enough to support a family.

On the other hand, it is only fair to take note of a vigorous countercurrent to the depression of living standards, primarily in the field of social welfare. Both Russian and Chinese governments made the most vigorous efforts to improve the health of the people during the period of early industrialization. In Russia, the personnel in health services more than tripled in about twelve years; so did the number of hospital beds. Mortality from many diseases dropped sharply,[21] and the life expectancy of ordinary citizens rose. China also claims to have reduced the death rate sharply through improvements in health and sanitation.

Welfare provisions have been made available to Russian and Chinese industrial workers at a far earlier point in the nation's economic development than was the case in the bourgeois nations. Though working conditions were poor, more attention was paid to safety. And though the

---

[21] Lorimer, *op. cit.*, pp. 120–21.

general level of wages was low, sick benefits, maternity benefits, and retirement pensions eased the lot of those who could no longer work.

For Russia there has always been dispute about the price paid by the Soviet people for the program of rapid industrialization. Certainly it was high. The picture brought back by eyewitnesses of the early days of industrialization is grim: the scarce and almost inedible food, the endless queues, the lack of medicines, the worn-out clothes, the canvas shoes worn even in the big cities and in winter, the obvious overcrowding, the houses rotting from lack of repairs, the unpaved streets, the near-famine in much of the countryside, the anxiety about the future.

How many Soviet citizens paid with their lives for Russian industrialization? How many died in labor camps? How many died of famine? How many peasants died during transportation away from their land in the collectivization drive? How many workers died in industrial accidents? How many died of diseases that could have been cured? How many babies were never born in the hard years of famine and overwork? And, in comparison, what would the death toll have been from want and disease and repression if there had been no industrialization in Russia? It is impossible to answer these questions. Lorimer has estimated that the rigors of industrialization and collectivization may have cost the U.S.S.R. more than five million lives,[22] but this is a guess, albeit an informed one. We can only conclude that the figure was high. There is, of course, no count at all of those who suffered but did not perish.

Now the Chinese have embarked upon the same course, and the price they pay will in all probability be even higher, for China faces even more difficult problems than

[22] *Ibid.*, pp. 133–34.

Russia faced. For those at the bottom of Chinese society life has always been hard—far harder than anything European peasants ever experienced. For them industrialization has probably brought some improvement, even in the early years. But the masses of Chinese, always a little hungry, always badly dressed and badly housed, now bear the additional burdens of vast overwork, stifling regimentation, constant indoctrination, and fierce repression. China's first sprint of industrial expansion has been followed by a period of exhaustion and recuperation, but the worst still lies ahead, for China's stalinist rulers are determined to drive the Chinese through whatever hardships are required to reach the promised land of industrial plenty.

CONCLUSION

Russia, like the bourgeois nations before her, has passed through the difficult process of industrialization and achieved full industrial status. She did so more rapidly and probably more painfully than her Western predecessors. This fact, which we all take for granted today, presents the West its greatest challenge, for it proves something now obvious although once highly doubtful: that a totalitarian political system and a government-controlled economy can accomplish economic modernization. China has elected to follow the same path, and it is probable that at least some other nations will make the same choice.

The Soviet Union today is poised in the middle between her adversaries. China, her rival for leadership within her own international order, is one stage behind her: the Chinese have completed their primitive unification and embarked upon the politics of industrialization. Russia's Western antagonists, on the other hand, have left the stage of the politics of industrialization and are now nearing the end of the stage of the politics of national welfare.

Thus Russia is one stage ahead of one of her adversaries and one stage behind all the rest. It will be interesting to see what innovations the Soviet Union introduces into the politics of national welfare, just as it will be interesting to see what variations China offers on the Communist style of the politics of industrialization. Contrary to current belief, there seems some justification for believing that China's political system will show more resemblance to Russia's after her administrators come to full power. On the other hand, there seems little reason for believing that Russia's course through the politics of national welfare will parallel that of the West any more closely than her path to industrialization has followed that of Europe. Broad similarities there are, but the Communist path is a new and distinctive one.

However, the bourgeois and stalinist paths to industrial growth and power are not the only ones. History has already recorded a third way: that of fascist politics. It is to this third alternative that we shall now turn our attention.

V

SYNCRATIC POLITICS

More often than not, the term *fascist* is today an insult. It is used by the left to describe almost any regime that meets with disfavor, and even more cautious souls of the center find *fascist* a handy term for any authoritarian, nationalistic, aggressive political system that is not clearly Communist. Using the word in this general fashion, one may call fascist such diverse political systems as those of Hitler, Mussolini, Franco, Salazar, Perón, Nasser, Batista, and Trujillo. Such use, however, does not reveal much about the nature of fascism.

For my part, I prefer to use *fascist* more narrowly. The men named above have ruled nations at very different stages of political development. The Dominican Republic under Trujillo and Italy under Mussolini had little in common except for some elements of repression. And refugees from the Nazis who escaped into Italy noticed immediately the very profound differences between National Socialism and fascism. It was usual to suggest that differences in national character were responsible, and certainly the difference between Teuton and Latin is great. But such explanations account for only part of the difference. For a more complete explanation, one must consider the levels of modernization.

Fascism will be used in this book to refer to one of the varieties of the politics of industrialization: a system that arises only in stage two, that springs from fundamentally similar social and economic conditions in each case; that represents, as we shall see, a peculiar compromise between two ruling elites; and that contributes in recognizably similar ways to the shape and the pace of industrialization.

Viewed in this light, Hitler was an authoritarian dictator, a nationalist, an aggressor, a represser, and a madman, but he was not a fascist, for Germany was fully industrial when Hitler came to power. In terms of the stages of political development presented in this book, the Nazi system was not a form of the politics of industrialization but a variant of the politics of national welfare, and it is as such that we shall consider it later.

Nor can Trujillo be included as a fascist in this narrower meaning. To admit that his rule was autocratic and repellent to democrats does not make it fascist—any more than Nero's rule in Rome was fascist. Trujillo's rule does not belong to stage two either, but is one of the personal or family autocracies so common in the politics of primitive unification.

For Italy, Spain, and Argentina, on the other hand, the relationship between fascist politics and industrialization is quite clear. It is no accident that Italy became industrial under Mussolini, that Spain gained industrial status under Franco, or that Perón sailed into power on the same wave that lifted Argentina into industrial life.[1] Each of these

---

[1] The indicator used for industrialization is the percentage of economically active males in nonagricultural pursuits, a country being considered industrial when more than 50 per cent are so employed.

cases differs from the others (and this is especially so for *Perónismo*, which represents a mutation in the fascist genes), but the role of fascist politics is similar in each.

It is also necessary to broaden the fascist category to include current and future examples of political systems that resemble the earlier fascist states in some regards but not in others. It appears likely, for example, that a considerable number of the industrializing nations will adopt political systems that are neither bourgeois nor stalinist and certainly not socialist, despite their occasional claims. Some of these governments will closely resemble fascist governments in their structure, in their support, and in their handling of industrialization, but they may embrace ideologies which differ considerably from the old model. Fashions in politics change with the times, and the downfall of Hitler and Mussolini, combined with the unquestioned supremacy in power and prestige of the United States and the Soviet Union, have virtually guaranteed that no modern government will call itself fascist or consciously model its institutions after those of Italy, Spain, or Argentina. There are, however, in the world today nations that stand at the same point as those nations did when they became fascist, nations that share the same problems and may adopt similar solutions, whatever they may be called.

For the sake of simplicity, let us invent a new word and call all these fascist and fascistlike systems *syncratic*,[2] reserving the term *fascist* for the politics of Italy, Spain, and Argentina. The reader may use words as he chooses,

---

[2] From the Greek *syn* (together) and *cratic* (rule), in reference to the compromise between two ruling elites that lies at the heart of this form of government—not to be confused with *syncretic*, which is used in other contexts and implies a closer union or fusion of conflicting beliefs.

but he should remember the way in which they are used here.

THE SYNCRATIC SETTING

Syncratic politics usually begin when a country is not yet industrial but when industrialization has already started and the economy is well along the path to full industrialization. Italy and Spain were economically relatively underdeveloped countries when fascism began (with Spain the more backward of the two), while in Argentina, on the other hand, fascism finally "took" when the country had almost become industrial. The span of economic development during which a syncratic political system may make its appearance is therefore fairly broad. However, as we have noted, syncratic politics do not occur in a country that is highly nonindustrial or in one already fully industrialized.

The span of the developmental process in which syncratic politics may occur is determined first by the shifting distribution of power among major groups within the developing nation, a shift that is directly attributable to economic and social modernization, and second by the fact that there are three major conflicts within every society that industrializes. The first conflict is between the industrial and the agricultural elites: in Marxian terms, between the owners of capital and the owners of land— or between the new industrialists and the old landlords, to use more common terms. The second conflict is between each of the elites and its respective employees or tenants. A third conflict, less important for our analysis, exists between the peasant villagers and the industrial workers. (See diagram, page 126.) Let us examine these conflicts, beginning with the struggle between the elites.

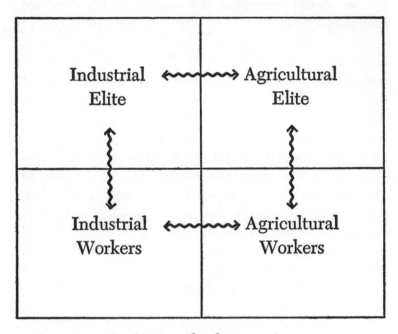

Conflicts in a developing nation.

Conflict between the Elites

Of the three conflicts, it is the antagonism between the industrial and agricultural leaders that is most significant, so far as development is concerned. This conflict is of course not limited to syncratic countries. It existed in stalinist countries, where revolution annihilated the old agricultural elite, and it existed in bourgeois countries, where the old landed aristocracy and the new industrialists struggled for power for nearly a century.

In the syncratic countries, however, the conflict has been particularly acute and in most cases has still not been completely resolved. Consider the often-noted alienation of Italy's peasant south from her industrial north, the similar hostility between the industrial north and the agricultural south in Spain, and the bitterness between the *porteños* and the *provincianos* of Argentina.

There is, not surprisingly, some overlap of personnel and attitudes between the two elites. Some of the landlords have invested in industry and some of the new industrialists have purchased large estates. Some of the landlords use industrial and commercial techniques in the management of their land, and some of the industrialists retain attitudes toward their labor that stem directly from the attitudes of landlords toward their peasants. Both elites will unite in putting down any attack from below.

Beneath this surface unity, however, the two elites stand in deep antagonism to each other. Their economic roles are almost antithetical, for the main function of the early industrialist is to save and to invest part of the savings, while the landlord in a peasant society is primarily a consumer. Moreover, the proper performance by each section of the elite of its economic role is profoundly disturbing to the other.

Much the same is true of the social values the two elites hold and encourage. For example, in the crucial matter of work values, the attitudes of each portion of the elite spells doom for the other. The industrialists place a high value on work, even toil, and consider the leisured landed gentry parasitical. The gentry, for its part, by and large regards "practical" work, and certainly all manual labor, demeaning.

The industrialists initially require labor possessing new skills and eventually come to require a mass market possessing the desire for a higher standard of living. However, the diffusion of economic skills and experience among the population represents a deep threat to the important class divisions of the old agricultural world, and dissatisfaction of the peasantry with its traditional living standard is the last thing the landed aristocracy wishes to create.

In two important respects the industrial sector of the economy grows at the expense of the agricultural sector. The industrial sector steals the peasants away from the fields and the villages and turns them into factory hands. Rural-to-city migration, as we have seen, is a crucial element of industrialization, and movement off the farms and into urban life is important both in shifting the labor force away from agricultural work and in destroying the peasant system of values that dominates the countryside.

The loss of their peasants galls the agricultural elite, not simply because they are needed to work the land, for unemployment and underemployment are rife in the countryside and, at least at the beginning, there is usually plenty of surplus labor available. It galls the landed elite because the departure of the few upsets the many who remain behind. Those who leave return to visit or write and tell of the life outside the village, and this disturbs the stability and upsets the inevitability of village life and the firmness of the landlord's rule. The possibility of leaving also offers an alternative to the peasants and they begin to speak up, to complain, and to "forget their place." The first way in which the industrial sector of the economy grows at the expense of its adversary, then, is by taking away part of agriculture's labor and creating discontent among the rest.

Second, the industrial sector forces the agricultural portion of the economy to save and to invest most of its savings in the underpinnings of an industrial society. This is accomplished through taxation. In developing countries in the twentieth century it is governments that build the base required for an industrial economy. Taxes go at least in part for roads, schools, health measures, hospitals, and the development of urban centers.

All of these are essential to the industrializing portion of the economy, but they are not needed—indeed, they are highly disturbing—in the life of a peasant society. What need is there for roads in the countryside when peasants have nowhere to go but to their fields and can walk or ride their mules? What need is there for literacy when a peasant can learn all he needs to know from his father? What need is there for hospitals to keep the sick alive when life is cheap and food is scarce and there is not even enough work for healthy men? The very payment of taxes also irritates the landed gentry, although they do not pay much. Why should they pay at all for purposes of which they do not approve? Why should they pay for the destruction of their own society?

Deep-seated hostility between the two elites exists from the first appearance of the industrialists to the last gasp of the landed aristocracy, but the relative power position of the two is an important factor in providing the preconditions for a syncratic system. Syncratic governments have typically come to power at a time when the country was not yet industrial and the industrial elite was still weaker than the agricultural elite.

Consider the influence of the two elites on the machinery of government in the years preceding syncratic rule. Both elites may be represented in the legislatures, but the agricultural elite always holds an important advantage over its rival, in both numbers and influence. In the executive, the advantage of the agricultural elite is even greater, with some departments of government reserved entirely as the private preserve of the landed aristocracy: the officer corps of the armed services, for example, and the diplomatic corps. In both Italy and Spain, the advantage of the agricultural elite was substantial in the years preceding the advent of fascism. In Argentina, the industrial elite had almost drawn abreast with the agricultural elite in wealth and economic power in the years preceding the military *coup* that opened the way for fascism, but even here the government was dominated by agriculturalists. It is interesting that the more even distribution of power between the two elites in Argentina was later influential in turning the course of Argentine fascism in a different direction from that of Italy and Spain.

Finally, it is important to note not only the relative power of the two elites in the presyncratic era but also their future prospects. The industrial elite, though weaker, is catching up with the landed aristocrats in wealth and power, and although the present may not be satisfactory to the industrialists, they can look forward to a time when they will be in control of the state and will run it their own way. The agricultural elite, on the other hand, may be satisfied with the existing situation but fears the future. As we shall see, both the actual circumstances of the two elites and their own perception of the future are important elements in the development of the syncratic system.

Conflict between Proletariats

The conflict between the two elites is reflected and continued in a lesser conflict between their followers. The residue of the hostility between peasant villagers and urban workers is still to be observed, even in the most industrial societies, where the clash between the value systems of the two worlds continues to echo.

The differences are real. On the part of the villager, they stem from the fact that the peasant is the repository

of tradition and therefore deeply conservative in his outlook. His feelings about the city are ambivalent, however.
On the one hand, it has deep attractions for him: witness
the wholesale desertion by peasants of the land. On the
other hand, the city and its ways seem to him wicked and
frightening. The uncertainty, the pace, and the pressure
of urban life are deeply unsettling.

For urban people, country life is often the object of
pleasant fantasies. They say that they envy the villager the
slow pace, the serenity, and the beauty of his environment.
In his dealings with the villager, however, the urban
dweller often shows ill-disguised contempt for the peasant's slowness, for the poverty and drab monotony of his
life, and for his provincialism.

Such attitudes run deep and sometimes have important
political consequences. Peasant troops and peasant feelings have often proved a strong bulwark against modernization or revolution or both.

Conflict with Those Below

In any industrializing country the conflict between the
elites is complemented and obscured by the even sharper
conflict between each of the elites and its supporting
workers. Particularly in the industrial sector, the old battle
between rich and poor assumes new forms and new
proportions.

A similar struggle goes on in the agricultural sector as
peasants seek to safeguard their rights and improve the
terms on which they work the land, while the landowners
seek new freedom to do as they please while retaining the
old high rents. The conflict here is less sharp than in
industry, for the peasants are restrained by tradition, weak
organization, and a fatalistic failure to realize the degree
to which they might manipulate their social environment.

Furthermore, in an industrializing society, those peasants who are most dissatisfied "solve" the peasant question by migrating to the cities and ceasing to be peasants.

In the industrial sector the conflict is more marked, first, because so many of the industrial occupations and situations are new with no tradition of docility—indeed with no tradition at all; second, because industrial workers work and live in a proximity which makes their eventual organization into unions easier; and third, because the early industrialists squeeze them right down to and sometimes below the level of subsistence. Low living standards for the mass of workers are perhaps unavoidable in a period of early industrialization, when productivity is low and sufficient savings for reinvestment can hardly be gathered without scrimping on labor costs, but as both the bourgeois and stalinist cases attest, early industrialists have come close to the limits of human endurance in the sacrifices they have imposed upon their workers. Under both systems, the savings for investment in capital goods have been created in large part at the expense of the living standards of the working population. Presyncratic industrialists have done the same, following for the most part the bourgeois path.

Presyncratic society, then, is split in four by a combination of class conflict and conflict between the two elites and between the two proletariats. Of the three conflicts, the fight between the two elites is the most divisive because it can end only in the defeat of one elite by the other. In the long run there cannot be coexistence and there cannot be two winners and, on the basis of all previous experience, it is the agricultural elite that perishes in the struggle. The conflict between the industrial elite and its workers is of a different nature, for not only do both survive but the hostility between them abates when productivity rises to the point at which there is enough to raise standards of living as well as to invest and maintain industrial growth.

It is important for the growth of syncratic government that these conflicts become acute and come to the surface, but it is also important that attention be focused mainly on the struggle between the elites and the working class: on the strikes, the lockouts, the street disorders, and the revolutionary talk. This serves to hide from public view (and from the participants themselves) the bitter struggle between the two elites.

The Surfacing of the Conflicts

In the three major historical cases of syncratic politics (Italy, Spain, and Argentina), the circumstances which rendered these conflicts acute and brought them to the surface were an initial massive surge in the modernization of the country followed by a sudden and sharp slowdown in industrial growth. It was rapid industrial growth which accelerated the move away from an agricultural way of life and roused the agricultural elite to new alarm and to new political action in its war with the industrial elite. While industrial expansion heightened the conflict between the two elites, the attempts at retrenchment which followed were primarily responsible for turning the latent war between industrialists and workers into open economic warfare complete with strikes, street brawls, and talk of revolution.

In each case the fundamental cause of the speedup in industrialization was war, and the cause of retrenchment was the adjustment to peacetime when the war ended. World War I served to start Italy and Spain on the road to fascism, and World War II put Argentina on the same track. Let us review the case of Italy as an example.

Italy before the first world war was still largely an underdeveloped country moving toward industrial status at a rapid pace. With the war, however, the modern and industrial portion of the country received a different stimulus, for the war provided an insatiable market for a wide variety of military goods. Moreover, the war with its draft and the war work with its need for labor provided a double stimulus to migration off the farms. Peasant Italy was rudely shaken, and the shift from peasant to industrial life became quite visible, though the needs of war prevented the conflict between the elites from erupting into the open. After the war ended, other social strife kept the attention of the nation away from this central struggle.

The end of the war brought new social and economic problems. Foremost was the need to reabsorb into society both the war veterans and the large number of civilian workers who had moved to the cities in search of better jobs and were now returning home. Both veterans and recent urban dwellers faced difficulties in settling back into agricultural and village life.

In addition to these difficulties, industry was forced to retrench and did so in large part by holding down wages and by trimming its labor rolls. Commercial agriculture followed suit. Organized labor responded by enlisting new members and by joining with militant political parties to resist the threat of re-establishing *ante bellum* labor conditions. Strikes and disorders broke out both in the cities and in the Italian countryside.

The strikes and the revolutionary talk (which was considerable, though not in responsible quarters) and the revolutionary activity (which was not great)[3] took on a

---

[3] Evidence of this is presented by Gaetano Salvemini, *Under the Axe of Fascism* (New York: Viking, 1936), pp. 144–53.

sinister tinge in the popular mind, where they were connected with revolutionary activities in Russia. There was, in fact, no danger of revolution in Italy, but the strikes and the threats frightened the middle classes, especially the lower middle class, for they were at the edge of the great social divide and their fear of becoming declassed was (and still is) real and potent.

Perhaps more important, the strikes frightened and angered the latifundists and the industrialists, who were the real and immediate targets of the strikers. The revolutionary talk distressed the Church by its antireligious bent and angered the Army with its rejection of the sacrifices of the recent war. Right or wrong, the social and economic unrest alarmed all these elements of the elite, who feared the disorders were the first step to revolution. Faced with new dangers from below, the elites found it possible to compromise their differences to make common cause against the enemy. In short, they were able to make the peculiar compromise that characterizes syncratic government.

The situation in Spain was not dissimilar, although fascism arrived in Spain in two stages: first the dictatorship of Primo de Rivera, and second the civil war of Franco. Here, too, World War I stimulated a need for Spanish goods, though Spain was not a combatant, and the end of the war ushered in a period of stagnation and unrest. In the republican interlude after Rivera's dictatorship ended, the industrial sector of the economy again jumped forward and aggravated the differences between the two elites. And in Spain also the conflict between agriculturalists and industrialists was smothered by the fear of the fury from below, particularly in the period preceding the rise of Franco.

In Argentina, events were slightly different, though

Argentina's first experience with fascism, the dictatorship of General Uriburu, follows the classic pattern, coming as it did after a period of industrial expansion followed by a cutback caused by the depression of the 1930s. World War II again stimulated Argentine industry but there was no slowup. Indeed, the industrialists were within sight of dominance when the revolution of Rawson, Ramirez, Farrel, and Perón ushered in a new era of fascism.

SYNCRATIC GOVERNMENT TAKES OVER

This, then, is the situation at the moment syncratic regimes take over. Industrial expansion has greatly increased the power, the wealth, and the future prospects of the new industrialists and has sharpened their conflict with the old agricultural elite. The latter, however, remains in control of the government though it feels its dominance slipping away. Economic reverses caused by peacetime readjustment or by economic depression have caused industry to retrench. This has aroused social protest from the workers, whose riots and strikes frighten all elements of the elite and the middle classes as well.

The immediate reason for the rise of syncratic leaders to political power is that the syncratic party takes the side of the elite groups against the protest from below. This was certainly the case in Italy and in Spain, and it was intended to be the case in Argentina, where Perón was made Secretary of Labor to keep unions and strikes in check, though (as we shall see) *Perónismo* later veered off the prescribed course.

It is an error, therefore, to see fascism as a lower-middle-class movement oriented toward the benefit of the lower classes. It is an error to think of Perón's fascism as a movement of the left. It is true that many individual leaders and members of the fascist movement in Italy, Spain, and Argentina came from the lower middle classes, but this did not determine the direction of party politics, any more than the bourgeois origins of many Russian and Chinese Communists made communism a bourgeois movement. The fascist movements operated within the framework established by the interests of the elites and supported those interests as effectively as if the elites had ruled directly.

In Italy, for example, it is difficult to explain the rise of Mussolini in any other terms. Fascist nationalism had appeal, but there were other nationalists with greater renown and greater support—D'Annunzio, for example. The opposition to fascism was certainly better led and better organized. The Communists, the Socialists, and the Christian Democrats were all numerically superior to the fledgling Fascists, and all had leaders of ability. Moreover, each of these parties represented significant social and economic forces within Italian society. Why, then, did Mussolini, who had a party of no more than 17,000 members in 1919, achieve control of the government a short three years later?

The answer lies in the fact that between these two dates Mussolini won over important elements of the elite: specifically, he won the support of important segments of the Church, the Army, the landed gentry, and the bourgeoisie, and he won them in large part because the Fascist Party had played the role of strikebreaker and antirevolutionary fighter. The breaking of strikes and the beating and terrorizing of strikers, reformers, and revolutionists gained for the Fascists the support of both the agricultural and industrial elites, who saw in the Fascist bands an effective obstacle to any challenge to their own power position. Fascist anticommunism appealed to the

(137)

Church, and Fascist nationalism appealed to the Army. In addition, the Fascists' promise of a return of law and order gained them the support of the middle classes.

SYNCRATIC REGIMES

Syncratic government is made possible by the fact that the syncratic party sides with the elites in the conflict between the elites and the workers. Equally important is "the syncratic solution" to the conflict between the agricultural and industrial elites.

Looking back on the three main fascist regimes, one is struck by the fact that they appear to be the political expression of a crude but fundamental economic and social bargain between the agricultural and industrial elites. The compromise that syncratic politics legitimizes and executes is to give each elite complete sway within its own economic and social sector.

A crucial part of this bargain, however, is to make it difficult for the industrial elite to raid the agricultural sector for manpower and for savings. This, it can be logically concluded, must slow the pace of industrialization somewhat. Certainly it helps preserve the waning power and privileges of the agricultural elite.

In Italy, in Spain, and in Argentina the agricultural world was extolled as the foundation of the nation, and in all three nations the protection afforded by the government to the landowners and to the peasant sector was substantial. In Italy and Spain, landowners were favored in taxation and were given privileges that helped them preserve their holdings. In Italy, the government even went so far as to hold down rural-to-city migration, thus helping stop the wound that was draining away the lifeblood of the old agricultural system.

In Argentina, the case was slightly different. Here more

than elsewhere agriculture was made to underwrite the plans for industrialization, but even in Argentina, the hold of the landed aristocracy within its own domain was left untouched. In spite of all the fulminations from Casa Rosada, Perón never touched the privileges and the power of the landed oligarchy within the peasant world.

This protection of the agricultural sector represents one of the most fundamental differences between the syncratic method of industrialization on the one hand and the bourgeois and the stalinist methods on the other. Under bourgeois politics, all of the country was made to contribute to economic modernization, and under stalinist politics, the agricultural sector was squeezed even harder to provide manpower and capital for economic modernization.

The fact that syncratic regimes protect the agricultural sector from having to make a major contribution to the capital for economic growth raises an important question: Where does capital come from under the syncratic political compromise? There must be some source for it, because industrial growth continues under syncratic politics (though probably at a slower rate than would otherwise be the case).

The heart of the answer is as follows: Under a syncratic system, the savings for investment in industry are squeezed primarily out of the industrial sector itself, not gathered from the entire country. To a very large extent, the savings in the industrial sector are created by increases in productivity in the modern portion of the economy and by decreases in the living standard of the industrial proletariat.

Aid to Industry

The second part of the syncratic compromise takes the form of governmental assistance to the industrial elite in order to help it expand industry despite the hands-off-agriculture policy. In the three fascist countries, such assistance took many forms: direct loans and financial assistance to industrial enterprises, government purchases of industrial goods. Less obvious but nevertheless effective in stimulating industrial expansion were the high military expenditures that characterized the fascist governments. In Argentina, a country that had never fought a major war, Perón devoted almost one third of the governmental investment to defense.[4] Spanish armed forces were not highly effective, but expenditures were high, and although Mussolini's pose as a military leader was grotesque, he spent a good deal of money on arms and armies. Such expenditures encouraged the growth of industry and at the same time were acceptable to the agricultural elite with its long military tradition.

More important than any of these measures, however, was the attitude of the fascist governments toward wages, working conditions, and labor-management disputes in industry. It was here that the governments of Italy and Spain gave their greatest assistance to the industrialists, allowing them virtually a free hand in creating savings by shearing their workers.[5]

Again Italy furnishes the clearest example, though Spain does not differ in essentials. The power of the state was used unsparingly to lower the wages of the workers, in agriculture as well as in industry. In Italy the "corpora-

---

[4] Robert J. Alexander, *Labor Relations in Argentina, Brazil and Chile* (New York: McGraw-Hill, 1962), p. 146, Table 8.
[5] The situation in Argentina was different and will be discussed separately below, pp. 151–55.

tions" were the governmental organs with chief responsibility in this matter, but the government played this role even before the corporations came into existence. Strikes were forbidden by law and arbitration of disputes by the government was compulsory. The government, however, almost invariably decided in favor of management; the record is monotonous in this regard.

The immediate effect of fascism was to reduce real wages and consumption by the Italian working classes.[6] Stable boys in Cremona had their wages reduced after the Fascists took over. In Foggia in 1926 women and boys who worked at the harvest had their daily wages reduced to half the amount they had earned in 1920. Wages in the silk industry dropped by 50 per cent from 1926 to 1933, and bank clerks lost more than one third of their salaries between 1927 and 1932.[7]

Welfare Measures

There is one point that needs to be raised. How are we to reconcile the syncratic role of reducing living standards with the emphasis on welfare policies that all the fascist regimes proclaimed? The welfare programs of the fascist regimes are well known: cheap housing for needy families, hot soup for the poor at fascist centers, a dole for the unemployed, summer holidays at the seaside and in the mountains at fascist camps for the children of the urban poor.

In the light of such programs is it accurate to say that standards of living are lowered by syncratic regimes? Is it not more likely that living standards remain the same or even rise, with the government giving back in welfare measures the equivalent or more of what is taken away

---

[6] Gaetano Salvemini, *op. cit.*, pp. 159ff., 346ff.
[7] *Ibid.*, pp. 161, 163, 221–22.

by low wages? The answer is no: what is given and what is taken away are not the same. First, only a small portion of the fascist welfare programs were of such a nature as to spend potential investment funds. Second, a good part of the money spent on welfare was obtained by taxing the working classes. Third, perhaps most important, the welfare programs were relatively small and touched only a small part of the population. Though excellent politics, fascist welfare was not nearly as large, costly, or successful as fascist propaganda portrayed it.

The shouldering of the welfare problem by the government, even in a token fashion, represents a major difference between syncratic politics and bourgeois politics. In bourgeois politics the government took no appreciable responsibility for the welfare of the general population. Fully sensitive to the interests of those who controlled the economy, it took no steps that would have siphoned off savings into mass consumption. Nor did employers ever take any responsibility for aiding those who suffered from the immense social changes that made increasing productivity possible. It was government that eventually undertook the task, but only *after* industrialization was well advanced, and it did so then because in the process of industrialization the masses had been politicized and had turned to government for protection against the hardships of industrial life.

The politics of industrialization in the twentieth century are perforce different, for the people are politicized *before,* not after, industrialization. Indeed, economic development is much more a result than a cause of such politicization. This difference can be seen clearly in syncratic as well as stalinist politics. Unlike their bourgeois predecessors, syncratic and stalinist governments have had to deal with masses already aroused. The existence of other societies with industrial economies and democratic ideologies raises the expectations of ordinary people everywhere. In addition, totalitarian dictatorships are often the result of revolutions which have made direct appeals to the masses, as in the case of the stalinist governments, or which have involved the masses in the political struggle which preceded their coming to power, as in the case of the fascist governments. Once in power, these totalitarian dictatorships have kept the masses stirred up with parades, mass meetings, sports competitions, and endless talk of the greatness of the nation and the accomplishments of the regime.

Inevitably, governments presiding over industrialization must contribute in significant ways to the hardships of life for many of their citizens, probably the majority, and just as inevitably the governments of industrializing nations where the masses are politicized must take up at least in token form the burden of welfare. As a twentieth-century product, syncratic politics straddles to some extent stages two and three of political development, the politics of industrialization and the politics of national welfare. Syncratic and stalinist governments alike have taken up the welfare burden earlier than bourgeois governments did. All governments industrializing their nations in the twentieth century, whatever their political complexion, will be forced to do the same.

Rate of Industrialization

In summary, then, the syncratic compromise protects agriculture from paying its full share of the costs of industrialization and compensates industry for the loss of the savings of a large part of the nation by helping it squeeze capital out of the industrial proletariat. Thus capital accumulation in syncratic nations is carried on from a restricted base.

It seems likely, therefore, although it is difficult to prove, that syncratic politics slows the pace of industrialization, for it slows down the rate of capital accumulation, the key to industrialization. One can arrive at this same conclusion in yet another way. Syncratic politics is a compromise between the two wings of the elite, arrived at because of the revolutionary attack upon their privileges from below. The two elites are interested in stemming revolutionary change. The agricultural elite, indeed, is opposed to almost any change, since it can look forward only to a further deterioration of its own position. The position of the industrial elite differs, but for purposes of government it joins the agricultural elite at least for a time and acquiesces in its efforts to slow the rate of change, including most importantly the rate of economic modernization.

SYNCRATIC SELF-DESTRUCTION AND ITS AFTERMATH

Syncratic politics are built upon a fundamental compromise, but the compromise does not and cannot last, and in a surprisingly short period of time the system crumbles and falls. It is not an accident of history that the fascist regimes of the past have all been so short-lived.

The reasons for their collapse are fairly obvious. There are three preconditions for syncratic government: (1) the industrial elite is weaker than the agricultural elite but gaining ground; (2) the agricultural elite is aware that it is losing power; (3) both elites are attacked from below. The syncratic compromise is one that attempts to freeze politically the socioeconomic position of the two elites at the time the syncratic political system is constructed. But the underlying social and economic trends that have strengthened the industrial elite continue as time goes on, since industrialization is not stopped by a syncratic system, only slowed down. Eventually the industrial elite, which agreed to the initial compromise because it was the weaker party, grows to become the stronger party, refuses to continue to compromise, and the syncratic political system falls apart.

In general, a syncratic system cannot be expected to last long. Perhaps if the compromise were made very early in the industrial development of the nation, syncratic institutions might last through the political lifetime of their originators and one set of successors, but probably no longer than that. In most instances it is more probable that the syncratic system will not outlive its originators. This was the case in Fascist Italy, and it is my contention that fascism would not have survived the eventual death of Mussolini even had Italy not become involved in World War II. This was the case in Perón's Argentina. And this, I predict, will be the case with Franco's *falangismo* when the old dictator dies and a change can be brought about without bloodshed.

It is also predictable what kind of political system will succeed a syncratic regime. Until now, when syncratic systems have come to an end, they have, with one exception, been replaced by mass democracies. This is what happened in Italy and in Argentina, although the latter is having a difficult time, and this is what will happen in Spain.

These democracies, however, are less than complete. They have parliaments and constitutions, elections and mass parties which compete for public favor. But a closer look reveals severe weaknesses in the operation of these democracies in comparison with the mass democracies of an earlier vintage. One can observe in countries that have industrialized in the syncratic manner a persisting inability to bring together the major groups—class, occupational, and religious groupings—into one economic, social, and political community. As a result, the democracies of Italy and Argentina lack a part of the content of the democratic system.

The crucial problem seems to be the lack of national values and a truly national ideology. In part this is the inevitable result of the fact that under syncratic rule traditional values and existent power groupings received greater protection from the encroachments of modernity than under bourgeois politics. K. H. Silvert, writing of syndicalism rather than fascism, nevertheless describes in a brilliant passage the core problem of the weakness we are discussing:

> Public decisions . . . result from the interplay of the institutional oligarchs, and not from the deliberations of groups and men elected at large from a citizenry escaping its occupational bonds in an act of political selection and decision formally and somewhat substantially indicative of equality.
>
> . . . The weakness of the state, the strength of competing institutions, and the accent upon class-bound politics wedded to hierarchy and obedience within the occupational function . . . all are incompatible with the fluidity and self-adjustment required for the voluntaristic human mobilization of democratic development.[8]

In this passage Silvert refers to the syndicalist and falangist state, of which he considers Argentina a modified example, whereas he feels that fascism of the Italian variety differs in attempting to establish the supremacy of the state. It seems to me, however, that the fascist claim of

[8] K. H. Silvert (ed.), *Expectant Peoples: Nationalism and Development* (New York: Random House, 1963), p. 360.

unity was an attempt to mask disunity, for in the fascist system it was the elites of the various groupings (Silvert's institutional oligarchs) that brought unity *at the top* by mediating differences and presenting a national compromise. The fascium is a perfectly accurate symbol of the fascist state, for the rods in it have no cohesion other than that imposed by external bonds.

It is to be expected, then, that the mass democracies that replace syncratic systems will be flawed. Their weaknesses, however, need not be permanent, for in the course of time modernization will continue to erode the remaining strongholds of tradition and spread truly national values throughout the population. It seems probable that eventually these descendants of syncratic rule will become mass democracies as fully in content as in form.

An Interesting Exception

We have noted that there is one exception to the generality that syncratic systems are replaced by mass democracies. The exception is Cuba, which industrialized along syncratic lines under Batista, then overthrew her syncratic system and turned Communist, not democratic. Such a dramatic exception demands a word of explanation.

It is a common belief that a Communist system cannot be grafted onto a country that is already industrial. Such a view assumes that the fundamental function of Communist (or what is here called stalinist) politics is to force the rapid accumulation of capital in very poor countries, and that communism has little to offer to countries that are already industrial. When Cuba went Communist, perceptive observers expressed regret that such a regression should have taken place, for Cuba had passed the point where a Communist system made any sense. I fully share this view.

Nevertheless, Cuba went Communist. Part of the explanation no doubt lies in unique historical circumstances: first in the fact that Castro, once in power as a charismatic leader with immense popular support, could swing his country in almost any direction he chose and that he chose to swing it in a direction which had been unanticipated by most of those who put him in power originally; and, second, in the fact that Cuba, as an economic dependency of the United States, was a reservoir of hostility toward the United States.

Such conditions, of course, may come to exist in other Latin American nations. If anti-Americanism and charismatic leadership were all that were required to prepare the ground for communism, we could expect a large number of Latin American countries to go Communist in the future. I do not believe this will happen. It seems to me that there is at least one other factor that predisposed Cuba to a Communist solution, a factor that stems directly from her syncratic past.

Syncratic industrialization consists of letting the industrial sector of the country move ahead while the agricultural sector remains as it was. This means that as industrialization progresses the two portions of the country, the old and the new, move farther and farther apart. In many cases the point is reached where there is little communication between the two parts, and the peasant sector is alienated from the national community. The country that has traveled the syncratic path to industrial status has two countries within its borders.

Thus syncratic politics leaves in its wake a fundamental problem which must be solved by its successor. To complete the economic and social modernization of the country, the two parts must be brought back together again. The old agricultural elite must finally be dislodged from power, even within its own sector. Large numbers of peasants must be absorbed into industrial work and into city life, and those who remain on the land must shed their old ways and learn to work more efficiently at the same time they are being permitted to earn enough to raise their living standards.

The dislodging of the agricultural elite and the modernization of agriculture are made particularly difficult in cases such as Cuba, where large agricultural interests are foreign-owned and beleaguered landowners can count on the support of such a powerful nation as the United States. Let us recall that in Cuba the agricultural and the industrial elites were equally strong, that they were tied to foreign interests, and that some portions of the elite itself were American. Under such circumstances the government that follows a syncratic regime is highly likely to turn against the United States (or other foreign owner of its land or industry), though it need not necessarily become a Communist state.

In industrial countries where the agricultural and industrial sectors are split apart and the old agricultural elite is still powerful, a Communist system is functional in at least one respect. It provides an ideology that may shock the peasant out of his torpor and hastens the final destruction of the power of the agricultural elite.

If there is any validity to such a line of reasoning, it should be possible to offer two hypotheses: (1) that the probability of an industrial nation adopting a Communist system (in the absence of foreign conquest) is extremely low, but (2) that this low probability is maximized in the case of a nation that has industrialized under a syncratic system and that has a substantial portion of its agricultural enterprises owned or controlled by foreign interests.

Cuba, then, is an exception. The usual aftermath of a

syncratic system is the restoration of parliamentary democracy; at least this has been the case in the past. It could be argued that a determining role was played by external factors: the Allied victory in World War II and the predominant position of Western democracy vis-à-vis communism at the present time. However, internal factors also helped bring about this result and probably would have been sufficient in themselves. Under a syncratic system, the essentially capitalistic nature of industrial enterprise is not seriously tampered with, although industrial management is deprived of some of its influence on government. When the industrial elite becomes strong enough to terminate its compromise with the agricultural elite and to dispense with the harassments and limitations to which syncratic government has exposed it, it supports that form of government most conducive to its interests—parliamentary democracy. With the fall of syncratic government the politics of national welfare begins, following for the most part the pattern common to the other Western democracies which have developed without a syncratic interlude.

THE CASE OF ARGENTINA

It has been noted that the rule of Perón in Argentina, although fundamentally a syncratic system, provides an exception to some of the above generalizations. It will be useful at this point to deal with Argentina in more detail. It has been stated, for example, that syncratic politics represents a compromise between the two elites at the expense of industrial workers. How, then, is one to understand the enthusiasm of the Argentine working classes for Perón and the cold shoulder industrialists turned to Perón and his regime? And how was the capital for Argentine industrialization accumulated, if not at the expense of the industrial workers?

Let us begin by noting the many ways in which the syncratic system in Argentina was much the same as those of Italy and Spain: (1) In Argentina the conflict between industrial and agricultural elites was both acute and clearly visible. (2) The industrial elite was the weaker of the two but was growing rapidly in power. (3) The agricultural elite, though stronger, was slipping and knew it was losing control of the economy and of the nation. (4) Both of Argentina's experiences with fascist governments, the dictatorship of Uriburu in 1930 and the revolution of Ramirez and Perón in 1943, were preceded by periods of rapid industrial expansion, followed in the first case (but not in the second) by a period of retrenchment. (5) Once in power, fascist leaders did not diminish the power of the agricultural elite within its own sector. (6) Perón encouraged industry by planning, by buying back control of industry owned by foreigners, by large military expenditures, and by using for industrial expansion the high profits from the sale of primary commodities during World War II. (7) Industrial development continued under Perón, and by 1955, when Perón was overthrown, the industrial elite was stronger than the agricultural elite. (8) The major regimes which followed Perón were parliamentary governments. These were the similarities.

Now the differences: Perón's advent to power was not preceded by a period of retrenchment or by the worker protest that such retrenchment engendered elsewhere. Perhaps in part for this reason, the two elites in Argentina did not draw close together. More important, the industrial elite never gave Perón the support one would expect in a syncratic system; because of this, Perón turned to labor for the support necessary to maintain his regime in power. Finally, Perón did not permit industrial management to squeeze labor harder in order to accumulate capital. On the contrary, he raised the living standards of the industrial and urban masses. The capital for industrial expansion was drawn from other sources.

An important reason for these last two major differences in Argentina fascism lay in the *lateness* of the Perónista revolution, which came at a time when Argentina was already newly industrial. A brief sketch of Argentine history may help make clearer the significance of this fact.

By the 1930s Argentina had progressed considerably in her industrialization and, thanks to the worldwide depression, presented a more or less classic setting for fascism. General Uriburu took control by force and established an openly fascist government and talked of a corporate state. After two years, however, the agricultural elite took power directly, and a government more constitutional in form ran Argentina for the next decade, with the help of massive fraud at the polls. This government tried to slow industrial growth and was successful for the first few years. Then World War II undid its work.

The war cut off European supplies from Argentina and provided a tremendous stimulus to Argentine industry. An avalanche of industrial production carried Argentina over the dividing line between agricultural and industrial status and produced fears among the agricultural elite that the next election would produce a government far more responsive to industrial needs. The agricultural elite therefore favored forestalling the coming election and, though it would be difficult to prove that the military acted as its agent, it was in this context that the military *junta* including Perón took over and did in fact forestall the election.

Thus the power position of the two elites at the fascist

takeover was quite different in Argentina than it had been in Italy and Spain. There the industrial elites were far weaker and thus more ready to compromise. In Argentina, however, the industrial elite was almost as strong as the agricultural elite and was looking forward to a government that would favor its interests. Why should it support a *junta* that had come to power to forestall this government? It is hardly surprising that the industrial elite turned a deaf ear to the overtures of the *junta* for support.

As a result, the *junta* was left in an exposed position and badly needed new major sources of support. Perón, who had originally been put in the labor department to control the unions and to prevent strikes, used his position to search for a common ground with union leaders and to win their support. This support raised Perón to supreme power and changed the direction of Argentine fascism.

Under Perón, the standard of life of Argentine labor went up, not down. However, this deviation from the usual syncratic pattern should not be overemphasized. Perón never went so far as to endanger savings for investment. In truth, the lives of Argentine peons were so miserable and the wages of industrial workers so low, while profit margins were so high, that the modest wage increases imposed by the government did not seriously alter the economy although they won much gratitude from the masses. Moreover, the improvements were greatest at the beginning—when they were needed to assure labor's support. Once labor was captured, it was held in check, strikes were discouraged, and wage increases tapered off. Finally, Perón, unlike other fascist leaders, was able to raise the living standards of the working population without seriously slowing the pace of industrialization because Argentine industry was already well advanced and generated considerable capital, and the war raised sharply the prices for Argentine primary commodities on the world market and provided a great stimulus to Argentine industry.

It is important not to confuse the attitude of the two elites toward Perón with the actual functioning of his government. Although both industrial and agricultural elites expressed contempt and even hostility toward Perón, he nevertheless aided and protected them both in the manner common to syncratic regimes. Despite the publicity surrounding his prolabor measures, he provided a governmental framework within which Argentine industry could expand, and despite the hostility of the agricultural elite (who particularly resented his efforts to grant a semblance of humanity to the peons), Perón safeguarded the power of the agricultural elite in the agricultural world.

What happened in Argentina after the fall of Perón conformed to the syncratic pattern. After a brief interregnum, power passed to a government primarily responsive to industrial needs and wishes. The government seemed to want to turn history back to 1943. After waiting for twelve years, the industrial elite had its way, and the cut in the standard of living of the workers was deep and sharp. Indeed, the Frondizi government went too far, for no government could act in Argentina again as if Perón had not existed.

It becomes clear that the Perón regime was not so different from other fascist governments as is sometimes believed. What differences there were seem to have been the result largely of the advanced position of Argentine modernization when Perón came to power. One can only speculate whether these differences would have existed had the fascist system created by Uriburu remained in power and had the agricultural elite been willing to compromise before it had clearly lost.

The syncratic system is not a fixed and unalterable

pattern. It has varied in the past and will vary more in the future. An important source of variation appears to be the level of economic development at which the syncratic regime comes to power.

CONCLUSION

Marxists are wrong when they claim that fascism is a creature of the bourgeoisie. As we have seen, syncratic systems represent an attempt by the agricultural elite to slow the pace of industrialization and to control its consequences. Syncratic government is a last victory for the landed aristocracy. Faced with certain defeat, they nevertheless manage to maximize their power and postpone its final shift into other hands.

The effect of syncratic government is not, however, to stop the process of economic modernization. Industrialization continues, though probably at a somewhat slower pace. The main effect of syncratic government is typically to exempt the agricultural elite from paying the economic and social cost of industrialization and to lessen the cost paid by the peasantry. Though their life remains hard and their exploitation at the hands of their landlords is often great, the peasants do not suffer the brutal displacement and abrupt change that afflicted their brothers in bourgeois Europe or in stalinist Russia and China. The burden of paying the price for economic progress is shifted almost entirely onto the backs of the industrial workers, whose lot is harder than it would have been in the absence of a syncratic regime.

It does not follow, nevertheless, that the industrial workers of syncratic countries have suffered more than those of bourgeois or stalinist countries. Industrialization in the nineteenth century was necessarily a more difficult business than it is today in nations that can take advantage both of the technology and of the social experience of those who preceded them, and industrialization at breakneck speed is more painful than modernization spread over many years. Syncratic industrialization has the advantages of taking place in the twentieth century and of proceeding at a relatively slow pace. Also, it is only fair to note that syncratic systems occur in relatively advanced countries, where the difficult early accumulation of capital has already taken place. Thus it is pointless to compare the lot of workers in these countries with that of workers under early bourgeois or early stalinist systems. The comparison must be made at the comparable stage of economic advance.

Syncratic politics, indeed, is a temporary phenomenon. Unlike bourgeois and stalinist politics, which see the industrialization process through from start to finish, syncratic politics emerges in the middle of the process and disappears once the nation has become industrial. In this sense, and in this sense only, the syncratic system is a variant of the bourgeois pattern, for syncratic politics is preceded by a period of bourgeois development and is followed by a resumption of the bourgeois pattern.

At this point, however, the nation enters a new stage of political growth, and it is no longer appropriate to refer to bourgeois politics. With industrialization achieved, the politics of national welfare begins, bringing great changes to all the developed nations—by whatever path they have reached that position. It is to this third stage of political development that we now turn.

STAGE THREE

The Politics of
National Welfare

VI

THE POLITICS OF
NATIONAL WELFARE

With the beginning of the third stage of political development, a curious phenomenon occurs: the function of government reverses itself as men finally achieve the industrial riches for which they have struggled so long.

The dividing line between stage two and stage three is hard to find—indeed it is not a line at all—but the difference between them is fundamental. In the politics of industrialization the job of government is to direct the accumulation of capital or to clear the way for those who accumulate it. In either case, the state plays a repressive role, exacting from those least able to defend themselves a disproportionately large share of the social and economic cost of modernization.

In the politics of national welfare, the primary function of the state is the exact opposite. The major task of government in stage three is to protect the very people who were the greatest sufferers in stage two. To put it another way, the fundamental function of national government in stage two is to protect capital from the people, while in stage three it is to protect the people from capital. The reversal of functions is complete.

Let me make one thing clear: by the politics of national welfare I do not mean simply that a government puts on its books some welfare legislation; virtually all governments do that today. To qualify as a welfare state, a government must not only espouse such programs as social security, health programs, education, and the regulation of working conditions. It must also adopt as its prime concern a responsibility for the economic and social welfare of ordinary citizens. This means intervening in various ways to raise the living standards of the masses and particularly of the underprivileged; it also means taking major steps to keep the economy running smoothly enough to provide relatively full employment.

For the first group of countries that industrialized, the bourgeois nations, the change in functions was fairly complete. Responsibility for welfare was neither widespread nor significant until industrialization was fairly well under way and stage two was nearing its end. The timing differed from country to country. Germany, for example, was relatively early in initiating welfare programs, the United States exceptionally late, but the generalization holds for the bourgeois nations as a group.

The stalinist and syncratic systems, on the other hand, introduced some elements of the welfare state while they were still industrializing. Neither, however, devoted such a large share of the national income to this purpose as to detract seriously from the accumulation of capital. Living standards were kept very low. Thus the primary function of government remained the formation of capital, but the idea of welfare was taking root, and the national government had assumed, at least in theory, the responsibility of protecting the general population from hardship.

Nations industrializing today (such as Brazil and Egypt) are attempting to introduce extensive social legislation even earlier. Indeed, even some of the most underdeveloped countries, still emphatically in stage one, are beginning to talk and to legislate social welfare. The very fact that developed countries exist makes it inevitable that underdeveloped countries will seek to imitate them in this respect as in others. It does not matter perhaps that their welfare programs are small and their welfare laws most often honored in the breach. It does not matter that modern trappings are often used to window-dress old realities. It is significant that such programs exist at all.

It is probable that as the twentieth century progresses, developing nations will try increasingly to carry out the political functions of all three stages at once. It is not likely that this will prove possible, but the overlap among the three stages, minimal in the European and the Japanese experience, should continue to expand in the case of the developing countries of today.

The countries that have reached stage three are nearly all mass democracies. In the past both Germany and Japan have combined totalitarian governments with welfare politics, but defeat in war brought a turn to mass democracy. Today three Communist countries are in the third stage of political development, but two, Czechoslovakia and East Germany, have had communism imposed upon them by external force, and the remaining one, Russia, has just entered stage three. We begin, then, with consideration of mass democracy, the dominant form of the politics of national welfare.

MASS DEMOCRACY

The connection between mass democracy and bourgeois politics can be seen clearly, for the roots of the modern democratic systems that flourish today in Western Europe and in the European countries overseas extend far back into the preceding period. Indeed, the first causes of the eventual change that transformed bourgeois politics into the politics of national welfare can be found even before the bourgeoisie came to power, in the days when the landed aristocracy was still the dominant force in politics. The eventual emergence of the politics of national welfare is rooted in the poverty and cruelty of life for the mass of people at the very beginning of the industrial period and in the rage and despair of the masses at the harshness of their lot. A revelation of the violence of their feelings can be seen in the furious outbursts when the masses were organized and directed by the bourgeoisie against the monopoly of power of the aristocracy, as in the French Revolution.

The accession of the bourgeoisie to power, did not bring plenty to the masses, nor could it possibly have done so. On the contrary, early industrialization with its disorganization of life in the countryside, its huge migration into unplanned cities, and its inhuman utilization of industrial labor increased the misery of the masses and added to the squalor and the injustice of their lives. The industrial workers of that day were in reality masses of raw peasants fresh from the countryside, still relatively few in number and lacking in leadership and in organization. They were helpless to correct the harsh conditions of their own lives, nor could the economies of that day have afforded significant improvements in the general standard of living.

Leadership, organization, and higher productivity were required before the masses could improve their lot.

The Masses Rise to Power

Industrialization provided these essentials. Thus bourgeois politics contained within it the seeds of its own destruction: the very conditions of its operation were also the ones that led the masses to political power. The climb of the masses to power is too well known to require great elaboration here. Let it simply be noted that several factors played an important part.

Increasing urbanization pulled the vast numbers of the working population into close proximity, where they were for the first time susceptible to organization. Worker organization took many forms, but inevitably workers used the factory organization to unite outside the factory walls. Unions and political-reform movements were fought by the bourgeoisie, but continued to grow. Unions in particular gave the masses experience in working together as well as a weapon with which to fight and a voice with which to speak to the broader community. In the democratic systems, geared as they were to respond to group pressures rather than individual pressures, numbers plus organization provided the common people with a key to power.

Increasing skills and the spread of education, both required for industrial progress, were also important in increasing the power of the masses, for skilled workers had greater bargaining power than unskilled labor, and in school the masses not only learned literacy and patriotism but also began to gain an acquaintance with the political environment and the ways of manipulating it.

Citizen armies, necessary for the external defense of the bourgeois nation, also helped unite and arouse the masses.

Citizen armies made their first appearance with the French Revolution, where they carried Napoleon to victory and then defeated him, but it is significant that throughout the rest of the nineteenth century the bourgeoisie resisted the use of such armies. The dangers of arming the masses and organizing the veterans were obvious. Indeed, it is more than coincidence that World War I in many ways marked the end of the period of bourgeois politics in Europe.

The primary means through which the masses achieved a voice in the direction of government was not, of course, either mass revolt or general strikes, but rather expansion of the franchise. Electoral reform had been a major battleground between the bourgeoisie and the landed gentry when the former rose to power, and it was again important in the battle between the masses and the bourgeoisie. Once the masses obtained a powerful voice in government, they used it to set limits within which national governments had to operate, and as a result the substance and the style of government were radically altered.

It comes down to this: under bourgeois political direction the new economy mobilized the people and made them dependent upon the national economy for their survival. Though the population was dependent upon the economy, it could not control it, and so the masses turned to government for protection. Political and industrial leaders alike found themselves increasingly dependent upon at least the tacit support of the mass of workers to run the system they headed and in consequence were forced to grant the common people an increasingly important voice in the determination of national policy.

Welfare First

The accession of the masses to political power was gradual, as that of the bourgeoisie had been, and like the bourgeoisie before them they shared their new power with the previous ruling group. Indeed, they share it still. At first there was no change in the people in power, but the new governments became increasingly sensitive to working-class needs. Even today, the majority of the top governmental officials in such countries as the United States, England, France, and Germany are drawn from the business community rather than from labor, but the governments they run have of necessity taken on the tasks of social welfare and the regulation of the economy.

As the political and economic power of the masses grew, the activity of the national governments increased, and the increase was taken up almost entirely with shielding the working population from the worst consequences of industrial development. The worst blights of unregulated industrial worklife began to be attacked. The workday was shortened, women and children received more protection. Old people whose children could no longer care for them in the new urban setting were increasingly recognized as a responsibility of the state. The right of labor to organize was grudgingly granted. Unemployment insurance, health benefits, the regulation of workrules and the provision of jobs, the stimulation of the economy and the regulation of economic transactions became part of governmental activity. Increasingly, governmental power intervened in the economic process. Inevitably, impelled by its dependence upon mass support, the government became centrally concerned with the welfare of the population.

The Rejection of Socialism

Why is it, then, that demands for thorough government control of the economy have been rejected in the politics of national welfare? Why is it that democratic socialism has not caught hold in the mass democracies? Not one government of the many countries that have industrialized under the tutelage of bourgeois politics has taken over completely the running of the economy which is so important in shaping the lives of the people.

To be sure, government ownership and control of major enterprises and even of entire industries is not unknown. In Germany, Italy, and France, and particularly in Scandinavia, direct participation of government in the economy is extensive, but there and elsewhere government has played a supporting role to private industry. In the mass democracies it has most often been bankrupt, not healthy, industries that fall under and remain under government ownership.[1]

Political parties that have taken a strong stand advocating government ownership of the economy have not found favor with the voters. Most significant of all, such important socialist parties as those of Britain and Germany in hoping to return to power have jettisoned much of the core of the socialist creed: government ownership of most means of production.

Now that the masses appear to have the power to establish socialism, the appeal of socialism is dying. Why is it that the drive of the masses to protect themselves through government has stopped far short of its logical conclusion?

In part, the reason socialist programs failed at the very time the masses rose to political power is the fact, often forgotten, that in the politics of national welfare the masses do not rule alone but share power with the bourgeoisie. Particularly at the beginning of the period the bourgeoisie enjoys far greater power, making it possible for industrial leaders to defend successfully their traditional role in the economic sphere. Certainly the power position of the bourgeoisie has been of primary

---

[1] For example, the British coal industry.

importance in shaping governmental attitudes and actions toward the economy. It is due largely to the ability of the bourgeoisie to resist the encroachments of government that the governments of the mass democracies have only regulated the economies, not run them. And it is due to the power of the bourgeoisie that these governments have regulated the economies only in certain areas.

However, it is the success of the developed economies in raising mass living standards that has been the most important factor in preserving private control of the economy. The answer of capitalism to the threat of socialism has been to raise the standard of living of the masses, and especially since World War II its success has been so phenomenal that socialist parties have found their creed a positive obstacle to success. Why should the European worker who has acquired for the first time a car, a refrigerator, and his own home interfere with the control of those who have made this possible? Like their American counterparts before them, the rich industrial workers whose unions are the voice of labor are losing interest in tampering with the system that has granted them such wealth.

It is these three factors, then—bourgeois power in government, the success of government regulation rather than direct control in achieving some measure of the reform desired, and finally the immense rise in productivity and in mass living standards—that have diverted the initial drive of the masses to protect themselves through government and have stopped the movement far short of its logical conclusion.

The Growth of Executive Power

With the politics of national welfare, the center of political power shifts from the legislature back to the executive, from which it had moved to the legislature a century before. The reasons for this shifting back and forth seem fairly clear. In the stage of primitive unification, governmental power resided entirely in the crown and in the bureaucracy developed by the crown to oversee the possessions of the king.

With the coming of industrialization, political and economic power came to rest in the hands of two different elites, an unusual historical situation but one which the nineteenth century took for granted because of its obvious existence. The bourgeoisie gained its first political toehold in the legislature, and as a result the attacks of the legislature on the executive were in large measure attacks by the new elite on the old. If the executive was the stronghold of the aristocracy, then the executive was to be subordinated to the legislature, which was in the hands of the bourgeoisie.

Legislative control was favored in still another way. Under bourgeois politics, the main responsibility for creating capital was in private rather than public hands. Executive action in this prime area, therefore, was not the main job of government. Legislative supremacy was particularly fitting for a government whose main function was to permit rather than to direct.

As the masses sought political power, conditions changed again, for the people turned to the executive for protection against the hardships of industrial life—inevitably, since the legislature was the citadel of bourgeois power. The alliance between people and executive forms the inner core of the union between people and government as a whole in the politics of national welfare.

The vast expansion of governmental activity that has occurred with the coming of stage three is probably sufficient in itself to account for the growth of executive power, for the expansion has occurred primarily in the departments of defense and in the departments charged with regulating the economy and with putting into practice the plans of welfare. While the expansion of welfare programs is to be expected, it is not so natural—indeed, it is ironic— that the politics of national welfare should be so tempestuously and extravagantly military.[2] The reasons for the military emphasis of welfare politics probably lie more in the shifting international distribution of power than in internal changes.[3] Nevertheless, extremely high expenditure on arms programs is a major characteristic of stage-three governments, both democratic and totalitarian; this too has favored the growth of executive power.

The shift in power from executive to legislature and back again was much clearer in some countries than in others. In Germany, for example, executive power was never weakened as much as in the United States, and in Germany important features of welfare were part of the picture as early as the 1880s.

Interdependence of People and Government

The stage of the politics of national welfare finds the people of a nation more dependent than ever upon the national government for welfare assistance, for regulation of the economy upon which their jobs and their livelihood depend, and for defense against foreign attack. At the same time, it finds the national government more dependent than ever upon the bulk of its citizenry for its wealth and for its power. Rulers in the stage of primitive unification depend for support only upon a relatively small number of important lords or chiefs and landowners.

---

[2] The point is Rupert Emerson's.
[3] See A. F. K. Organski, *World Politics* (New York: Knopf, 1958), chap. xii.

Government in the politics of industrialization comes to depend also upon the support of the major industrialists, and under bourgeois politics the nation is enlarged to include the bourgeoisie as well as the aristocracy. In the politics of national welfare, the building of the nation is complete: it is enlarged to include virtually the entire population,[4] and the government comes to depend upon the support of the working, fighting, and voting public.

In the modern world, a nation's wealth and power are in large part determined by the economic productivity of its people and by the availability of its men for military service, and it is the government's degree of success in mobilizing its people to work and to fight for national purposes that serves as a measure of the development of any political system.

Again one is reminded that World War I marked a turning point. The decades preceding the war saw the first effective use of governmental power by the masses in defense of their economic lives, but it was in the war itself that the dependence of the state upon the masses of the population for its defense as well as for its wealth and power became obvious. Only in World War I were the military, economic, and manpower needs of modern war fully understood.

Thus the ties between people and state were forged in politics, in work, and in war. The people needed the vote to bring the government to protect them from economic hardship, and once enfranchised, they placed the government in a position of dependence upon their support. The workers in an industrial, nationwide economy required government regulation to keep that economy running

---

[4] Virtually, since it might be argued that the American Negroes, for example, are not yet fully included in the nation, since many are disenfranchised.

smoothly, and the government required the revenues produced both by individual taxpayers and by prosperity in business as a whole. The entire population depended upon the government to protect it from mass destruction in modern war, and the government could not provide that protection without mass armies and mass citizen support. With the politics of national welfare, the interdependence and the unity of people and government reach their highest point. With the next stage of political development they will begin to disintegrate.

THE NAZI STATE

Nazi Germany serves as a reminder that even within the stage of national welfare there are other possible alternatives to mass democracy. National socialism and mass democracy are at opposite poles of the world of developed politics. One might say that mass democracy represents the functioning of the ego in modern politics while national socialism represents the activity of the id. Yet the two are tied together by the fact that one political system arises out of the failure of the other, and by the fact that the welfare state serves as the base of both systems. In other words, the Nazi system was a welfare state that brought to the surface the irrational drives of man.

To date, democratic systems have proved extremely sturdy. Rarely have democratic systems fallen in fully developed societies, even in countries defeated in war and occupied by the enemy. The Weimar Republic is the only mass democracy which collapsed for internal reasons, and Germany is the only instance of a totalitarian dictatorship that arose from internal causes in a fully industrial society.

To speculate on the basis of one case is obviously rash, but one is all we have. This single example suggests that the consequences of a fundamental breakdown in mass democracy are different from what is generally believed. If the politics of national welfare in a mass democracy are no longer able to afford the population that minimum protection for which the welfare state had been created; if large-scale unemployment arises, if terrible inflation takes place, if conditions of want and privation obtain for large portions of the population—in short, if mass democracy fails—the result of the breakdown is not communism, as is often maintained, but something resembling National Socialism. The two are very different indeed. Let us look at the case history of Germany in more detail.

The Breakdown of Mass Democracy

Mass democracy came to Germany with the Weimar Republic in 1918. An essential element of the new political system was mass participation in politics and worker participation in some direction of the economy. The masses had come to power, and the system created was one that guaranteed them some freedom and a measure of protection against the worst hardships of industrial life. Democracy was crushed when the great depression made this guarantee inoperative.

As in the other mass democracies, the masses in the German republic did not rule alone. They shared power with the bourgeoisie, with the bureaucracy, the German army, even with the landowners. Each of these groups had won from the new political system important concessions and the guarantee that their old privileges would be maintained. The Weimar Republic, as in the case of other democracies, was based on a bundle of compromises. We shall never know whether the compromises could have survived *if* the massive inflation that traumatized the German economy in the early 1920s and the great worldwide depression of the early 1930s had not struck at the foundations of the German welfare state.

But strike they did, and the basic relationships upon which German democracy rested began to fall apart. Vast unemployment eroded the very core structure of the welfare state and severely strained the allegiance of the masses to democracy, for it demonstrated that this democratic government at least was unable to carry out its part of the bargain. The trade unions, a pillar of support for the Republic in its early years, were themselves weakened by a decline in membership and revenues that resulted from unemployment. The increasing idleness of the country's industrial plant weakened the confidence of the bourgeoisie in the new political system.

The breakdown of the German welfare state led those who had unwillingly agreed to share power with the masses to attempt to exclude them again from control. It was not alone the totalitarian parties, the Communists and the National Socialists, who worked for the end of mass democracy. Many wished for its death: the landed gentry, the army, the bureaucracy. Each had a hand in the death of the Weimar Republic.

Reconstitution of the Welfare State

The first thing the Nazis did after assuming power was to reconstitute the welfare state. People had to be put to work again; the industrial might of Germany had to be put to full use. Confidence in the economy had to be restored, German unity reaffirmed, and the loyalty of the people to the government re-established.

All this the Nazis did. The nation was put back to work; in four years unemployment dropped from six million to less than one million. Agriculture, prostrated by the

depression, was rejuvenated, farm prices rose, and fore-
closures for debt stopped. The entire industrial plant, so
long idled by the depression, began to hum.

There can be no doubt that the base of Nazi politics
was the politics of the welfare state. Vast social services
were instituted. We need not list them all; it is enough to
remember the vacations for workers, the maternity benefits, or the *Führer* shrieking at his engineers to design an
inexpensive car for the German people, a people's car.

With the Nazis in power the government was again fulfilling the major tasks of the welfare state: the protection
of the population against economic and social hardship.
In so doing, the Nazis re-established the basic unity of
the nation. It did not seem to matter that workers could
no longer organize or strike, or that peasants were once
more bound to the soil. It did not seem to matter that
taxes were high or that the product of the economy was
channeled largely into war goods. Each of the major
groups had obtained what it wanted most. The workers
worked. The farmers farmed, and sold their produce at
high prices. The bourgeoisie ran an industrial machine
at full throttle. There was no labor trouble, profits were
high, and the government was certainly aggressive about
finding new markets. The landed aristocracy and the
bureaucracy kept their old privileges. And the Army could
hardly keep pace with arming.

We shall never know how much of Germany's allegiance
to the Nazis was due to the dementia that had swept the
country and how much was due simply to the fact that in
fundamental ways, to most people, the Nazi state was
acting in the initial period as any successful welfare state
must act. It seems logical and reasonable to assume that
a good deal of the allegiance of the Germans to the Nazi
regime stemmed from the fact that economic and social

life had been brought back to the order and security which are the first items of the politics of national welfare.

What was different, of course, was that the welfare state had been put back together out of quite different elements, and the end result was total disorder and insecurity.

Irrationality and Self-Destruction

Gone were the humane qualities and the rationality that characterize the mass democracies. In their place terror and irrationality—even madness—held sway. Terror was an important ingredient in the forces that held the Nazi state together. The Nazis bullied, terrorized, and murdered their opponents. But terror alone does not sustain the kind of support they received. There is no question that the Nazis forced a minority of the German people to do their bidding, but there is also no doubt that a majority of the Germans were willing to do as they were told.

Extreme irrationality also marked the Nazi system, nowhere clearer than in the demented ideology of which racism was the core. The body of Nazi beliefs was both shapeless and incoherent. It was summarized by one high Nazi theorist:

> Blood against formal reason; race against purposeful rationality; honor against profit; unity against individualistic disintegration; martial virtue against bourgeois security; the folk against the individual and the mass.[5]

One is almost embarrassed to quote such imbecilities today.

---

[5] Ernst Krieck, quoted in Franz Neumann, *Behemoth* (New York: Oxford, 1942), p. 464.

Yet in the short run they were politically effective. The Nazi system was stronger because of them, for Nazism represented not only the conscious and rational desires of the Germans, which democracy had also represented; it also put to work the force of the irrational and deep-seated hostilities that the democratic system had run harmlessly into the ground. Once set in motion they proved powerful forces.

Anti-Semitism, which is quite prevalent today, was widespread and deeply held long before Hitler came on the scene, and his anti-Semitic rantings helped him reach the German masses and bring them to his side as no rational promise or argument could have done. Anti-Semitism helped unify the country behind Hitler's aggressive moves. For example, hatred of the Jews served as a substitute for class antagonism, which had become acute during the depression. Much of the divisive emotion behind other internal conflicts was also channeled into anti-Semitism. The Jews in addition served as an external enemy; Nazi propaganda charged that the Western democracies were Jewish-controlled plutocracies. Anti-Semitism thus served many functions for the Nazis.

Take another example of Nazi irrationality turned to a purpose. One of the pet hatreds of the Nazis was Marxism, yet Nazism was full of Marxist symbolism and slogans. The Nazi flag was red. To the Nazis, Germany was proletarian (which she was not) and a have-not nation (which she was even less) struggling against plutocracies for her rights (which was untrue). All of this was nonsense, but it helped tie the heavily Marxist working population to Nazism, for it turned the Marxist symbols to the Nazi cause.

Equally irrational was the extreme aggressiveness which eventually brought the Nazi system to its destruction.

Here again the roots of aggressiveness stretched back into German history, back before the Weimar period, deep into the German empire. But under National Socialism all the political and social institutions that could have acted as a brake on excessive aggressiveness were destroyed, and military aggression came to occupy a central place in the system.

A large *rentier* class, always a steadying hand in the actions of modern nations, had disappeared in the early 1920s. Parliament ceased to exist as an independent voice. Voters had no control at all over the direction of politics, and the economy of the nation was highly centralized and controlled by giant industries that badly needed the foreign markets Hitler promised to win them through war. It is ironic that the German General Staff was the only place where feeble attempts were made to stop Hitler from going to war, but the Army was worrying about timing, not peace.

Aggression was not peripheral but central to the Nazi system, for the whole economy, its prosperity, its full employment—indeed, the whole welfare structure rebuilt so quickly by the Nazis—rested upon rearmament and the preparations for war. Hitler re-established the German welfare state, revitalized the German economy, and restored German unity, but all for the purpose of plunging Germany into a war she could not win, for Hitler was mad, and the same forces that drove Germany to the greatest power in her history also drove her over the brink to destruction.

The self-destructiveness of the Nazis becomes obvious when one remembers that the countries Germany defied and attacked were much stronger than she and that the world had had previous proof of this in World War I. The irrationality is equally clear when one reflects that Germany today, defeated by the democracies she hated and split in two, is richer than at any time in Hitler's reign.

The case of Nazi Germany, although unique, is suggestive of what might happen in other welfare states should mass democracy collapse. Some very tentative hypotheses can be fashioned: (1) The breakdown of mass democracy leads to the immediate re-establishment of welfare politics. (2) The new system is undemocratic. (3) The new system attempts to meet some of the rational welfare needs of the masses, but at the same time it gives expression to the irrational drives that the previous rational system kept below the surface. And one is tempted to a last hypothesis: (4) There is something incompatible in trying to represent both the rational and the irrational forces within man in a political framework. The irrational forces take over and bring the whole system to destruction.

COMMUNISM AND WELFARE POLITICS

Communism in an industrialized country appears to present still another alternative form of the politics of national welfare. The shifts in Communist politics away from stalinism are in some respects parallel to the changes that occurred as the West shifted from bourgeois politics to mass democracy, though the differences are also significant.

A word of caution must be extended at the outset. A good deal of the evidence has yet to develop, for most of the Communist countries are still in the stage of industrialization. Furthermore, with the exception of the Soviet Union and China, the form and substance of politics in Communist nations today are shaped far more by the demands of the big Communist countries than by internal forces. Of all the Communist countries, only Russia has emerged as a fully industrial nation after having undergone industrialization Communist style, and Russia herself is still in the period of transition from stage two to stage three of political development. Thus Russia is just a beginner in the politics of national welfare. Nevertheless, her example provides some interesting suggestions of things to come.

It seems increasingly clear that the accomplishments of Khrushchev's era are not to be found so much in foreign policy (where his much-discussed departures brought grief to the Communist camp) as at home. There Khrushchev presided over the fundamental shift in the basic function of politics: from the facilitation of rapid accumulation of capital at almost any cost in human welfare to improvement of the welfare of the general population.

That this is the goal of the present rulers of the Soviet Union there can be little doubt. In a visit to Hungary in 1964 Nikita Khrushchev pinpointed the nature of Russian politics and the heart of his dispute with the Chinese in his own inimitable style:

> "There are people in the world who call themselves Marxist-Leninist and at the same time say there is no need to strive for a better life. According to them, only one thing is important—revolution.
>
> "What kind of Marxism is this?" he asked scornfully.
>
> "Communism will achieve little if it cannot give the people what they want," Mr. Khrushchev said, and he added:
>
> "The important thing is that we should have more to eat—good goulash—schools, housing, and ballet. How much more do these things give to the enlargement of man's life? It is worth fighting and working for these things."[6]

---

[6] *The New York Times* (April 2, 1964), p. 1, col. 4.

Much of Russia's conflict with the Chinese Communists stems precisely from the fact that Chinese politics is still stalinist while Russia has entered upon the politics of national welfare. The divergent ideologies of stage two and stage three are also causing a conflict within the Soviet Union such as might be expected during this transitional period. The decade since the death of Stalin has been a period of struggle between those who wished to follow the old policies and those who are seeking new ones. It is highly probable that the shift will not be completed for some time and that the two trends, one gaining strength and the other weakening, will be fundamental in Soviet politics for some time to come.

The differences between stage two and stage three in the Soviet Union are basically these: The repressive system that Stalin fashioned and headed for almost thirty years was correlated with a highly unproductive labor force and a peasant system hostile to the modern world. The difference between the politics of Khrushchev and that of Stalin rests not only on the differential sanity of the two leaders but also on the fact that Russia was already an industrial nation when Stalin died, and repression was becoming an impediment to further economic modernization.

One of the reasons for the recent Russian "thaw" and the greatly increased concern with the living standards of the Soviet people is that substantial increases in economic productivity were no longer possible through the politics of the past. For one thing, further growth of the urban labor force could not be brought about without a substantial improvement in housing, food, and greater availability of consumer goods in general. The government under Khrushchev attempted to raise mass living standards in all these ways, and, if this analysis is correct, Russian politics in the third stage of political development ought to be characterized by a firm continuation, not a decrease, of the present policy of raising the low standards of Russian life.

The full meaning of the politics of national welfare becomes apparent as one watches the Soviet government do for its people what the mass democracies have done for theirs—protect the population from the hardships of industrial life and create the higher living standards which provide the setting for further economic growth. This function is at the heart of the politics of national welfare.

An important difference between Russia and the West can be found, however, in the motive power behind the changes now occurring. In the West the new welfare function of government came into existence in response to demands of the masses, who had gained political power. In the Russian dictatorship, however, the same function is exercised not as a result of the demands of the population but as a result of the demands of the economy.

It begins to appear that any government in an economically developed country—democratic, Nazi, or Communist—if it wishes to obtain the full contribution that the population can make to the nation's wealth and power, must undertake the welfare function, must see that the economy runs at relatively full production, that there is relatively full employment, and that a large portion of the product is widely shared. All developed politics, then, are politics of national welfare.

Trend toward Democratization?

There remains an important debate concerning the meaning of the changes that are occurring in the Soviet political system. There has been a lot of speculation about future democratization in the Soviet Union as an expected result of the demands of the rapidly growing and increasingly powerful intelligentsia and managerial classes. It is sometimes argued that well-fed and well-educated people will demand and obtain not only more material advantages but also more freedom of inquiry, more freedom of discussion, and more control over their government.

It is certainly true that the Russians are liberalizing their political as well as their economic practices. The more obvious signs of repression are gone: most of the labor camps are closed, most forced labor abolished, the secret police have been subjected to tighter controls and shorn of many of their powers. Thousands of political prisoners have been rehabilitated, and there is increased official tolerance of divergent opinions and their expression.

If these are indeed the beginning moves toward genuine democratization—if Russia is fulfilling her part of Maxim Litvinov's prediction to President Roosevelt that Russia would move toward the right and the United States would move toward the left until they would not be far apart—the implications for the West and for the world are very great indeed. If Russia is indeed moving toward a political system not dissimilar in its fundamental operation from that of the Western democracies, it is perfectly plain that a new evaluation of communism, and of stalinism in particular, will be required. In such a case, stalinist politics would turn out to be nothing more than violent pressure to open a bottleneck so that industrialization could proceed more rapidly; there would be no evil after-effects, because once the country had successfully industrialized, its political and economic path would rejoin that of the Western nations. Communism, like fascism, would then prove to be nothing more than a deviation from the regular democratic pattern.

The idea is attractive, but I do not believe that this will prove to be the case. Those who believe in the democratizing power of economic growth rely perhaps too heavily upon such examples as the United States and Britain. Nazi Germany, after all, was also fully developed economically. It is ironic that in the United States, where economic determinism is intellectually a capital crime, there exists an abiding faith in economic forces and an implicit belief that if economic forces are left free to operate everything will turn out for the best. In the Soviet Union, on the contrary, where belief in economic determinism is dogma, no economic force is ever left unsupervised and uncontrolled by politics.

In any case, the American hope that economic wealth will lead the Soviet Union to democracy appears a bit of misplaced economic determinism. Let us accept once and for all that totalitarianism is compatible with a high standard of living and that high productivity is compatible with dictatorship. There is no reason why the concentration of power in the Soviet Union and the authoritarian character of government need change much in the decades ahead.

There probably will continue to be increased liberalization of government—less repression, less stifling dogma, more recognition of individual rights—but I see no likelihood of increased political control for the masses or of formal government responsibility to voters with a choice between competing groups of officials. This, after all, is the essence of political democracy and there are no steps in that direction to be seen. We should make a distinction between freedom and democracy. The two quite often go together, but they are not the same.

It is my belief that political democracy requires decentralization of economic power and its separation from political power, conditions which are surely lacking in the Soviet Union. The masses in the West struggled to win a voice in government in order to use political institutions to protect themselves from unregulated economic forces. For the Russian masses such possibilities were much more remote. In the days of greatest hardship the government and the economy of industrializing Russia were in the hands of the same small, unified elite and there was nowhere to turn for protection. Now that the days of hardship are past, there is no economic need for political democracy, for the welfare state is being created from above.

Finally, the trend toward automation, already beginning in the Soviet Union, should further increase the centralization of power and reinforce the identity of economic and political leadership, thus making the achievement of political democracy even less likely than it is at present. Indeed, automation will pose grave threats to democracy in the West as well.

STAGE FOUR

The Politics of

Abundance

VII

THE POLITICS
OF ABUNDANCE

With automation we cross the thin line that separates
stage three from stage four of political development. We
also cross the line between present and future. Our analysis of political development up to the present is complete.
Now we enter the realm of speculation.

I hasten to add that speculation about the future is
grounded at least to some degree in fact. The reader is reminded of a now-familiar thought: that the roots of the
present lie in the past and the roots of the future are dis-
cernible today if we dig in the proper place. But certain
evidence as to what will grow from these roots does not
exist.

A handful of nations—a small handful at that—are nearing the end of stage three and beginning the difficult
transition to a new variety of national politics. Perhaps in
retrospect we shall date the beginning of stage four in the
West at the time of World War II. It is probably not an

accident that the beginnings of new periods of politics are so often marked by war. In Western Europe the politics of industrialization arrived in a burst of wars culminating in the French Revolution and the Napoleonic Wars, and in Russia industrialization was ushered in by World War I and the Revolution. The politics of national welfare entered with World War I. Perhaps a new outbreak of international violence will set the stage for stage four, but let us adopt the more optimistic view that it has already begun.

This fourth stage of political development, as closely linked to automation as the second stage was linked to industrialization, may bring an end to the nation-state. Certainly it will force political leaders to deal with a new set of human problems. All of the political systems of the past have been concerned in one way or another with the problems of economic scarcity; the politics of stage four, however, will face the problems of abundance. The difference is revolutionary, and for this reason stage four is called *the politics of abundance*.

ASSUMPTIONS

The analysis that follows of the politics of stage four is based upon four assumptions about the economy, that there will be:

1. *Greatly increased productivity in the peacetime economy.* The efficiency of the already developed economies will surely increase through automation, and the rise in productivity should be sharper than any that has occurred to date. The automated systems that have already been installed or designed have proved immensely efficient, and there seem to be no fundamental technical reasons for believing that such efficiency will not increase

or that automation cannot be applied to additional areas of the economy. It is assumed therefore that the efficiency of automated systems will increase.

It is also assumed that, despite the resistance of opposing interests, automation will spread throughout the economy. Obviously the entire economy can never be automated, but the bulk of manufacturing probably can be. Purchasing, accounting, bookkeeping, record-keeping, most routine clerical jobs, and many lower-management decisions can and probably will be turned over to the computers of the future.

At the present time, automation of the peacetime economy has barely started.

2. *Increased efficiency of war machines.* As is often the case, new technology and new economic organization have received their first welcome and major stimulus in the production of weapons. Atomic power, radar, guided missiles, satellites, and space ships are technological developments more typical of stage four than of stage three. Warfare and defense as exercised by the largest and most powerful nations today are already highly automated. They will almost certainly become more so and the use of such automated systems will spread to other large, wealthy nations.

3. *Economic abundance.* It is a major assumption that the full utilization of the automated portions of the economy will result in an era of material abundance. For the first time in the history of man it will be entirely possible for the productive system to stay ahead of man's economic needs. This is hard to accept intellectually, for our whole conditioning has been to deal with problems of economic scarcity. Problems of scarcity will remain the major interest of the underdeveloped and developing nations for some time to come, but *for those nations in stage four* they will

be well on their way to solution. We have already seen tremendous strides in the creation of plenty in our own lifetimes. (Compare the Gross National Product or the living standards of the United States in 1900 with those of today, for example.) In agricultural production the United States has already achieved a surplus, though rational distribution and pricing would decrease it considerably.

Abundance will bring its own problems, of course, but there is no doubt that they will be preferable to problems of scarcity. From this point of view, it is nonsense to think of stopping automation.

4. *A smaller labor force.* The final assumption is that the spread of automation will mean large-scale displacement of men and women from the productive process by machines. As a result of the first industrial revolution, machines have taken over most of the unskilled jobs performed by human muscle. Now they will take over most of the routine jobs performed by human minds. Even middle-management jobs will be capable of being performed by machines, though management will probably protect its own position. Blue-collar workers and ordinary white-collar workers will not be in a position to protect the majority of their jobs.

No doubt the production of the new machines will create some new jobs, and no doubt there will be an expansion in professional and service occupations that do not lend themselves to automation. Finally, there will remain old-fashioned pockets of the economy which continue to function on the old basis, though such areas will be noncompetitive and badly paid.

It is not possible to say with accuracy what degree of total job displacement there will be, but in view of the potential of the machines it is hard to believe that the labor force will not shrink drastically. It is assumed here as a conservative estimate that from one quarter to one half of the present labor force will be displaced from paid employment once automation has reached its full development.

It must be acknowledged immediately that there is no agreement on the assumptions advanced here. In particular, disagreement centers on the matter of the displacement of labor by machines. This is true in part because the first three assumptions are desiderata while the fourth, of course, is not; here the battle rages. Economists and sociologists disagree bitterly and widely among themselves. There are those who argue that automation will create as many jobs as it destroys and that dislocation can be handled by relocation. I for one do not think that this will be the case, but there is no way yet to settle the argument.

A major problem lies in the fact that there is no clear-cut evidence one way or the other. Existing data do not clarify the relationship between rising productivity and falling employment, and it is certainly not clear how many people are losing jobs through automation. Estimates by responsible sources vary from 5,000 to 80,000 a week in the United States, and even here it is not known how many of these people find other jobs—or where. An even more basic source of uncertainty lies in the fact that automation itself is in its infancy. Even accurate data on the present would show us little about the future.

It must also be acknowledged that the range of possible institutional solutions to the problems raised by automation is wide. It is by no means certain that the changes in economic power, class structure, and government sketched in the following pages will, in fact, occur. Prediction is surely rash. Nevertheless it seems useful to set forth what appear to me to be the most probable changes. If this discussion stimulates disagreement, so much the better. At the least it will help focus consideration on important problems that must be solved.

THE PERIOD OF TRANSITION

Finally, the reader should be warned that the growth and expansion of automation are not inevitable. Before automation comes into its own, a difficult period of transition must be successfully traversed. This period, which lies immediately ahead for the United States and which will occupy at least the next fifty years, is highly interesting in its own right and deserves far more detailed study than it will receive here. In keeping with the broad scheme of this work, emphasis here will be on the patterns typical of stage four, which appear when automation has reached relatively full development. A word, however, should perhaps be said about the period of transition, for it will be characterized by its own changes and by its own problems.

During the transition period, increased productivity in automating industries will increase living standards for some while causing unemployment for others. In the economy there will be a decrease in the number of workers engaged in manufacturing and a great increase in the number employed in services. Indeed, such trends are already evident in the United States.

There should also be a decrease in the proportion of workers and product in competitive, profit-making enterprises and an increase in the proportion in non-profit enterprises such as education, government health services, and social work. This development in itself will produce great changes in the nature of the economy in the West and may in the end result in the loss of the free competitive market as a rationale for production and of prices as a primary means of allocating goods in what will continue to be an economy of scarcity.[1]

New mechanisms will also be developed for dealing with the faster rate of change. In the private economy there may well be a swing from the sale of goods to the rental of goods, with a consequent increase in the predictability of markets for the manufacturer who must plan far in advance of automated production.

An increased role for government can also be easily foreseen as the necessity arises for such services as a truly national employment service to help displaced workers find new jobs.

Political ferment aimed at stopping or controlling automation will also increase. Automation can indeed be stopped, but probably will not be. Past writers have generally underestimated the rapidity of technological and social change; I think that most present writers on automation are making the same mistake.

Let us turn, however, to the examination of stage four as it develops further, *assuming that the transition has been successfully made*. And as we do so, let the reader bear in mind the four assumptions about the economy: greatly increased productivity in the peacetime economy, increased efficiency of the war machine, economic abundance, and large-scale "non-employment."

CHANGES IN THE POWER STRUCTURE

Economic changes of great magnitude can be made only if the political system permits them to be made and presides over the distribution of the social "costs" of such major readjustment. Interests opposed to rapid automation

---

[1] The author is indebted to Victor R. Fuchs of the National Bureau of Economic Research for stimulating discussion of these transitional problems.

will naturally make every effort to enlist the national governments to prevent it, and groups that will suffer in the readjustment will turn to government to cushion the shock. Thus government will in one sense control the course of automation.

At the same time, automation will bring about significant changes in the power structure that underlies government, even in a democracy. These changes will have great repercussions in the functioning of national governments and will perhaps alter their form. Let us begin by looking at some of the shifts in power.

Concentration of Economic Power

First and most noticeable, there should be a sharp increase in the concentration of economic power in fewer hands. The economic demands of an automating economy would accelerate the tendency toward larger production units than has prevailed in the developed economies for almost a century. The cost of the new computers and self-regulated machinery in itself guarantees that only very large enterprises will find it economical to automate. A newly developed computer slated for delivery in 1966, for example, will have a monthly rental charge of $115,000. Once in possession of such machinery, the large firms will have a competitive advantage that should make it virtually impossible for their smaller competitors to stay in business.

Trends toward monopoly will be encouraged by the necessity for planned production if the giant systems of machines are to be used rationally. From the point of view of economic efficiency it would seem to make sense not only that there be at least close cooperation between the various manufacturers competing for the same market but also that there be some kind of organized control extending through the whole chain of related industries, from the supplier of raw materials to the final distributor to the buying public.

Automation, then, would encourage larger production units, outright monopolies or monopolistic agreements within each industry, and monopolistic controls extending from raw-material production to consumer distribution. All of these tendencies already exist, but they are consistently opposed and hindered by national governments such as those of the United States (though not the Soviet Union). Rapid automation would seem to require some easing up of government opposition to mergers and monopolies and perhaps a shift to some sort of price regulation as a means of protecting consumers from the dangers inherent in such concentration of economic power. Such regulation is already commonplace among monopolistic public utilities.

If automation comes to pass, economic power will be concentrated in still another way, for the power of management will expand while that of labor unions should diminish sharply as the men they represent are replaced by machines. Unions, of course, are well aware of this; the major opposition to automation today comes from organized labor. Even in its infancy, the head of the AFL–CIO has labeled automation "a curse." One can imagine what labor's attitude will be once automation begins to make serious inroads into employment.

It seems probable that labor unions will slow the pace of automation in the Western democracies—indeed, they have already done so. But they have not stopped the process, nor is it likely that they will be able to do so in the future. At most, unions can only protect those already employed. They probably will not be able to force management to replace each worker when he quits or retires (though they may be able to keep him on the payroll long after he is needed), and they cannot protect the people who are never hired because industry is able to increase production without hiring additional personnel. Automation promises to be the problem of the unhired people, and there is little that labor unions can do to prevent the occupations they represent from gradually disappearing.

It is possible, of course, that unions such as the automobile workers' and the steel workers' will expand to include at least the lower personnel who manage, program, and check the new machines. In this case a union might continue to exist as an important power in industry though with membership reduced and in different occupations than at present. There will no doubt be bitter battles over the classification of new positions opening up in automating industries with union shop agreements, management maintaining that the new personnel are engineers and management and the unions claiming that they are labor. However, even under optimum conditions it is difficult to see how organized labor can maintain anything approaching its present power in an automated society. The telephone system in the United States does not shut down during a strike, but continues to operate with supervisory personnel. Someday a strike will not shut down the steel or auto industries either, and the power of their unions—so heavily based on the ability to strike—will suffer accordingly.

New Class Structure

Automation would also bring great changes in the class structure, though probably not as dramatic as those produced by the original industrial revolution. Most obvious would be tremendous alterations in the occupational structure, with whole categories of jobs virtually disappearing. One can foresee, for example, a significant decline in the number of private managerial personnel because of economic concentration in large concerns, a vast increase in government personnel, a significant increase in certain categories of engineers and other technical workers, an expansion in such professions as teaching, social work, and medicine, and a drastic decline in the number of clerical workers, agricultural workers, and industrial workers, both skilled and unskilled.

The power structure would also be changed. The positions of greatest power would be those of top government and business management, as they are today, but the power of government would probably be much greater, for reasons to be explained below, while labor leaders would probably be excluded almost completely from major positions of influence.

There would also be new sources of wealth and a different distribution of wealth among the population. This is perhaps the most difficult matter of all to predict, for much will depend upon the degree to which socialism replaces private operation of the economy and upon government policies regarding taxation, price controls, and welfare measures to support the vast number of unemployed.

It seems safe to say that in an abundant society the entire class system will be oriented much more toward power and prestige and much less toward wealth as a basis for differentiation. Since power and prestige are more directly related to occupation than is wealth (which can be passed down for several generations or spread through such means as ownership of stock in corporations over which no direct control is exercised), one can expect continued high social mobility—both up and down—as individuals are promoted or demoted in the highly competitive scramble for the top positions. Marx was wrong; the abundant society will be far from classless.

Particularly sharp differences should separate those who work from those who do not. Presumably some means of supporting the permanently unemployed at a relatively high standard of living must be found, but they will surely lose out in power and in prestige. It seems likely that the "lower classes" of the automated society will be those who do not work, but it is also possible that unemployment will be spread throughout the social pyramid from top to bottom and that the choice to work at a paid job will be more a psychological than a social choice.

The whole distinction between working and nonworking members of society raises some extremely interesting problems which merit much more extended consideration than they will receive here. If indeed one quarter to one half of those who now work are no longer needed in the labor force, there will be great need of new values to give their lives some meaning. As my wife and I have written elsewhere:

> Modern man devotes his life to work. Not only his wages but also his social standing, his way of life, his friends, his amusements, and his self-respect are tied to the work he does. Men spend their lives and break their hearts scrambling for occupational success, not only for the money involved, but for power and prestige, for the approval of wives and neighbors, and as proof of their competence and their manhood.[2]

Such values would appear as necessary as ever for those who work in an automated society, perhaps even more necessary than at present if able individuals are to be made to prefer employment to well-paid leisure.

On the other hand, the same values would be absolutely useless—worse, they would be psychologically and socially

---

[2] Katherine Organski and A. F. K. Organski, *Population and World Power* (New York: Knopf, 1961), p. 23.

destructive—for those who do not work. Is half the population to strive and fail and consider itself misfit and rejected because it cannot find employment which does not exist? This hardly seems a reasonable expectation.

It seems more likely that new values (or old values) will appear that place a value on leisure and on personal qualities other than occupational success. It is interesting to speculate what these qualities might be. On the other hand, how are two contradictory sets of values to exist compatibly side by side? Will we be led to a society of Alphas and Gammas conditioned to two different ways of life? This indeed would be a revolutionary change in class structure and seems too farfetched to be considered seriously, but the problem of the unemployed remains.

GOVERNMENTAL CHANGES

One of the most significant changes to be expected from the rise of automation would be an increasingly close identification between government and industry. It seems inevitable that giant corporations such as we have envisaged would exercise great influence upon government. It seems equally unavoidable that government will increase its intervention in the operation of the economy, for no representative government can allow such great and concentrated economic power to be wielded by private hands for private purposes without, at the very least, extensive regulation in the common interest. Moreover, the need to coordinate the operation of huge private economic enterprises with the activity of the public sector of the economy will make it imperative that there be a good deal of planning as well as regulation and may lead some governments to take over directly certain key industries.

The result, which sounds somewhat paradoxical today, should be on the one hand increased control of government by businessmen and on the other hand increased governmental operation and control of the economy. In all probability there will be such an enlarged interchange of personnel between government and business that it will not be altogether clear whether big business is running the government or the government running big business.

In the end, the concentration of economic power in itself should prove more significant than the distinction between private and public economic power. The sharp narrowing of the number of men who make economic decisions combined with the close cooperation between private and public sectors of the economy and the large exchange of personnel between the two should make the distinction between private and public enterprise less meaningful than it is today.

Concentration of Political Power

The concentration of political power should also be marked in an automated society, for the control of the economy and the government will rest in the same few hands, and this new elite will find itself relatively freed from dependence upon the mass of the population.

Just as industrial leaders will no longer require the labor of masses of workers to keep the economy running, so governmental leaders will no longer require the active participation of the mass of the citizenry to make the nation rich and powerful.

The change should be particularly marked in the military sphere, where automated weapons of immense destructive power should remove the necessity for citizen armies. Large standing armies in peacetime are no longer a nation's best defense. Antimissile missiles and "second strike capability" are more important. If nuclear war should occur, the strike will be sudden and the major battles fought long before large armies can be drafted. In the absence of nuclear war, there will still be smaller conflicts, but large-scale armies are unnecessary in limited wars, fought as they are in fear and trembling of escalation.

Footsoldiers will probably always have their functions, but the main point is that in an automated future, citizens will have much less control over the decisions of war and peace, since the cooperation of most of them will not be required either to launch an attack upon an enemy or to retaliate. Indeed, we have already reached the point where a handful of men in any one of the several most powerful nations could start a world war if they chose.

The foundation of the welfare state, and in particular of mass democracy, is the mutual dependence of people and government. The government depends upon the masses to produce, to pay taxes, and to fight. The people in turn depend upon the government to regulate the economy, to protect them from economic hardship, and to guard them against foreign attack.

Automation will loosen and unbalance this mutual dependence, for while it decreases the dependence of the government upon the people for the execution of its policies, it will greatly *increase* the dependence of the masses upon the government—not only for defense and for the regulation of the economy but also for a guarantee that those who do not work shall nonetheless eat.

Problems for Democracy

It should be fairly clear that if the trends described above have been accurately foreseen, the prospects for a continuation of mass democracy are not good. In the past, decentralization of economic power and the separation of economic and political power have been the prerequisites of mass democracy.[3] The masses have used political institutions to protect themselves against the actions of the industrial elite, a situation clearly impossible if government and industry are closely identified. Furthermore, voters have had a choice (within a framework, but still a choice) between competing groups of politicians in large part because different parties could turn to different sources of economic power for support. If the entire economy becomes highly centralized, the political party supported by the industrial elite will have an overwhelming advantage.

The increasing independence of the elite from the people's services in the economy and the military forces also bodes ill for continued popular control, as does the probable direct dependence of the unemployed upon governmental support. Finally, the effect of splitting the population into a large, permanently leisured group and a hard-working, directing minority at the controls of government and industry can only be viewed as disastrous for democracy. It is likely that, even in such circumstances, some of the forms of mass democracy would be continued in the United States and in most of Western Europe, but how much actual popular control would continue to exist remains to be seen.

Expanded Welfare Measures

Oddly enough, the welfare state, so hard-won by the masses in the West, would probably continue in an automated society even if mass democracy perished or were diluted into meaninglessness. There are at least three reasons why national governments would probably continue to be heavily occupied in guaranteeing decent living

---

[3] Robert MacIver, *The Web of Government* (New York: Macmillan, 1947), chap. viii.

standards for the masses. Indeed, government would probably take a more direct hand than ever in providing services and paychecks for the public.

First of all, the production of abundance would make no sense unless living standards were raised and the abundance were widely shared. In the absence of such arrangements there would be no social reason for producing so many goods.

Second, to put the matter even more strongly, automation will not occur unless the public retains purchasing power to buy the enlarged production of industry. Governmental defense needs may keep a portion of the automated economy running, but an immense expansion of mass consumption will also be required if there are to be markets for the products of automated industry. Thus a high degree of mass consumption would be the concern not only of the masses themselves but also of the elite who are charged with running the economy and the government. The bulk of the common people may no longer be needed as workers or fighters, but they will still be needed to purchase the tremendous outpouring of goods and services.

Third, the maintenance of internal peace, mass loyalty to the government, and national unity will also require the provision of decent living standards for the masses, including the unemployed. It would be difficult if not impossible for any group to remain in power or for any system to remain in operation that permitted as much as a quarter of the population to live in destitution and uncertainty in the midst of plenty.

For all these reasons, the continuation of a wide distribution of wealth and of welfare measures by the government can be assumed even in the absence of popular democracy. The economic functions of government will in all probability be vastly expanded as the government seeks to regulate and control the economy more closely, and welfare measures will almost certainly be expanded as the government faces the task of providing for the needs of millions and millions of able-bodied nonworking citizens. The state will not wither away in this new stage of political development. Quite the contrary; it is likely that the amount and the complexity of political activity will increase.

Providing for the Unemployed

The problem of providing for the welfare of the permanently unemployed raises some particularly ticklish problems. In all of the welfare states, capitalist and Communist alike, practically the entire population is forced to work for a living, and the size and the nature of the living are related directly to the work performed. How is wealth to be distributed if a large part of the population no longer works? How is the increased wealth of the country to be passed on to the common people if many or most of them are not on any payroll?

The idea of a guaranteed wage for all, regardless of work, smacks of "something for nothing" and is apparently repugnant to Western values at the present time, but it is difficult to avoid the conclusion that some kind of government stipends, pensions, or expanded social security will be necessary if a large percentage of the population is displaced from employment by machines.

Perhaps the widespread ownership of stock would solve the problem of distributing income to those without paid employment, but unfortunately the people most likely to be thrown out of work by machines are not those most likely to purchase stocks and bonds. The shares would have to be given to them, in which case their income could not be rationalized by the assumption that they had given up the use of their capital. Could people legitimately be given government bonds simply by virtue of being citizens? Or does the answer lie in making many goods and services "free" (paid for by the government out of taxes or other revenues, as is the case with schools and socialized medicine)?

In the Communist world there exists at least the ideology for solving this problem—"from each according to his ability, to each according to his need." Communes would provide a form of economic organization in which all could consume although all did not produce, but the Communist world, too, is a long way from social organizations that would give reality to such a solution. The necessity for productive labor as almost the only form of social usefulness and the linking of different income to different work is emphasized among the Communist nations even more than it is in the West.

It is far easier to envisage arrangements far in the future than it is to work out the transition to them from existing practices and attitudes. All of the measures suggested here run counter to the dominant values of the present day and would surely be opposed by powerful interests. But the problem is real and if automation is to succeed, some solution must be found.

The problem is made more difficult by the gradual nature of most social change, automation probably included. Once we have achieved an age of economic abundance there will not be much quarrel about passing out a few dollars (or rubles) to those on the bottom of the economic pyramid, but in order to achieve economic abundance it will first be necessary to automate the major industries. In the process, large numbers of people will be thrown out of work *before* abundance is achieved, and in an economy of scarcity there is always great resistance to sharing with the have-nots. The problem of supporting the unemployed is not one to pose difficulties once automation is complete. The great problem is immediately ahead of us in the period of transition.

THE FUNCTIONS OF GOVERNMENT

As nations move into this fourth stage of political development, government will have two new functions to fulfill. First, it will be a major function of national government to make automation possible, just as it was the function of government in stage two to encourage industrialization in spite of the hardship and the social dislocation it caused.

The nature of the problem will be somewhat different this time, however. It will not be necessary to grant political power to those who wish to modernize the economy; they already possess it. No shift comparable to the shift from feudal landlords to the bourgeoisie will be required, for industrial leaders already have an important voice in governmental councils. Nor will it be necessary to make major social rearrangements to facilitate the accumulation of capital. The highly industrial economies of the welfare states generate enough capital as things stand to permit the installation of automated equipment. Nor will physical movements and social reorganization comparable to that produced by rural–urban migration be necessary. The hardships of the past need not be repeated for this new industrial revolution.

There will, however, be major groups whose interests will suffer in the shift to automation: small and even middle-sized businesses, small farmers, organized labor, and of course the great mass of clerical and agricultural workers, most of whom will either lose their jobs, be forced to seek new occupations, or continue the old work at reduced pay in marginal enterprises. To reach the age of plenty, the majority of the population will first have to undergo a transitional period of anxiety and unemployment; and unemployment, at least in the early years, will carry the consequences it carries today: loss of self-respect and loss of income. The pains of transition for the majority must be eased substantially through governmental action if automation is not to be stopped in its tracks by political and economic protest.

Let me repeat: the degree of automation foreseen here is in no way inevitable. It will take place only if the majority of the population will put up with the dislocations and the suffering of the changeover, for there is a profound difference between the power distribution in the industrial countries today and the situation when the Luddites smashed machinery in the first industrial revolution. At that time the people had no political power; today they do.

It is possible, of course, that the political power of the masses will never be used to oppose automation, particularly if the change occurs slowly and if only a minority are adversely affected at any one time. However, it would seem that organized labor in particular must be brought to share immediately in the benefits of automation if social protest is not to slow the process of change excessively.

Dictatorial systems such as that of the Soviet Union, it should be noted, will probably be able to automate their economies more rapidly, thanks both to their ability to override social protest and to their control of occupational selections.

The first function of government in stage four, then, will be to make automation possible by cushioning the adjustments for those who suffer in the vast social reorganization required. The second function will be to make an automated economy politically responsible.

In retrospect, it is relatively easy to describe the functions of government in past periods for what they were, but in thinking about the future it is always tempting to describe as necessary that which is merely desirable. Certainly it would be Utopian to insist that the governments of all, or even most, automated nations will be politically responsible in the sense of being democratic. Throughout the history of the nation-state, in all its stages of political development, democracy and its precursors have been only one of several alternative forms.

It does seem, however, that if the long-run interests of the nation are to be served, the immense concentrations of economic power produced by automation must be made responsible, if not to the masses, at least to the state. It is hard to see how such national or even international economic organizations could be permitted to be operated for private purposes alone. It is not enough to say that the masses would naturally be paid enough to allow them to consume the products of industry. There are other rights which government, in the politics of national welfare, has traditionally guaranteed. The successful operation of the economy and the maintenance of decent living standards for all are not the only goals of man, even in the most materialistic of societies. The awesome power of tomorrow's captains of industry must be controlled by more than voluntary public-mindedness. Some means must be found through which this power can be used to serve the interests of the nation and of all its people. This is the task of government.

Though the material welfare of the public will probably be assured by the governments of stage four whether they are democratic or not, there are other reasons for preferring mass democracy to an authoritarian political system. Authoritarian governments may be benevolent, but *need not be*. They may be reasonable in their approach to problems of war and peace but *need not be*. They may spare the common people unnecessary sacrifices, and then again they may not. Making a government accountable to the public for what it does imposes checks upon governmental activity both in matters of war and peace and in matters affecting the distribution of wealth. It assures a higher degree of common welfare *as the common people see it themselves* than does any other form of government.

It remains a major question, however, whether a democratic system can be maintained in the face both of a tremendous concentration of political and economic power in the hands of a small elite and of a virtual guarantee that welfare measures will be continued even in the absence of democracy. It comes down to this: if democracy is to be maintained in stage four of political development, it will be the result of conscious effort. The trends foreseen here all press in the opposite direction.

THE FORM OF GOVERNMENT

It is perhaps curious that democratic socialism, rejected as inappropriate in stages two and three of political development, should emerge as a likely form for the political system in stage four; or perhaps I should say that socialism emerges as a likely form and democratic socialism as desirable form. The reason for this belated preference for socialism lies in the difference of governmental functions at the various stages of development.

The function of government in stage two, it will be remembered, was to facilitate industrialization by protecting the accumulation of capital from the needs and demands of the masses, hardly a task for a democratic socialist government, though one that a socialist regime of the stalinist variety might perform. In stage three it was the function of government to protect the masses from the hardships of industrial life. This might appear more suitable for a socialist government, but let us keep in mind that in the West the bourgeoisie has retained considerable political power in stage three and has been able to defend itself against governmental attempts to control the economy. Moreover, in stages two and three the problem is still scarcity—the allocation of scarce resources and the creation of wealth.

The whole meaning of socialism, on the other hand, is centered not upon the creation of wealth but upon its distribution. This, of course, is precisely the major problem in stage four of political development. The major preoccupation of the politics of the time will be not the running of the economy and the production of wealth, but the immensely complex problem of distributing the economic abundance produced by the high efficiency of the economy. To this purpose a system of governmental ownership of the means of production is admirably suited.

Socialism also provides for an identity between government and industry which, as was suggested above, would probably be a natural outcome of automation in any case, though of course it would not be necessary to formalize the relationship or to make it as close as would government ownership of industry. In addition, government ownership and direction of the major automated enterprises would facilitate the national planning which would also be a logical outgrowth of automation.

Equally important, socialism *if democratic* would provide a bridge between ordinary individuals and the system of economic production by making that system ultimately responsible to the people not only as consumers but as voters. Such a bridge would be particularly important in a society in which a large leisured minority (or even majority) played no part in economic production and could easily become totally alienated from the mainstream of society.

To say that democratic socialism seems well suited to the tasks of government in an automated society is not, of course, to say that it will in fact become the dominant political form in stage four. There are problems inherent in the nature of socialism that may prevent it from being genuinely democratic—problems posed by the immense concentration of power in the hands of government. In addition, resistance to socialism is strong, particularly in the United States, and may well continue to be so on into the age of automation. It is possible, perhaps even likely, that in the United States private ownership, government regulation, and a close relationship between big business and big government will manage to cope with the problems of automation under *forms* that are not significantly different from those of the stage of national welfare. In the Soviet Union, the other major world power that faces automation in the relatively near future, the form of government is almost certain to be socialistic but not democratic. If these two giants automate their economies successfully under such differing political systems, the chances for democratic socialism may not be so great after all, for surely each will have a powerful influence upon the form of government adopted by other members of its bloc.

END OF THE NATION-STATE?

It is possible that blocs may replace nation-states, that United States of Europe and United Republics of Africa, Unions of this and Federations of that may become the dominant form of political organization in stage four.

If the efficiency of automated war machines is ever put to use in the full-scale nuclear war for which they have been designed, one of the first victims will surely be the nation-state. With the world in ruins, the survivors may well decide to place their hopes in some new and less explosive form of government.

Even without war there will be forces at work to expand the political unit. The needs of defense and the demands of trade are already pushing in this direction, and with automation the international character of these needs will grow. The new economies of scale will require the largest markets in which to distribute products and the largest community from which to draw investment. Such needs may make an anachronism of the nation-state, particularly among the smaller countries.

It may well be that the nation-state, built with such toil and flourishing as it is today, contains in its heart the seeds of its own destruction. As stage three has brought the nation to its full development, so stage four may bring its short and violent life to an end.

VIII

THE CHOICE
OF NATIONS

This, then, is the course of nations: a struggle for unity; the steep, hard climb of industrialization; a turn to common welfare and, for some, democracy; and finally automation and the battle to make it a blessing instead of a curse.

No nation can skip these stages, leap straight from stage one, for example, into stage three, or skip two and three altogether, for the national government has important work to do at each stage and by executing its function at one stage lays the necessary groundwork for the next. Without primitive unification, a nation cannot industrialize. Without industrialization it cannot provide decent living standards and mass democracy. Without a society of high consumption it cannot have automation.

It can, of course, speed up the pace, condense the stages, even overlap them and start on one task before the last is finished. The world today is in a hurry, and those who started last seem anxious to reach—or at least not lose sight of—the nations that started so long ago and arrived at their own goals in a solid and leisurely fashion.

Nations also can choose, as they hurry along, which path to follow, for the nations ahead have left clearly blazed trails. The choices in stage one have largely been made: the choice, for example, of independence over colonial status, of narrow nationalism over regional federation. As they enter stage two, however, they must decide whether to industrialize in the bourgeois tradition, to take the stalinist short cut with its promise of speed and its heavy price, to take the syncratic detour, or to find a new path of their own. Stage three presents the choice of communism, mass democracy, or irrational totalitarianism, and the choices for stage four are still wide open. The choices nations make will be of great importance both for their future and for ours. Let us see if we can locate some of the determinants of the choice.

First, a word of warning. Prediction of the exact course for any particular nation assumes a knowledge of all the significant variables determining that course. This book makes no attempt to locate all the variables. It does not, for instance, consider the effect of external influences upon the choice of political system, although such influences may be decisive. Consider the case of Hungary or postwar Japan. Nor does it identify all the many subtle variables included in the national culture. What, for example, caused bourgeois democracy to originate in Western Europe or syncratic systems to be limited thus far to Latin cultures? Much ground remains for further study.

We can, however, trace the background against which these changes and differences occur and suggest some of the points at which one choice becomes more likely than another.

CHOICES FOR INDUSTRIALIZATION

All of the nations that industrialized in the nineteenth century followed the bourgeois pattern, while all the major countries that have industrialized in the twentieth century have had at least a protracted period of totalitarian rule at crucial points in their modernization. What is the setting in which this rejection of bourgeois democracy has taken place? Is it the trend of the future or simply a coincidence of history?

Comparing in broad terms the situation of the bourgeois nations with that of the later stalinist and syncratic states, one is struck by certain obvious contrasts. Stalinism has appeared only in very poor countries at a very low level of economic modernization. Syncratism has appeared only after bourgeois politics has already brought the nation to a fairly high level of economic advance. Nations industrializing under bourgeois democracy obviously have made the whole transition from poor peasant agriculture to rich industrial status without turning to totalitarianism.

If we consider bourgeois democracy as the mainstream of industrialization—and the idea is not altogether biased if we remember that most of the world's present industrial nations arrived by that route—it appears that there are two points in the process at which a nation is most likely to go astray. One is at the very beginning.

When the nation is still at a very low level of economic development there are at least two factors that make industrialization extremely difficult: the power position of the traditional elite and the general low productivity. Where a traditional elite is firmly entrenched, in full control of the government and of the economy, rapid industrialization is simply not possible. Such a nation has two choices: to overthrow such an elite or to postpone industrialization until the slow growth of the tiny industrial sector has gradually undermined the power of the preindustrial elite.

The latter alternative was that of the bourgeois democracies, the former that of the stalinist states. It may, of course, be possible to overthrow the landed aristocracy, even in violent revolution, without becoming a stalinist state in the Marxist-Leninist tradition, but at present the only major ideology preaching such overthrow is Marxism, especially Marxism of the Chinese (or stalinist) variety. It stands to reason, then, that men determined to industrialize extremely backward nations *in a hurry* will find stalinism most attractive, unless some new variety of politics is developed.

Even where the men who would lead the drive for industrialization prefer to do so under stalinism, their rise to power is far from assured where the opposing power of the traditional elite (and the fledgling private industrialists) is great. The overthrow of an agricultural elite is not likely, precisely because the elite *is* so well entrenched—unless its position is severely weakened by a collapse of the agricultural society it leads. This is precisely what happened, in both Russia and China, where wars against modern, industrial nations strained the old society to the breaking point.

The optimum conditions for the rise of a stalinist system seem to include a low level of economic modernization *plus* a strongly entrenched landed aristocracy *plus* a desire by the would-be new elite to industrialize rapidly *plus* a collapse of the old system in war.

The probabilities of a turn to stalinism may be somewhat less for some of the new nations, where a major fraction of the ruling elite consists of government officials who are modern intellectuals and the traditional elite consists of local chieftains rather than large landowners. Colonial rule and departure have had the fortunate outcome of granting governmental power to a modern elite without the necessity of ousting the old aristocracy by force. The traditional elite still retains a strong position, however, and continues to offer obstacles to those who wish to modernize the nation.

Once in power, the new industrializers of any extremely underdeveloped country face other problems that predispose them to reject bourgeois solutions in favor of stalinism. The general level of economic productivity is so low that the rapid accumulation of capital is possible only if the government directs it, and the general level of poverty is so great that further sacrifices can be wrung out of ordinary citizens only by totalitarian methods. Thus even benevolent bureaucrats of amiable intentions may eventually be led to stalinism.

The second point at which a nation is most likely to turn from bourgeois industrialization can be located again with reference to the level of economic modernization and, more specifically, the relative power of the agricultural and the industrial elites. It comes in the middle of the industrialization process, at that point where the power of the industrialists is almost but not quite equal to that of the landowners. The danger here is of a turn to syncratic politics.

Such danger may be avoided in some of the new nations (as in Africa) where modern bureaucrats drawn from the intelligentsia have achieved control of the government before the rise of a powerful landlord class. In much of Asia and Latin America, however, the power of the landowning elite is great.

The relatively equal distribution of power between the two elites in such countries makes it possible for them to agree on the "syncratic compromise," and the relatively high level of industrial development makes the compromise workable, for the economy is rich enough to permit the industrialists to continue to expand industry while drawing their capital mostly from the industrial sector.

Here again, there is no certainty that a syncratic system will arise simply because a nation stands at this point of its development. In the bourgeois democracies, the agricultural elite allowed the moment of possible compromise to slip by, in part because the pace of change was slow and in part because it could not foresee the eventual outcome in which it would be totally eclipsed. Unaware of the dangers, the agricultural elite began to share its power and was slowly but surely dislodged. Much also depends upon the strength of the threat from below, for in the syncratic nations it has been this threat that drew the two elites together.

The optimum conditions for a syncratic system to arise, therefore, include a strong landowner aristocracy *plus* a relatively high level of economic development with the industrial elite almost as strong as the agricultural elite *plus* an awareness on the part of the agriculturalists that they are losing power *plus* a willingness of the industrialists to compromise. The willingness to compromise has generally been stimulated by a strong threat from below, which has in turn been generated by industrial expansion followed by a period of retrenchment resulting from depression or readjustment after a war. These conditions seem somewhat rarer in the world today than those favorable to stalinism, but the possibility of their arising remains.

There are two other factors that operate in a way not altogether favorable to the future development of bourgeois politics. One, to which we have already alluded, is the speed of change. Consider first the speed of economic and social change *desired* by those who wish to modernize the country. Those who desire extremely rapid change at an early point in the nation's economic development are predisposed toward stalinism, because of the necessity for overthrowing the traditional elite instead of waiting for it to lose power.

We must also consider the actual rate of change. At the beginning of industrialization, rapid development greatly increases the difficulty of accumulating capital and increases the likelihood of government centralization of the economy and of totalitarian repression of the common people. Later in the industrialization process, rapid change heightens the awareness by the elites of their changing power position and encourages the agricultural elite to put up resistance, thus foreclosing the possibilities of that gradual and peaceful transfer of power from one elite to the other that characterized bourgeois industrialization.

The difficulty, of course, is that rapid industrialization is almost universally desired today by important groups within the underdeveloped nations. It is nothing new for nations to adopt the accomplishments of their neighbors as goals for themselves. In the eighteenth century, the fact that England had clearly passed France in modernization was a matter of anxiety to France, despite the fact that she was a rich and powerful nation. But today, when the differences in levels of economic development are greater than they have ever been before in human history and when even the most backward of lands has been exposed to comparison with its colonial masters, the felt need of hastening the pace of change in the underdeveloped countries is tremendous. Indeed, some of the aspirations are beyond realization by any political system known to man.

The second factor which operates against the prospects for bourgeois democracy is the degree of politicization of the masses. Under bourgeois politics the masses of the citizenry had little interest, knowledge, or power in politics until industrialization was almost completed. Though they suffered at the hands of private industry they did not revolt, for they knew no alternative. The industrializers, aided by a favorable government framework, were able to hold down mass consumption without the erection of vast, repressive government machinery.

In underdeveloped areas today, however, there is an increasing tendency to politicize the masses even before the beginnings of industrialization. Political parties and universal suffrage are used as means for unifying the country, but at the same time they arouse in the masses an interest in the political life of the nation and an illusion of governmental protection against hardship. High politicization before a country is industrialized favors a dictatorial system, for it places directly upon government the responsibility of imposing low consumption upon the masses and of keeping them under control.

CHOICES FOR THE WELFARE STATE

Stage three, in contrast to stage two, appears a very stable period in the political growth of nations. Most of the bourgeois democracies have evolved in an orderly fashion into mass democracies in stage three, as have the syncratic states, while the stalinist nations are evolving into Communist welfare states. Thus the major determinants of the form of politics in stage three appear to lie in the choice made for stage two.

There are, to date, no examples of Communist states forsaking communism of their own volition, nor do I find any clear indications that they are evolving into mass democracies.

Mass democracy seems also to be a most sturdy type of governmental system, capable of surviving the shocks of two world wars. Indeed, with the exception of Czechoslovakia and Germany, not a single mass democracy has disappeared. Even in these cases the causes of change were not political malfunctions but external force in the one case and failure of the economic system in the other.

The established mass democracies would seem to be safe unless they suffer economic breakdown or conquest. For the new nations, the chances of evolving into mass democracies will depend upon the choices they make in stage two.

CONCLUSION

Let the prophet beware of the future, for it ever unfolds new variety to confound the most careful prediction. Nothing I have written is intended to exclude the possibility of new forms of national politics. Nations faced with choices that seem to us narrow and even predetermined may break through the restrictions and invent new forms. Indeed, let us hope that they do.

Yet one is struck by the melancholy fact that analysis based on the factors to which we have devoted most attention does not seem particularly favorable to the prospects for bourgeois industrialization and mass democracy. If low levels of development, strength of traditional elites, high speed of change, and high politicization of the masses do indeed form a hostile setting for bourgeois politics and consequently for later mass democracy, there is trouble ahead, for all these conditions are widespread.

The mind resists the conclusions that must obviously be drawn from what has been written here. I feel, myself, that conclusions are entirely premature. We understand too little of what has happened, and too much of the future is still beyond the horizon. Yet we are duty-bound to consider the warning made earlier in this chapter. All of the nations that industrialized in the nineteenth century chose the path of bourgeois politics; the important ones that have industrialized in the twentieth have turned to totalitarianism. This alone provides much food for thought.

Selected Bibliography

The short list of books and essays which appears below represents some of those which have impressed me most in the years I have been working on this book.

Almond, Gabriel A., and James S. Coleman, eds., *The Politics of the Developing Areas* (Princeton, N.J.: Princeton University Press, 1960).

Carr, E. H., *Nationalism and After* (New York: Macmillan, 1946).

Hagen, Everett E., *On the Theory of Social Change* (Homewood, Ill.: Dorsey Press, 1962).

Kautsky, John H., *Political Change in Underdeveloped Countries* (New York: John Wiley, 1962).

Mannheim, Karl, *Ideology and Utopia* (New York: Harcourt, Brace, 1946).

Rostow, W. W., *The Stages of Economic Growth* (Cambridge, Eng.: Cambridge University Press, 1961).

Schumpeter, Joseph A., *Capitalism, Socialism and Democracy*, 3d ed. (New York: Harper and Bros., 1950).

Silvert, K. H., ed., *Expectant Peoples: Nationalism and Development* (New York: Random House, 1963).

Staley, Eugene, *The Future of Underdeveloped Countries: Political Implications of Economic Development* (New York: Harper and Bros., 1954).

Truman, David B., *The Governmental Process* (New York: Alfred A. Knopf, 1951).

I. On the Stage of the Politics of Primitive Unification

Almond, Gabriel A., and James S. Coleman, eds., *The Politics of the Developing Areas* (Princeton, N.J.: Princeton University Press, 1960).

Apter, David E., *The Political Kingdom in Uganda. A Study in Bureaucratic Nationalism* (Princeton, N.J.: Princeton University Press, 1961).

——, *The Gold Coast in Transition* (Princeton, N.J.: Princeton University Press, 1955).

Ashford, Douglas E., *Political Change in Morocco* (Princeton, N.J.: Princeton University Press, 1961).

Benda, Harry J., "Non-Western Intelligentsias as Political Elites," *The Australian Journal of Politics and History*, VI, No. 2 (November, 1960).

Blanksten, George I., "Political Groups in Latin America," *The American Political Science Review*, LIII, No. 1 (March, 1959).

Bretton, Henry L., "Current Political Thought and Practice in Ghana,"

Selected Bibliography

The American Political Science Review, LII, No. 1 (March, 1958).

Carr, E. H., *Nationalism and After* (New York: Macmillan, 1946).

Deutsch, Karl W., *Nationalism and Social Communication* (Cambridge, Mass.: Massachusetts Institute of Technology Press, 1963).

———, "The Growth of Nations," *World Politics*, V (January, 1953).

Dupree, Louis, "Tribalism, Regionalism, and National Oligarchy: Afghanistan," in K. H. Silvert, ed., *Expectant Peoples: Nationalism and Development* (New York: Random House, 1963).

Eisenstadt, S. N., "Sociological Aspects of Political Development and Cultural Change," *Economic Development and Cultural Change*, V, No. 4 (July, 1957).

Emerson, Rupert, "Paradoxes of Asian Nationalism," *The Far Eastern Quarterly*, XIII, No. 2 (February, 1954).

———, *Political Modernization, The Single Party System* (Denver: The Social Science Foundation and Department of International Relations, University of Denver, 1964).

———, *From Empire to Nation* (Cambridge, Mass.: Harvard University Press, 1960).

Hanson, Simon, *Economic Development in Latin America* (Washington, D.C.: Inter-American Affairs Press, 1951).

Heckscher, Eli F., *Mercantilism*, rev. ed., 2 vols. (London: Allen & Unwin, 1955).

Johnson, John J., *The Military and Society in Latin America* (Stanford, Calif.: Stanford University Press, 1964).

Karpat, Kamal, *Turkey's Politics* (Princeton, N.J.: Princeton University Press, 1959).

Khadduri, Majid, "The Role of the Military in Middle Eastern Politics," *The American Political Science Review*, XLVII, No. 2 (June, 1953).

Kling, Merle, "Toward a Theory of Power and Political Instability in Latin America," *The Western Political Quarterly*, IX, No. 1 (March, 1956).

Lerner, Daniel, *The Passing of Traditional Society* (Glencoe, Ill.: Free Press, 1958).

Lerner, Daniel, and Richard D. Robinson, "Swords Into Plowshares: The Turkish Army as a Modernizing Force," *World Politics*, XIII, No. 1 (October, 1960).

Lichtblau, George E., "The Politics of Trade Union Leadership in Southern Asia," *World Politics*, VII, No. 1 (October, 1954).

Lieuwen, Edwin, "The Military: A Revolutionary Force," *The Annals of the American Academy of Political and Social Science*, CCCXXXIV (March, 1961).

———, *Arms and Politics in Latin America* (New York: Frederick A. Praeger, 1960).

Lockwood, William W., "Japan's Response to the West: The Contrast with China," *World Politics*, IX, No. 1 (October, 1956).

Marshall, Charles B., "Reflections on a Revolution in Pakistan," *Foreign Affairs*, XXXVII, No. 2 (January, 1959).

Nolte, Richard H., "From Nomad Society to New Nations: Saudi Arabia," in K. H. Silvert, ed., *Expectant Peoples: Nationalism and Development* (New York: Random House, 1963).

SELECTED BIBLIOGRAPHY

Pauker, Guy J., "Southeast Asia as a Problem Area in the Next Decade," *World Politics*, XI, No. 3 (April, 1959).

Pye, Lucian W., *Politics, Personality and Nation Building* (New Haven, Conn.: Yale University Press, 1962).

Rustow, Dankwart A., "The Army and the Founding of the Turkish Republic," *World Politics*, XI, No. 4 (July, 1959).

————, *Politics and Westernization in the Near East* (Princeton, N.J.: Princeton University Center for International Studies, 1956).

Safran, Nadav, *Egypt in Search of a Political Community* (Cambridge, Mass.: Harvard University Press, 1961).

Schachter, Ruth, "Single-Party Systems in West Africa," *The American Political Science Review*, LV, No. 2 (June, 1961).

Silvert, K. H., *A Study in Government: Guatemala, Part I* (New Orleans: Middle American Research Institute, Tulane University, 1954).

United Nations, Department of Economic Affairs, *Economic Development of Latin America 1953* (New York: United Nations, 1954).

Wiener, Myron, *The Politics of Scarcity: Public Pressure and Political Response in India* (Chicago: The University of Chicago Press, 1962).

Wriggins, Howard, *Ceylon* (Princeton, N.J.: Princeton University Press, 1960).

II. On the Stage of the Politics of Economic Growth

(a) On Bourgeois Politics:

Ashton, Thomas S., *An Economic History of England: The 18th Century* (London: Methuen, 1955).

————, *The Industrial Revolution 1760–1830* (New York: Oxford University Press, 1948).

————, *An Eighteenth-Century Industrialist* (Manchester: Manchester University Press, 1939).

Beckmann, George M., *The Modernization of China and Japan* (New York: Harper and Row, 1962).

Brontë, Charlotte, *Jane Eyre* (New York: Modern Library, 1950). First printed in 1847.

Cole, G. D. H., and Raymond Postgate, *The British [Common] People 1746–1946* (New York: Barnes and Noble University Paperbacks, 1961).

Dulles, Foster R., *Labor in America* (New York: Thomas Y. Crowell, 1949).

Dunham, Arthur L., *The Industrial Revolution in France, 1815–1848* (New York: Exposition Press, 1955).

Engels, Friedrich, *The Conditions of the Working Class in England*, edited by W. O. Henderson and W. H. Chaloner (Oxford: Basil Blackwell, 1958).

Florence, P. Sargant, *Industry and the State* (London: Hutchinson's University Library, 1957).

Josephson, Mathew, *The Robber Barons* (New York: Harcourt, Brace and World, 1962).

Letwin, William, ed., *Documentary History of American Economic Policy Since 1789* (Garden City, N.Y.: Doubleday, 1961).

Lockwood, William, *The Economic Development of Japan* (Princeton, N.J.: Princeton University Press, 1954).

Selected Bibliography

——, "Japan's Response to the West: The Contrast with China," *World Politics*, IX, No. 1 (October, 1956).

Pipkin, Charles W., *Social Politics and Modern Democracies*, 2 vols. (New York: Macmillan, 1931).

——, *The Idea of Social Justice* (New York: Macmillan, 1927).

Toynbee, Arnold, *The Industrial Revolution* (Boston: Beacon Press, 1956).

Ward, Robert E., and Dankwart Rustow, eds., *Political Modernization in Japan and Turkey* (Princeton, N.J.: Princeton University Press, 1964).

Wendel, Hugo C. M., *The Evolution of Industrial Freedom in Prussia 1845–1849* (Allentown, Pa.: H. Ray Haas, 1918).

(b) On Stalinist Politics:

Bergson, Abram, ed., *Soviet Economic Growth* (Evanston, Ill.: Row, Peterson, 1953).

——, *The Real National Income of Soviet Russia Since 1928* (Cambridge, Mass.: Harvard University Press, 1961).

——, and Simon Kuznets, *Economic Trends in the Soviet Union* (Cambridge, Mass.: Harvard University Press, 1960).

Brzezinski, Zbigniew K., *The Permanent Purge* (Cambridge, Mass.: Harvard University Press, 1956).

Churchill, Winston, *The Second World War*, Vol. IV, *The Hinge of Fate* (London: Cassell, 1951).

Deutscher, Isaac, *Russia in Transition and Other Essays* (New York: Coward-McCann, 1957).

——, *Stalin: A Political Biography* (New York: Oxford University Press, 1949).

Dobb, Maurice, *Soviet Economic Development Since 1917* (New York: International Publishers, 1948).

Ehrlich, Alexander, *The Soviet Industrialization Debate 1924–1928* (Cambridge, Mass.: Harvard University Press, 1961).

Friedrich, Carl J., and Zbigniew K. Brzezinski, *Totalitarian Dictatorship and Autocracy* (Cambridge, Mass.: Harvard University Press, 1956).

Grossman, Gregory, "National Income," in Abram Bergson, ed., *Soviet Economic Growth* (Evanston, Ill.: Row, Peterson, 1953).

Hubbard, L. E., *Soviet Labour and Industry* (London: Macmillan, 1942).

Hughes, T. J., and D. E. T. Luard, *The Economic Development of Communist China, 1949–1960*, 2d ed. (London: Oxford University Press, 1961).

Inkeles, Alex, and Raymond A. Bauer, *The Soviet Citizen, Daily Life in a Totalitarian Society* (Cambridge, Mass.: Harvard University Press, 1959).

Kaplan, Norman, "Capital Formation and Allocation," in Abram Bergson, ed., *Soviet Economic Growth* (Evanston, Ill.: Row, Peterson, 1953).

Kingsley, Susan M., and Mildred Fairchild, *Factory, Family and Woman in the Soviet Union* (New York: G. P. Putnam's Sons, 1935).

Koestler, Arthur, *Darkness at Noon* (New York: Signet, 1961).

Lorimer, Frank, *The Population of the Soviet Union* (Geneva: The League of Nations, 1946).

SELECTED BIBLIOGRAPHY

Milbank Memorial Fund, *Population Trends in Eastern Europe, the USSR and Mainland China* (New York: Milbank Memorial Fund, 1960).
Moore, Barrington, *Terror and Progress USSR* (Cambridge, Mass.: Harvard University Press, 1954).
———, *Soviet Politics: The Dilemma of Power* (Cambridge, Mass.: Harvard University Press, 1950).
Tang, Peter S. H., *Communist China Today*, 2d ed., Vol. I (Washington, D.C.: Research Institute on the Sino-Soviet Bloc, 1961).
Wiles, P. J. D., *The Political Economy of Communism* (Cambridge, Mass.: Harvard University Press, 1962).

(c) *On Syncratic Politics:*

Alexander, Robert J., *Labor Relations in Argentina, Brazil, and Chile* (New York: McGraw-Hill, 1962).
———, *Prophets of the Revolution* (New York: Macmillan, 1962).
Argentina 1930–1960 (Buenos Aires: SUR, 1961).
Blanksten, George I., *Perón's Argentina* (Chicago: The University of Chicago Press, 1953).
Carocci, Giampiero, *Storia del Fascismo* (Milano: Garganti, 1959).
Casucci, Costanzo, *Il Fascismo* (Bologna: Società Editrice Il Mulino, 1962).
Finer, Herman, *Mussolini's Italy* (New York: Henry Holt, 1936).
Guérin, Daniel, *Fascism and Big Business* (New York: Pioneer Publishers, 1939).
Issawii, Charles, *Egypt at Mid-Century* (London: Oxford University Press, 1954).
Johnson, John J., *Political Change in Latin America* (Stanford, Calif.: Stanford University Press, 1958).
La Palombara, Joseph A., *The Italian Labor Movement: Problems and Prospects* (Ithaca, N.Y.: Cornell University Press, 1957).
———, "I Gruppi d'Interesse in Italia," *Studi Politici*, VII (January–March 1960).
Lipset, Seymour Martin, *Political Man* (Garden City, N.Y.: Doubleday, 1959).
Portnoy, Leopoldo, *Análisis Crítico de la Economía Argentina* (Buenos Aires: Fondo de Cultura Economica, 1961).
Rossi, Ernesto, *Lo Stato Industriale* (Bari: Editori Laterza, 1953).
Salvatorelli, Luigi, and Giovanni Mira, *Storia del Fascismo* (Rome: Edizioni di Novissima, 1952).
Salvemini, Gaetano, *The Fascist Dictatorship in Italy*, Vol. I (New York: Henry Holt, 1927).
———, *Under the Axe of Fascism* (New York: The Viking Press, 1936).
Sartori, Giovanni, ed., *Il Parlamento Italiano, 1946–1963* (Naples: Edizioni Scientifiche Italiane, 1963).
Silvert, K. H., "The Costs of Anti-Nationalism: Argentina," in K. H. Silvert, ed., *Expectant Peoples: Nationalism and Development* (New York: Random House, 1963).
Sturzo, Don Luigi, *Italy and Fascismo* (London: Faber and Gwyer, 1926).
Virgili, F., *L'Italia Agricola Odierna* (Milano: Hoepli, 1930).

Selected Bibliography

Warriner, Doreen, *Land Reform and Development in the Middle East* (London: Royal Institute of International Affairs, 1957).
Weil, Felix J., *Argentine Riddle* (New York: John Day, 1944).
Whitaker, Arthur P., *Argentine Upheaval* (New York: Praeger, 1956).

III. On the Stage of the Politics of National Welfare

Bullock, Alan, *Hitler—A Study in Tyranny* (New York: Harper & Row, 1952).
Ebenstein, William, *The Nazi State* (New York: Farrar & Rinehart, 1943).
Friedrich, Carl J., and Zbigniew K. Brzezinski, *Totalitarian Dictatorship and Autocracy* (Cambridge, Mass.: Harvard University Press, 1956).
Galbraith, John K., *American Capitalism* (Boston: Houghton Mifflin, 1962).
———, *The Affluent Society* (Boston: Houghton Mifflin, 1962).
Inkeles, Alex, and Raymond A. Bauer, *The Soviet Citizen: Daily Life in a Totalitarian Society* (Cambridge, Mass.: Harvard University Press, 1959).
Kerr, Clark, John T. Dunlap, Fredrick H. Harbison, and Charles A. Myers, *Industrialism and Industrial Man: The Problems of Labor and Management in Economic Growth* (Cambridge, Mass.: Harvard University Press, 1960).
Klein, Burton, *Germany's Economic Preparations for War* (Cambridge, Mass.: Harvard University Press, 1959).
Kornhauser, William, *The Politics of Mass Society* (Glencoe, Ill.: Free Press, 1959).
Meinecke, Friedrich, *The German Catastrophe* (Cambridge, Mass.: Harvard University Press, 1950).
Moore, Barrington, *Terror and Progress USSR* (Cambridge, Mass.: Harvard University Press, 1954).
———, *Soviet Politics: The Dilemma of Power* (Cambridge, Mass.: Harvard University Press, 1950).
Nathan, Otto, *The Nazi Economic System: Germany's Mobilization for War* (Durham, North Carolina: University of North Carolina Press, 1944).
Neumann, Franz, *Behemoth* (New York: Oxford University Press, 1942).
Roepke, Wilhelm, *The Solution of the German Problem* (New York: Putnam, 1947).
Schuman, Frederick L., *The Nazi Dictatorship* (New York: Alfred A. Knopf, 1935).
Trevor-Roper, H. R., *The Last Days of Hitler* (New York: Macmillan, 1947).
Tucker, Robert C., "The CPSU Draft Program: A Credo of Conservatism," *Problems of Communism*, X, No. 5 (September–October, 1961).
Ulam, Adam B., *The Unfinished Revolution* (New York: Random House, 1960).
Wheeler-Bennet, John W., *Wooden Titan: Hindenbenburg* (New York: W. Morrow, 1936).
———, *The Nemesis of Power: The German Army in Politics, 1918–1945* (New York: Macmillan, 1953).

IV. On the Stage of the Politics of Abundance

Auerhan, Jan, *Avtomatizatsiia i Obshchestvo* (Moscow, 1960).
Brady, Robert A., *Organization, Automation and Society: The Scientific Revolution in Industry* (Berkeley: University of California Press, 1961).
Bright, James R., *Automation and Management* (Boston: Division of Research, Graduate School of Business Administration, Harvard University Press, 1958).
Department of Scientific and Industrial Research, *Automation* (London: H. M. Stationery Office, 1956).
Diebold, John, *Automation: Its Impact on Business and Labor* (Washington: National Planning Association, 1959).
Dunlop, John T., ed., *Automation and Technological Change* (Englewood Cliffs, N.J.: Prentice-Hall, 1962).
Emelianov, Aleksei D., *Ekonomicheskaia Effektivnost Mekhanizatsii i Avtomatizatsii Proisvodstva* (Moscow, 1962).
Friedmann, George, *Industrial Society* (Glencoe, Ill.: Free Press, 1955).
Hilton, Alice M., *Logic, Computing Machines and Automation* (Washington, D.C.: Spartan Books, 1963).
Honeywell, George F., *Automation, Cybernetics and Society* (New York: Philosophical Library, 1959).
Mann, Floyd C., and L. Richard Hoffman, *Automation and the Worker* (New York: Holt, Rinehart & Winston, 1960).
Michael, Donald N., *Cybernation: The Silent Conquest* (Santa Barbara, Calif.: Center for the Study of Democratic Institutions, 1962).
Pollock, Fredrick, *Automation: A Study of Its Economic and Social Consequences*, translated by W. O. Henderson and W. H. Chaloner (New York: Frederick A. Praeger, 1955).
Pyke, Magnus, *Automation: Its Purpose and Future* (London: Hutchinson Scientific and Technical Publications, 1956).
Strauss, Eric, *The Ruling Servants* (New York: Frederick A. Praeger, 1961).
Teani, Renato, *Aspetti della Automazione Nella Produzione Industriale* (Genova: SIAG, 1956).
United States Congress, Joint Economic Committee, *Instrumentation and Automation*, Hearings before Subcommittee on Economic Stabilization of the Joint Economic Committee (Washington, D.C.: U.S. Government Printing Office, 1957).
United States President's Advisory Committee on Labor-Management Policy, *The Benefits and Problems Incident to Automation and Other Technological Advances* (Washington, D.C.: U.S. Government Printing Office, 1962).
World Health Organization, *Mental Health Problems of Automation* (Geneva: World Health Organization, 1959).

Index

A Note on the Type

THE TEXT of this book is set in *Caledonia,* a typeface designed by W(illiam) A(ddison) Dwiggins for the Mergenthaler Linotype Company in 1939. Dwiggins chose to call his new typeface Caledonia, the Roman name for Scotland, because it was inspired by the Scotch types cast about 1833 by Alexander Wilson & Son, Glasgow type founders. However, there is a calligraphic quality about this face that is totally lacking in the Wilson types. Dwiggins referred to an even earlier typeface for this "liveliness of action"—one cut around 1790 by William Martin for the printer William Bulmer. Caledonia has more weight than the Martin letters, and the bottom finishing strokes (serifs) of the letters are cut straight across, without brackets, to make sharp angles with the upright stems, thus giving a "modern face" appearance.

W. A. Dwiggins (1880–1956) was born in Martinsville, Ohio, and studied art in Chicago. In 1904 he moved to Hingham, Massachusetts, where he built a solid reputation as a designer of advertisements and as a calligrapher. He began an association with the Mergenthaler Linotype Company in 1929, and over the next twenty-seven years designed a number of book types for that firm. Of especial interest are the Metro series, Electra, Caledonia, Eldorado, and Falcon. In 1930, Dwiggins first became interested in marionettes, and through the years made many important contributions to the art of puppetry and the design of marionettes.

Composed, printed, and bound by
AMERICAN BOOK–STRATFORD PRESS, INC., NEW YORK, N.Y.
Typography by Margaret F. Plympton